RE
IN
WESTERN
CIVILIZATION

MW01504005

Fourth Edition

Don C. Rawson
Alan F. Wilt
Iowa State University

McGraw-Hill, Inc.
College Custom Series

*New York St. Louis San Francisco Auckland Bogotá
Caracas Lisbon London Madrid Mexico Milan Montreal
New Delhi Paris San Juan Singapore Sydney Tokyo Toronto*

READINGS IN MODERN WESTERN CIVILIZATION

1 2 3 4 5 6 7 8 9 0 MALMAL 9 0 9 8 7 6 5 4 3 2 1

ISBN 07-051291-4

Editor: John K. Earl

Printer/Binder: Malloy Lithographing, Inc.

This book is printed on recycled paper.

Foreward

The selections in this book emphasize the major trends and issues in Western Civilization since the mid-seventeenth century. We are convinced that such readings do not go out of fashion but in fact epitomize the bedrock of our modern Western heritage. Therefore, we encourage students to become familiar with the actual words of persons who have influenced and articulated these trends and issues.

The selections themselves represent a variety of ideas, from absolute monarchy to liberalism, communism, and fascism; and from questions of war and peace to reflections on population, human progress, and social justice. We have introduced each selection with a short passage giving its historical setting and, when appropriate, biographical information about the author. We have made no attempt to draw conclusions about the merits of these works, but have left this for students to discuss in class or to present in written form. We hope that this volume, when used to supplement a standard textbook, will deepen the reader's understanding of the issues, ambiguities, and achievements that have fashioned modern Western Civilization.

A.F.W.
D.C.R.

Table of Contents

Jacques Bénigne Bossuet

Potitics Drawn From the Very Words of the Holy Scriptures

The dominant political theory in early modern Europe was divine right monarchy. It reached its apogee during the reign of Louis XIV of France (1643-1715), and its most famous theoretician was the French bishop, Jacques Bénigne Bossuet (1627-1704). Bossuet, who tutored Louis XIV's only child, stated his ideas in a number of essays, including Politics Drawn from the Very Words of the Holy Scriptures.

There are four essential characteristics or qualities of royal authority.

First, royal authority is sacred.

Second, it is paternal.

Third, it is absolute.

Fourth, it is subject to reason.

This is necessary to establish in order in the following articles.

Royal authority is *sacred*.

God establishes kings as his ministers and reigns through them over the people. We have already seen that all power comes from God. "The prince," adds Saint Paul, "is the minister of God for the common good. If you do evil, tremble; for it is

Text: Bishop Jacques Bénigne Bossuet, Oeuvres Completès, *ed. F. Lachat (Paris: Librairie de Louis Vives, 1864), XXIII, pp. 539-533, 534, 535-536, 537-538, 539, 558-559, 579-581, 582, 644-645. Trans. by Alan Wilt.*

not in vain that he wields the sword; and he is the minister of God, the avenger of evil deeds."

Princes thus act as ministers of God and as His lieutenants on earth. It is through them that He acts upon His domain. "Do you think you have the power to resist the Kingdom of the Lord, which he rules through the Child of David?"

This is why we have seen that the royal throne is not the throne of a man, but the throne of God Himself. "God chose my son Solomon to be placed on the throne, from which the Lord reigns over Israel." And again: "Solomon sits on the throne of the Lord."

* * * * * * * *

The person of the king is sacred.

It appears from all this that the person of the king is sacred and that to attempt anything against him is a sacrilege. God had his prophets anoint kings with a sacred unction, just as He had His pontiffs and altars anointed.

But even without the external application of this unction, they [kings] are sacred because of their charge, as being the representatives of His divine majesty, deputized by His providence for the execution of His design.

* * * * * * * *

It is necessary to guard kings as sacred objects, and whoever neglects to guard them is deserving of death. "Long live the Lord," says David to the captains of Saul. "You are the children of death, all of you who do not guard your master, the anointed of the Lord."

* * * * * * * *

One should obey the prince on the principles of religion and conscience. Saint Paul, after having said that the prince is the minister of God, concludes thus: "It is therefore necessary to be submissive to him, not only through fear of his anger, but also through the obligation of your conscience. . . ." That is why it is necessary "to serve with an eye not for pleasing men, but with good will, with belief, with respect, and with a sincere heart for serving Jesus Christ."

If the Apostle [Paul] therefore speaks of servitude, an

* * * * * * * *

unnatural condition, what should we think of legitimate sub-jection to princes and to magistrates who are the protectors of public liberty?

This is why Saint Peter says: "For the love of God be thus submissive to the order that is established among men; be sub-missive to the king, as to Him who has the supreme power, and to those to whom He gives His authority as being sent by Him for the praise of good deeds and the punishment of bad."

Even when kings do not carry out their duties as they should, it is necessary to respect in them their charge and their ministry. "Obey your masters, not only those who are good and moderate, but also those who are troublesome and unjust."

There is thus something religious in the respect one renders a prince. The service of God and the respect for kings are things united; and Saint Peter put together the two duties: "Fear God; honor the king."

* * * * * * * *

Kings must respect their own power and ought to use it only for the public good.

Since their power comes from on high, as has been said, they should not believe that they are masters to use it as they please; but they must use it with fear and restraint, as a thing which comes to them from God and of which God will demand an accounting . . . .

Kings therefore ought to tremble when using the power which God gives them, and remember how horrible is the sacrilege of using for evil a power which comes from God.

We have seen kings seated upon the throne of the Lord, hav-ing in hand the sword that He Himself put in their hand. What profanation and what audacity of these unjust kings to sit on the throne of God in order to render decrees contrary to law and, by using the sword which He put in their hands, to do deeds of violence and to slaughter His children!

Let them thus respect their power, because it is not their power but the power of God, which ought to be used piously and religiously . . . . That is to say, govern as God governs, in a noble, impartial, charitable, in a word, divine manner.

Royal authority is *paternal*, and its inherent character is goodness.

After what has been said, this truth needs no further proof. We have seen that kings take the place of God, who is the true Father of the human race. We have also seen that the first idea of power among men was that of paternal power, and that kings have been made on the model of fathers. Also everyone agrees that the obedience which is due to public power is found only in the Ten Commandments, in the precept which obliges one to honor one's parents.

It appears from all this that the name of king is a name of a father and that goodness is the most natural characteristic of kings.

* * * * * * * *

Because God is great and sufficient unto Himself, He turns, so to speak, entirely to doing good to men, conforming to this word: "As is His greatness, so is His compassion."

He puts an image of His greatness in kings to force them to imitate His goodness. He raises them to a level where they desire nothing more for themselves. We have heard David saying: "What can your obedient servant add to this greatness in which You have clothed him?" And at the same time He declares to them that He gives them this greatness out of love for the people. "Because God loves His people, He makes you to reign over them."

* * * * * * * *

In effect, God, who formed the bodies of all men from the same earth and has distributed equally His image and His likeness in their souls, has not established among them such distinctions in order to place on the one side the haughty and on the other the slaves and the poor. He has made the great only to protect the little; He has given kings His power only to care for the public good and to be the support of the people.

* * * * * * * *

Royal authority is *absolute*.

In order to render this proposition odious and insufferable, many people try to equate absolute government with

arbitrary government. But there are no two things more dissimilar.

The prince need not account for his orders to anyone.

"Observe the commandments which come from the mouth of
the king, and listen to the oath which you have given him. Do
not think to escape from his sight, and do not continue in evil
works, because he will do whatever he desires. The word of the
king is powerful; and no one can say to him: Why do you do
this? Whoever obeys will not be harmed."

Without this absolute authority, he [a king] could neither do
good nor repress evil; his power must be such that no one can
hope to escape him; and finally the only defense of individual
persons against the public power ought to be their innocence.
This doctrine conforms to what Saint Paul says: "If you do not
want to fear power, then do good."

When the prince has judged, there is no other judgment. Sovereign judgments are attributed to God Himself. When Jehosh-
aphat appoints the judges to judge the people: "It is not," says he,
"in the name of men that you judge but in the name of God."

This is what is said in *Ecclesiastes*: "Do not judge the
judge," for even stronger reasons do not judge the sovereign
judge who is the king . . . . It is not that he judges all the time;
but it is that he is deemed capable of judging; and that no one has
the right to judge or to review after him.

It is thus necessary to obey princes as justice itself, without
which there is no order or end to matters.

They are of gods and share in a sense in divine independence.
"I have said: You are of gods, and you are all children of the
Most High."

* * * * * * * *

Royal authority is *subject to reason.*

Government is a work of reason and intelligence. "Now, 0
kings, listen; be instructed, you judges of the earth . . . ." God,
in installing Joshua, ordered him to study the Law of Moses,
which was the law of royalty. "To this end," He said, "that you
understand all that you do." And again: "Then you carry on your
plans, and you understand what you do."

David said as much to Solomon in the last instructions which he gave him before dying: "Take care to observe the law of God, so that you will understand all that you do, and what way you ought to turn."

Let no one bend you; bend yourself with knowledge; let reason direct all your movements; know what you do, and why you do it.

* * * * * * * *

He [the king] lives under the burden of affairs of the vast multitudes of people, whom he has to lead. So many moods, so many interests, so many artifices, so many passions, so many surprises to fear, so many matters to consider, so much of the world on all sides to listen to and to understand; what one mind can suffice . . . ?

He asks it [wisdom] of God, and God gives it to him; but at the same time He gives him all the rest which he has not requested, that is to say, wealth and glory. Kings learn that they lack nothing when they have wisdom, and that it alone attracts to them all the other blessings.

* * * * * * * *

Let us summarize the great and majestic things which we have said about royal authority. See a vast people united in a single person; see this sacred power, paternal and absolute; see the mystical reason which governs the entire body of the State, contained in a single head. You see the image of God in kings, and you have the idea of royal majesty.

God is holiness itself, goodness itself, power itself, reason itself. In these things is the majesty of God. In the image of these things is the majesty of the prince.

This majesty is so great that it cannot be in the prince as in its source; it is borrowed from God, who gives it to him for the good of the people, for whom it is good to be restrained by a superior force.

I do not know what attributes of divinity attaches itself to the prince and inspires fear in the people. The king himself should not forget this. "I have said to him: It is God who speaks. I have said: You are of God, and you are all children of the Most

High; but you will die like men and you will fall like the great."
* * * * * * * *

You are the children of the Most High; it is He who has established your power for the good of the human race. But, O gods of flesh and blood, O gods of clay and dust, you will die like men, you will fall like the great. Greatness separates men for a short time; a common fall makes all equal in the end.

Therefore, O kings, exercise your power boldly, for it is divine and beneficial to the human race; but exercise it with humility. You are endowed with it from beyond. In reality it leaves you weak, it leaves you mortal; it leaves you sinners: and lays on you a very great reckoning before God.

Thomas Hobbes

Leviathan

In contrast to the divine right theory, Thomas Hobbes (1588-1679) presents a secular argument for political absolutism. Published in 1651, the Leviathan *reflects Hobbes' aversion to the chaos of the English Civil War of the 1640s, and his general desire for an authoritarian political system, capable of ensuring stability and peace. In his treatise, he examines the nature of society, the reasons for forming commonwealths, and the irrevocable character of sovereign power once it is attained.*

Nature hath made men so equal, in the faculties of the body, and mind; as that though there be found one man sometimes manifestly stronger in body, or of quicker mind than another; yet when all is reckoned together, the difference between man, and man, is not so considerable, as that one man can thereupon claim to himself any benefit, to which another may not pretend, as well as he. For as to the strength of body, the weakest has strength enough to kill the strongest, either by secret machination, or by confederacy with others, that are in the same danger with himself.

And as to the faculties of the mind, setting aside the arts grounded upon words, and especially that skill of proceeding upon general, and infallible rules, called science; which very few have, and but in few things; as being not a native faculty, born with us; nor attained, as prudence, while we look after somewhat else, I find yet a greater equality amongst men, than that of strength. For prudence, is but experience; which equal time, equally bestows on all men, in those things they equally apply

---

Text: The English Works of Thomas Hobbes *(London: John Bohn, 1839), III, pp. 110-111, 112-113, 116-118, 152-154, 157-158, 159-161.*

themselves unto. That which may perhaps make such equality incredible, is but a vain conceit of one's own wisdom, which almost all men think they have in a greater degree, than the vulgar; that is, than all men but themselves, and a few others, whom by fame, or for concurring with themselves, they approve. For such is the nature of men, that howsoever they may acknowledge many others to be more witty, or more eloquent, or more learned; yet they will hardly believe there be many so wise as themselves; for they see their own wit at hand, and other men's at a distance. But this proveth rather that men are in that point equal, than unequal. For there is not ordinarily a greater sign of the equal distribution of any thing, than that every man is contented with his share.

From this equality of ability, ariseth equality of hope in the attaining of our ends. And therefore if any two men desire the same thing, which nevertheless they cannot both enjoy, they become enemies; and in the way to their end, which is principally their own conservation, and sometimes their delectation only, endeavour to destroy, or subdue one another. And from hence it comes to pass, that where an invader hath no more to fear, than another man's single power; if one plant, sow, build, or possess a convenient seat, others may probably be expected to come prepared with forces united, to dispossess, and deprive him, not only of the fruit of his labour, but also of his life, or liberty. And the invader again is in the like danger of another.

* * * * * * * *

Hereby it is manifest, that during the time men live without a common power to keep them all in awe, they are in that condition which is called war; and such a war, as is of every man, against every man. For war, consisteth not in battle only, or the act of fighting; but in a tract of time, wherein the will to contend by battle is sufficiently known and therefore the notion of time, is to be considered in the nature of war; as it is in the nature of weather. For as the nature of foul weather, lieth not in a shower or two of rain; but in an inclination thereto of many days together; so the nature of war, consisteth not in actual fighting; but in the known disposition thereto, during all the time there is no assurance to the contrary. All other time is peace.

Whatsoever therefore is consequent to a time of war, where every man is enemy to every man; the same is consequent to the time, wherein men live without other security, than what their own strength, and their own invention shall furnish them withal. In such condition, there is no place for industry; because the fruit thereof is uncertain: and consequently no culture of the earth; no navigation, nor use of the commodities that may be imported by sea; no commodious building; no instruments of moving, and removing, such things as require much force; no knowledge of the face of the earth; no account of time; no arts; no letters, no society; and which is worst of all, continual fear, and danger of violent death; and the life of man, solitary, poor, nasty, brutish, and short.

* * * * * * * *

The right of nature, which writers commonly call *jus naturale,* is the liberty each man hath, to use his own power, as he will himself, for the preservation of his own nature; that is to say, of his own life; and consequently, of doing any thing, which in his own judgment, and reason, he shall conceive to be the aptest means thereunto.

By liberty is understood, according to the proper signification of the word, the absence of external impediments; which impediments, may oft take away part of a man's power to do what he would; but cannot hinder him from using the power left him, according as his judgment, and reason shall dictate to him.

A law of nature, *lex naturalis,* is a precept or general rule, found out by reason, by which a man is forbidden to do that, which is destructive of his life, or taketh away the means of preserving the same; and to omit that, by which he thinketh it may be best preserved. For though they that speak of this subject, use to confound *jus,* and *lex,* right and law: yet they ought to be distinguished; because right consisteth in liberty to do, or to forbear; whereas law, determineth, and bindeth to one of them: so that law, and right, differ as much, as obligation, and liberty; which in one and the same matter are inconsistent.

And because the condition of man, as hath been declared in the precedent chapter, is a condition of war of every one against every one: in which case every one is governed by his own reason; and there is nothing he can make use of, that may not be a help unto him, in preserving his life against his enemies; it followeth, that in such a condition, every man has a right to every thing; even to one another's body. And therefore, as long as this natural right of every man to every thing endureth, there can be no security to any man, how strong or wise soever he be, of living out the time, which nature ordinarily alloweth men to live. And consequently it is a precept, or general rule of reason, that every man, ought to endeavour peace, as far as he has hope of obtaining it; and when he cannot obtain it, that he may seek, and use, all helps, and advantages of war. The first branch of which rule, containeth the first, and fundamental law of nature; which is, to seek peace, and follow it. The second, the sum of the right of nature; which is, by all means we can, to defend ourselves.

From this fundamental law of nature, by which men are commanded to endeavour peace, is derived this second law; that a man be willing, when others are so too, as far-forth, as for peace, and defence of himself he shall think it necessary, to lay down this right to all things; and be contented with so much liberty against other men, as he would allow other men against himself. For as long as every man holdeth this right, of doing any thing he liketh; so long are all men in the condition of war.

* * * * * * * *

The final cause, end, or design of men, who naturally love liberty, and dominion over others, in the introduction of that restraint upon themselves, in which we see them live in commonwealths, is the foresight of their own preservation, and of a more contented life thereby; that is to say, of getting themselves out from that miserable condition of war . . . .

For the laws of nature, as justice, equity, modesty, mercy, and, in sum, doing to others, as we would be done to, of themselves, without the terror of some power, to cause them to be observed, are contrary to our natural passions, that carry us to partiality, pride, revenge, and the like. And covenants, without the sword, are but words, and of no strength to secure a man at all.

* * * * * * * *

The only way to erect such a common power, as may be able to defend them from the invasion of foreigners, and the injuries of one another, and thereby to secure them in such sort, as that by their own industry, and by the fruits of the earth, they may nourish themselves and live contentedly; is to confer all their power and strength upon one man, or upon one assembly of men, that may reduce all their wills, by plurality of voices, unto one will: which is as much as to say, to appoint one man, or assembly of men, to bear their person; and every one to own, and acknowledge himself to be author of whatsoever he that so beareth their person, shall act, or cause to be acted, in those things which concern the common peace and safety; and therein to submit their wills, every one to his will, and their judgments, to his judgment. This is more than consent, or concord; it is a real unity of them all, in one and the same person, made by covenant of every man with every man, in such manner, as if every man should say to every man, I authorize and give up my right of governing myself, to this man, or to this assembly of men, on this condition, that thou give up thy right to him, and authorize all his actions in like manner.

This done, the multitude so united in one person, is called a *commonwealth,* in Latin *civitas.* This is the generation of that great *leviathan,* or rather, to speak more reverently, of that mortal god, to which we owe under the immortal God, our peace and defence. For by this authority, given him by every particular man in the commonwealth, he hath the use of so much power and strength conferred on him, that by terror thereof, he is enabled to perform the wills of them all, to peace at home, and mutual aid against their enemies abroad. And in him consisteth the essence of the commonwealth; which, to define it, is one person, of whose acts a great multitude, by mutual covenants one with another, have made themselves every one the author, to the end he may use the strength and means of them all, as he shall think expedient, for their peace and common defence.

And he that carrieth this person, is called *sovereign,* and said to have sovereign power; and every one besides his *subject.*

* * * * * * * *

A commonwealth is said to be instituted, when a multitude of men do agree, and covenant, every one, with every one, that to whatsoever man, or assembly of men, shall be given by the major part, the right to present the person of them all, that is to say, to be their representative; every one, as well he that voted for it, as he that voted against it, shall authorize all the actions and judgments, of that man, or assembly of men, in the same manner, as if they were his own, to the end, to live peaceably amongst themselves, and be protected against other men.

From this institution of a commonwealth are derived all the rights, and faculties of him, or them, on whom sovereign power is conferred by the consent of the people assembled.

First, because they covenant, it is to be understood, they are not obliged by former covenant to anything repugnant hereunto. And consequently they that have already instituted a commonwealth, being thereby bound by covenant, to own the actions, and judgments of one, cannot lawfully make a new covenant, amongst themselves, to be obedient to any other, in any things whatsoever, without his permission.   And therefore, they that are subjects to a monarch, cannot without his leave cast off monarchy, and return to the confusion of a disunited multitude; nor transfer their person from him that beareth it, to another man, or other assembly of men: for they are bound, every man to every man, to own, and be reputed author of all, that he that already is their sovereign, shall do, and judge fit to be done: so that any one man dissenting, all the rest should break their covenant made to that man, which is injustice; and they have also every man given the sovereignty to him that beareth their person; and therefore if they depose him, they take from him that which is his own, and so again it is injustice.   Besides, if he that attempteth to depose his sovereign, be killed, or punished by him for such attempt, he is author of his own punishment, as being by the institution, author of all his sovereign shall do: and because it is injustice for a man to do anything, for which he may be punished by his own authority, he is also upon that title, unjust. And whereas some men have pretended for their disobedience to their sovereign, a new covenant, made, not with men, but with God; this also is unjust: for there is no covenant with God, but by mediation of somebody that representeth God's person; which none doth but God's lieutenant, who hath the sovereignty under God. But this pretence of covenant with God, is so evident a lie, even in the pretenders' own consciences, that it is not only an act of an unjust, but also of a vile, and unmanly disposition.

Secondly, because the right of bearing the person of them all, is given to him they make sovereign, by covenant only of one to another, and not of him to any of them; there can happen no breach of covenant of the part of the sovereign; and consequently none of his subjects, by any pretence of forfeiture, can be freed from his subjection. That he which is made sovereign maketh no covenant with his subjects beforehand, is manifest; because either he must make it with the whole multitude, as one party to the covenant; or he must make a several covenant with every man. With the whole, as one party, it is impossible; because as yet they are not one person: and if he make so many several covenants as there be men, those covenants after he hath the sovereignty are void; because what act soever can be pretended by any one of them for breach thereof, is the act both of himself, and of all the rest, because done in the person, and by the right of every one of them in particular.

John Locke

Second Treatise on Government

Like Hobbes, a generation earlier, John Locke (1632-1704) discusses the nature of society and the purpose of commonwealths, but he emphasizes the limited power of government and the right of society to terminate its contractual relationship with those who abuse their delegated authority. Written in 1681 and published in 1690, Locke's Second Treatise on Government *provided a philosophical justification of the Glorious Revolution of 1688, as well as a foundation of classical liberalism.*

To understand political power right, and derive it from its original, we must consider what state all men are naturally in, and that is, a state of perfect freedom to order their actions and dispose of their possessions and persons, as they think fit, within the bounds of the law of nature; without asking leave, or depending upon the will of any other man.

A state also of equality, wherein all the power and jurisdiction is reciprocal, no one having more than another; there being nothing more evident than that creatures of the same species and rank, promiscuously born to all the same advantages of nature, and the use of the same faculties, should also be equal one amongst another without subordination or subjection; unless the Lord and Master of them all should, by any manifest declaration of his will, set one above another, and confer on him, by an evident and clear appointment, an undoubted right to dominion and sovereignty.

* * * * * * * *

But though this be a state of liberty, yet it is not a state of licence: though man in that state have an uncontrollable liberty to

Text: The Works of John Locke *(London: Thomas Tegg, 1823), V, pp. 339-340, 341-342, 394-396, 411-413, 469-470, 484-485.*

dispose of his person or possessions, yet he has not liberty to destroy himself, or so much as any creature in his possession, but where some nobler use than its bare preservation calls for it. The state of nature has a law of nature to govern it, which obliges every one: and reason, which is that law, teaches all mankind, who will but consult it, that being all equal and independent, no one ought to harm another in his life, health, liberty, or possessions: for men being all the workmanship of one omnipotent and infinitely wise Maker; all the servants of one sovereign Master, sent into the world by his order, and about his business; they are his property, whose workmanship they are, made to last during his, not another's pleasure: and being furnished with like faculties, sharing all in one community of nature, there cannot be supposed any such subordination among us that may authorize us to destroy another, as if we were made for one another's uses, as the inferior ranks of creatures are for ours. Every one, as he is bound to preserve himself, and not to quit his station wilfully, so by the like reason, when his own preservation comes not in competition, ought he, as much as he can, to preserve the rest of mankind, and may not, unless it be to do justice to an offender, take away or impair the life, or what tends to the preservation of life, the liberty, health, limb, or goods of another.

And that all men may be restrained from invading others' rights, and from doing hurt to one another, and the law of nature be observed, which willeth the peace and preservation of all mankind, the execution of the law of nature is, in that state, put into every man's hands, whereby every one has a right to punish the transgressors of that law to such a degree as may hinder its violation: for the law of nature would, as all other laws that concern men in this world, be in vain, if there were nobody that in the state of nature had a power to execute that law, and thereby preserve the innocent, and restrain offenders. And if any one in the state of nature may punish another for any evil he has done, every one may do so: for in that state of perfect equality, where naturally there is no superiority or jurisdiction of one over another, what any may do in prosecution of that law every one must needs have a right to do.

* * * * * * * *

Men being, as has been said, by nature all free, equal, and independent, no one can be put out of this estate, and subjected to the political power of another, without his own consent. The only way whereby any one divests himself of his natural liberty, and puts on the bonds of civil society, is by agreeing with other men to join and unite into a community, for their comfortable, safe, and peaceable living one amongst another, in a secure enjoyment of their properties, and a greater security against any that are not of it. This any number of men may do, because it injures not the freedom of the rest; they are left as they were in the liberty of the state of nature. When any number of men have so consented to make one community or government, they are thereby presently incorporated, and make one body politic, wherein the majority have a right to act and conclude the rest.

For when any number of men have, by the consent of every individual, made a community, they have thereby made that community one body, with a power to act as one body, which is only by the will and determination of the majority; for that which acts any community being only the consent of the individuals of it, and it being necessary to that which is one body to move one way; it is necessary the body should move that way whither the greater force carries it, which is the consent of the majority: or else it is impossible it should act or continue one body, one community, which the consent of every individual that united into it agreed that it should; and so every one is bound by that consent to be concluded by the majority. And therefore we see that in assemblies, empowered to act by positive laws, where no number is set by that positive law which empowers them, the act of the majority passes for the act of the whole, and of course determines, as having, by the law of nature and reason, the power of the whole.

And thus every man, by consenting with others to make one body politic under one government, puts himself under an obligation to every one of that society to submit to the determination of the majority, and to be concluded by it; or else this original compact, whereby he with others incorporate into one society, would signify nothing, and be no compact, if he be left free, and under no other ties than he was in before in the state of nature. For what appearance would there be of any compact? what new engagement, if he were no farther tied by any decrees of the society than he himself thought fit, and did actually consent to? This would be still as great a liberty as he himself had before his compact, or any one else in the state of nature hath, who may submit himself and consent to any acts of it if he thinks fit.

For if the consent of the majority shall not, in reason, be received as the act of the whole, and conclude every individual, nothing but the consent of every individual can make any thing to be the act of the whole: but such a consent is next to impossible ever to be had, if we consider the infirmities of health, and avocations of business, which in a number, though much less than that of a commonwealth, will necessarily keep many away from the public assembly. To which if we add the variety of opinions, and contrariety of interests which unavoidably happen in all collections of men, the coming into society upon such terms would be only like Cato's coming into the theatre, only to go out again. Such a constitution as this would make the mighty leviathan of a shorter duration than the feeblest creatures, and not let it outlast the day it was born in: which cannot be supposed, till we can think that rational creatures should desire and constitute societies only to be dissolved: for where the majority cannot conclude the rest, there they cannot act as one body, and consequently will be immediately dissolved again.

* * * * * * * *

If man in the state of nature be so free as has been said; if he be absolute lord of his own person and possessions, equal to the greatest, and subject to nobody, why will he part with his freedom, why will he give up this empire, and subject himself to the dominion and control of any other power? To which it is obvious to answer, that though in the state of nature he hath such a right, yet the enjoyment of it is very uncertain, and constantly exposed to the invasion of others; for all being kings as much as he, every man his equal, and the greater part no strict observers of equity and justice, the enjoyment of the property he has in this state is very unsafe, very unsecure. This makes him willing to quit a condition, which, however free, is full of fears and continual dangers: and it is not without reason that he seeks out, and is willing to join in society with others, who are already united, or have a mind to unite, for the mutual preservation of their lives, liberties, and estates, which I call by the general name property.

The great and chief end, therefore, of men's uniting into commonwealths, and putting themselves under government, is the preservation of their property. To which in the state of nature there are many things wanting.

First, there wants an established, settled, known law, received and allowed by common consent to be the standard of right and wrong, and the common measure to decide all controversies between them: for though the law of nature be plain and intelligible to all rational creatures; yet men being biassed by their interest, as well as ignorant for want of studying it, are not apt to allow of it as a law binding to them in the application of it to their particular cases.

Secondly, in the state of nature there wants a known and indifferent judge, with authority to determine all differences according to the established law: for every one in that state being both judge and executioner of the law of nature, men being partial to themselves, passion and revenge is very apt to carry them too far, and with too much heat, in their own cases; as well as negligence and unconcernedness, to make them too remiss in other men's.

Thirdly, in the state of nature there often wants power to back and support the sentence when right, and to give it due execution. They who by any injustice offend, will seldom fail, where they are able, by force to make good their injustice; such resistance many times makes the punishment dangerous, and frequently destructive to those who attempt it.

Thus mankind, notwithstanding all the privileges of the state of nature, being but in an ill condition, while they remain in it, are quickly driven into society. Hence it comes to pass, that we seldom find any number of men live any time together in this state. The inconveniencies that they are therein exposed to, by the irregular and uncertain exercise of the power every man has of punishing the transgressions of others, make them take sanctuary under the established laws of government, and therein seek the preservation of their property. It is this makes them so willingly give up every one his single power of punishing, to be exercised by such alone as shall be appointed to it amongst them; and by such rules as the community, or those authorized by them to that purpose, shall agree on. And in this we have the original right of both the legislative and executive power, as well as of the governments and societies themselves.

* * * * * * * *

The reason why men enter into society is the preservation of their property; and the end why they choose and authorize a legislative is, that there may be laws made, and rules set, as guards and fences to the properties of all the members of the society: to limit the power, and moderate the dominion, of every part and member of the society: for since it can never be supposed to be the will of the society that the legislative should have a power to destroy that which every one designs to secure by entering into society, and for which the people submitted themselves to legislators of their own making; whenever the legislators endeavour to take away and destroy the property of the people, or to reduce them to slavery under arbitrary power, they put themselves into a state of war with the people, who are thereupon absolved from any farther obedience, and are left to the common refuge, which God hath provided for all men, against force and violence.

Whensoever therefore the legislative shall transgress this fundamental rule of society; and either by ambition, fear, folly, or corruption, endeavour to grasp themselves, or put into the hands of any other, an absolute power over the lives, liberties, and estates of the people; by this breach of trust they forfeit the power the people had put into their hands for quite contrary ends, and it devolves to the people, who have a right to resume their original liberty, and, by the establishment of a new legislative (such as they shall think fit) provide for their own safety and security, which is the end for which they are in society. What I have said here, concerning the legislative in general, holds true also concerning the supreme executor, who having a double trust put in him, both to have a part in the legislative, and the supreme execution of the law, acts against both, when he goes about to set up his own arbitrary will as the law of the society.

* * * * * * * *

If a controversy arise betwixt a prince and some of the people, in a matter where the law is silent or doubtful, and the thing be of great consequence, I should think the proper umpire, in such a case, should be the body of the people: for in cases where the prince hath a trust reposed in him, and is dispensed from the common ordinary rules of the law; there, if any men find themselves aggrieved, and think the prince acts contrary to, or beyond that trust, who so proper to judge as the body of the people, (who, at first, lodged that trust in him) how far they meant it should extend? But if the prince, or whoever they be in the administration, decline that way of determination, the appeal then lies nowhere but to Heaven; force between either persons, who have no known superior on earth, or which permits no appeal to a judge on earth, being properly a state of war, wherein the appeal lies only to Heaven; and in that state the injured party must judge for himself, when he will think fit to make use of that appeal, and put himself upon it.

To conclude, the power that every individual gave the society, when he entered into it, can never revert to the individuals again, as long as the society lasts, but will always remain in the community; because without this there can be no community, no commonwealth, which is contrary to the original agreement: so also when the society hath placed the legislative in any assembly of men, to continue in them and their successors, with direction and authority for providing such successors, the legislative can never revert to the people whilst that government lasts; because, having provided a legislative with power to continue for ever, they have given up their political power to the legislative, and cannot resume it. But if they have set limits to the duration of their legislative, and made this supreme power in any person, or assembly, only temporary; or else, when by the miscarriages of those in authority it is forfeited; upon the forfeiture, or at the determination of the time set, it reverts to the society, and the people have a right to act as supreme, and continue the legislative in themselves; or erect a new form, or under the old form place it in new hands, as they think good.

Isaac Newton

Mathematical Principles Of Natural Philosophy

Sir Isaac Newton (1642-1727) was the most illustrious figure of the "scientific revolution." An English mathematician, physicist, astronomer, and philosopher, he discovered the law of universal gravitation, devised a system of differential calculus, and made important contributions to the field of optics. In The Mathematical Principles of Natural Philosophy, *published in 1687, he explains the law of gravitation as the unifying factor in a precisely operating universe; and he emphasizes the use of empirical evidence and mathematical reasoning as the basis of the new science.*

Preface to the First Edition

Since the ancients (as we are told by Pappus) made great account of the science of mechanics in the investigation of natural things, and the moderns, laying aside substantial forms and occult qualities, have endeavored to subject the phenomena of nature to the laws of mathematics, I have in this treatise cultivated mathematics so far as it regards philosophy. The ancients considered mechanics in a twofold respect; as rational, which proceeds accurately by demonstration, and practical. To practical mechanics all the manual arts belong, from which mechanics took its name. But as artificers do not work with perfect accuracy, it comes to pass that mechanics is so distinguished from geometry that what is perfectly accurate is called geometrical; what is less so is called

---

Text: Isaac Newton, The Mathematical Principles of Natural Philosophy *(London: Benjamin Notte, 1729), I, pp. i-iv; II, 202-205.*

mechanical. But the errors are not in the art, but in the artificers. He that works with less accuracy is an imperfect mechanics. Geometry does not teach us to draw these lines, but requires them to be drawn. For it requires that the learner should first be taught to describe these accurately, before he enters upon mechanic; and if any could work with perfect accuracy, he would be the most perfect mechanic of all. For the description of right lines and circles, upon which geometry is founded, belongs to geometry; then it shows how by these operations problems may be solved. To describe right lines and circles are problems, but not geometrical problems.

The solution of these problems is required from mechanics; and by geometry the use of them, when so solved, is shown. And it is the glory of geometry that from those few principles, fetched from without, it is able to produce so many things. Therefore geometry is founded in mechanical practice, and is nothing but that part of universal mechanics which accurately proposes and demonstrates the art of measuring. But since the manual arts are chiefly conversant in the moving of bodies, it comes to pass that geometry is commonly referred to their magnitude, and mechanics to their motion. In this sense rational mechanics will be the science of motions resulting from any forces whatsoever, and of the forces required to produce any motions, accurately proposed and demonstrated.

This part of mechanics was cultivated by the ancients -- in the five powers which relate to manual arts -- who considered gravity (it not being a manual power) no otherwise than as it moved weights by those powers. Our design not respecting arts but philosophy, and our subject not manual but natural powers, we consider chiefly those things which relate to gravity, levity, elastic force, the resistance of fluids, and the like forces, whether attractive or impulsive. And therefore we offer this work as mathematical principles of philosophy. For all the difficulty of philosophy seems to consist in this: from the phenomena of motions to investigate the forces of nature, and then from these forces to demonstrate the other phenomena. And to this end the general propositions in the first and second books are directed.

In the third book we give an example of this in the explication of the System of the World. For by the propositions mathematically demonstrated in the first books we there derive from the celestial phenomena the forces of gravity with which bodies tend to the sun and the several planets. Then from these forces, by other propositions which are also mathematical, we deduce the motions of the planets, the comets, the moon, and the sea.

I wish we could derive the rest of the phenomena of Nature by the same kind of reasoning from mechanical principles. For I am induced by many reasons to suspect that they may all depend upon certain forces by which the particles of bodies, by some causes hitherto unknown, are either mutually impelled towards each other and cohere in regular figures, or are repelled and recede from one another, which forces being unknown, philosophers have hitherto attempted the search of Nature in vain. But I hope the principles here laid down will afford some light either to that or some truer method of philosophy.

The Rules of Reasoning in Philosophy

Rule I

We are to admit no more causes of natural things than such as are both true and sufficient to explain their appearances.

To this purpose the philosophers say that Nature does nothing in vain, and more is in vain when less will serve. For Nature is pleased with simplicity, and affects not the pomp of superfluous causes.

Rule II

Therefore to the same natural effects we must, as far as possible, assign the same causes.

As to respiration in a man and in a beast; the descent of stones in Europe and in America; the light of our culinary fire and of the sun; the reflection of light in the earth and planets.

Rule III

The qualities of bodies which admit neither intensification nor remission of degrees, and which are found to belong to all bodies within the reach of our experiments, are to be esteemed the universal qualities of all bodies whatsoever.

For since the qualities of bodies are only known to us by experiments, we are to hold for universal all such as universally agree with experiments; and such as are not liable to diminution can never be quite taken away. We are certainly not to relinquish the evidence of experiments for the sake of dreams and vain fictions of our own devising; nor are we to recede from the analogy of Nature, which uses to be simple, and always consonant to itself. We no other way know the extension of bodies than by our senses, nor do these reach it in all bodies; but because we perceive extension in all that are sensible, therefore we ascribe it universally to all others also. That abundance of bodies are hard we learn by experience. And because the hardness of the whole arises from the hardness of the parts, we therefore justly infer the hardness of the undivided particles not only of the bodies we feel but of all others. That all bodies are impenetrable we gather not from reason, but from sensation. The bodies which we handle we find impenetrable, and thence conclude impenetrability to be an universal property of all bodies whatsoever. That all bodies are movable, and endowed with certain powers (which we call the inertia) of persevering in their motion, or in their rest, we only infer from the like properties observed in the bodies which we have seen. The extension, hardness, impenetrability, mobility, and inertia of the whole, result from the extension, hardness, impenetrability, mobility, and inertia of the parts; and thence we conclude the least particles of all bodies to be also all extended, and hard, and impenetrable, and movable, and endowed with their proper inertia.

And this is the foundation of all philosophy. Moreover, that the divided but contiguous particles of bodies may be separated from one another, is matter of observation; and, in the particles that remain undivided, our minds are able to distinguish yet lesser parts, as is mathematically demonstrated. But whether the parts so distinguished, and not yet divided, may, by the powers of Nature, be actually divided and separated from one another, we cannot certainly determine. Yet, had we the proof of but one experiment that any undivided particle, in breaking a hard and solid body, suffered a division, we might by virtue of this rule conclude that the undivided as well as the divided particles may be divided and actually separated to infinity.

Lastly, if it universally appears, by experiments and astronomical observations, that all bodies about the earth gravitate towards the earth, and that in proportion to the quantity of matter which they severally contain; that the moon likewise, according to the quantity of its matter, gravitates towards the earth; that, on the other hand, our sea gravitates towards the moon; and all the planets mutually one towards another; and the comets in like manner towards the sun; we must, in consequence of this rule, universally allow that all bodies whatsoever are endowed with a principle of mutual gravitation. For the argument from the appearances concludes with more force for the universal gravitation of all bodies than for their impenetrability; of which among those in the celestial regions we have no experiments, nor any manner of observation. Not that I affirm gravity to be essential to bodies. By their *vis insita* I mean nothing but their inertia. This is immutable. Their gravity is diminished as they recede from the earth.

Rule IV

In experimental philosophy we are to look upon propositions collected by general induction from phenomena as accurately or very nearly true, notwithstanding any contrary hypotheses that may be imagined, till such time as other phenomena occur, by which they may either be made more accurate, or liable to exceptions.

This rule we must follow that the argument of induction may not be evaded by hypotheses.

Charles de Secondat de Montesquieu

The Spirit of the Laws

Charles de Secondat, Baron de Montesquieu (1689-1755) was a wealthy French notable, who served as a judge until 1726, when he resigned to devote himself to writing. In 1748, he published his famous Spirit of the Laws, *a detailed study of the relationship of law and government. Although, in the excerpt below, he somewhat overestimated the achievements of the early 18th century governmental system in England, his "enlightened" views on the separation of powers had a pronounced influence on subsequent political theory in Europe and America, and still carry a fundamental significance today.*

Different Significations of the Word Liberty

There is no word that admits of more various significations, and has made more varied impressions on the human mind, than that of liberty. Some have taken it as a means of deposing a person on whom they had conferred a tyrannical authority; others for the power of choosing a superior whom they are obliged to obey; others for the right of bearing arms, and of being thereby enabled to use violence; others, in fine, for the privilege of being governed by a native of their own country, or by their own laws. A certain nation for a long time thought liberty consisted in the privilege of wearing a long beard. Some have annexed this name to one form of government exclusive of others: those who had a republican taste applied it to this species of polity; those who liked a monarchical state gave it to monarchy. Thus they have all applied the name of liberty to the government most suitable to

Text: Charles de Secondat de Montesquieu, The Spirit of the Laws, *trans. Thomas Nugent (London: George Bell and Sons, 1878), I, pp. 160-163, 164-168, 173-174.*

their own customs and inclinations: and as in republics the people have not so constant and so present a view of the causes of their misery, and as the magistrates seem to act only in conformity to the laws, hence liberty is generally said to reside in republics and to be banished from monarchies. In fine, as in democracies the people seem to act almost as they please; this sort of government has been deemed the most free, and the power of the people has been confounded with their liberty.

In what Liberty consists

It is true that in democracies the people seem to act as they please; but political liberty does not consist in an unlimited freedom. In governments, that is, in societies directed by laws, liberty can consist only in the power of doing what we ought to will, and in not being constrained to do what we ought not to will.

We must have continually present to our minds the difference between independence and liberty. Liberty is a right of doing whatever the laws permit, and if a citizen could do what they forbid he would be no longer possessed of liberty, because all his fellow-citizens would have the same power.

The same Subject continued

Democratic and aristocratic states are not in their own nature free. Political liberty is to be found only in moderate governments; and even in these it is not always found. It is there only when there is no abuse of power. But constant experience shows us that every man invested with power is apt to abuse it, and to carry his authority as far as it will go. Is it not strange, though true, to say that virtue itself has need of limits?

To prevent this abuse it is necessary from the very nature of things that power should be a check to power. A government may be so constituted, as no man shall be compelled to do things to which the law does not oblige him, nor forced to abstain from things which the law permits.

Of the End or View of different Governments

Though all governments have the same general end, which is that of preservation, yet each has another particular object. Increase of dominion was the object of Rome; war, that of Sparta; religion, that of the Jewish laws; commerce, that of Marseilles; public tranquillity, that of the laws of China; navigation, that of the laws of Rhodes; natural liberty, that of the policy of the Savages; in general, the pleasures of the prince, that of despotic states; that of monarchies, the prince's and the kingdom's glory; the independence of individuals is the end aimed at by the laws of Poland, thence results the oppression of the whole.

One nation there is also in the world that has for the direct end of its constitution political liberty. We shall presently examine the principles on which this liberty is founded; if they are sound, liberty will appear in its highest perfection.

To discover political liberty in a constitution, no great labor is requisite. If we are capable of seeing it where it exists, it is soon found, and we need not go far in search of it.

Of the Constitution of England

In every government there are three sorts of power: the legislative; the executive in respect to things dependent on the law of nations; and the executive in regard to matters that depend on the civil law.

By virtue of the first, the prince or magistrate enacts temporary or perpetual laws, and amends or abrogates those that have been already enacted. By the second, he makes peace or war, sends or receives embassies, establishes the public security, and provides against invasions. By the third, he punishes criminals, or determines the disputes that arise between individuals. The latter we shall call the judiciary power, and the other simply the executive power of the state.

The political liberty of the subject is a tranquillity of mind arising from the opinion each person has of his safety. In order

to have this liberty, it is requisite the government be so constituted as one man need not be afraid of another.

When the legislative and executive powers are united in the
same person, or in the same body of magistrates, there can be no
liberty; because apprehensions may arise, lest the same monarch
or senate should enact tyrannical laws, to execute them in a
tyrannical manner.

Again, there is no liberty, if the judiciary power be not separated from the legislative and executive. Were it joined with the
legislative, the life and liberty of the subject would be exposed
to arbitrary control; for the judge would be then the legislator.
Were it joined to the executive power, the judge might behave
with violence and oppression.

There would be an end of everything, were the same man
or the same body, whether of the nobles or of the people, to
exercise those three powers, that of enacting laws, that of
executing the public resolutions, and of trying the causes of
individuals.

* * * * * * * *

The judiciary power ought not to be given to a standing senate; it should be exercised by persons taken from the body of the
people at certain times of the year, and consistently with a form
and manner prescribed by law, in order to erect a tribunal that
should last only so long as necessity requires.

By this method the judicial power, so terrible to mankind, not
being annexed to any particular state or profession, becomes, as
it were, invisible. People have not then the judges continually
present to their view; they fear the office, but not the magistrate.

In accusations of a deep and criminal nature, it is proper the
person accused should have the privilege of choosing, in some
measure, his judges, in concurrence with the law; or at least he
should have a right to except against so great a number that the
remaining part may be deemed his own choice.

The other two powers may be given rather to magistrates or
permanent bodies, because they are not exercised on any private
subject; one being no more than the general will of the state, and
the other the execution of that general will.

But though the tribunals ought not to be fixed, the judgments ought; and to such a degree as to be ever conformable to the letter of the law. Were they to be the private opinion of the judge, people would then live in society, without exactly knowing the nature of their obligations.

The judges ought likewise to be of the same rank as the accused, or, in other words, his peers; to the end that he may not imagine he is fallen into the hands of persons inclined to treat him with rigor.

If the legislature leaves the executive power in possession of a right to imprison those subjects who can give security for their good behavior, there is an end of liberty; unless they are taken up, in order to answer without delay to a capital crime, in which case they are really free, being subject only to the power of the law.

But should the legislature think itself in danger by some secret conspiracy against the state or by a correspondence with a foreign enemy, it might authorize the executive power, for a short and limited time, to imprison suspected persons, who in that case would lose their liberty only for a while, to preserve it forever.

* * * * * * * *

As in a country of liberty, every man who is supposed a free agent ought to be his own governor; the legislative power should reside in the whole body of the people. But since this is impossible in large states, and in small ones is subject to many inconveniences, it is fit the people should transact by their representatives what they cannot transact by themselves.

The inhabitants of a particular town are much better acquainted with its wants and interests than with those of other places; and are better judges of the capacity of their neighbors than of that of the rest of their countrymen. The members, therefore, of the legislature should not be chosen from the general body of the nation; but it is proper that in every considerable place a representative should be elected by the inhabitants.

The great advantage of representatives is, their capacity of discussing public affairs. For this the people collectively are extremely unfit, which is one of the chief inconveniences of a democracy.

* * * * * * * *

All the inhabitants of the several districts ought to have a right of voting at the election of a representative, except such as are in so mean a situation as to be deemed to have no will of their own.

One great fault there was in most of the ancient republics, that the people had a right to active resolutions, such as acquire some execution, a thing of which they are absolutely incapable. They ought to have no share in the government but for the choosing of representatives, which is within their reach. For though few can tell the exact degree of men's capacities, yet there are none but are capable of knowing in general whether the person they choose is better qualified than most of his neighbors.

Neither ought the representative body to be chosen for the executive part of government, for which it is not so fit; but for the enacting of laws, or to see whether the laws in being are duly executed, a thing suited to their abilities, and which none indeed but themselves can properly perform.

In such a state there are always persons distinguished by their birth, riches, or honors: but were they to be confounded with the common people, and to have only the weight of a single vote like the rest, the common liberty would be their slavery, and they would have no interest in supporting it, as most of the popular resolutions would be against them. The share they have, therefore, in the legislature ought to be proportioned to their other advantages in the state; which happens only when they form a body that has a right to check the licentiousness of the people, as the people have a right to oppose any encroachment of theirs.

The legislative power is therefore committed to the body of the nobles, and to that which represents the people, each having their assemblies and deliberations apart, each their separate views and interests.

Of the three powers mentioned, the judiciary is in some measure next to nothing: there remain, therefore, only two; and as these have need of a regulating power to moderate them, the part of the legislative body composed of the nobility is extremely proper for this purpose.

The body of the nobility ought to be hereditary. In the first place it is so in its own nature; and in the next there must be a considerable interest to preserve its privileges -- privileges that in themselves are obnoxious to popular envy, and of course in a free state are always in danger.

But as a hereditary power might be tempted to pursue its own particular interests, and forget those of the people, it is proper that where a singular advantage may be gained by corrupting the nobility, as in the laws relating to the supplies, they should have no other share in the legislation than the power of rejecting, and not that of resolving.

By the power of resolving I mean the right of ordaining by their own authority, or of amending what has been ordained by others. By the power of rejecting I would be understood to mean the right of annulling a resolution taken by another; which was the power of the tribunes at Rome. And though the person possessed of the privilege of rejecting may likewise have the right of approving, yet this approbation passes for no more than a declaration, that he intends to make no use of his privilege of rejecting, and is derived from that very privilege.

The executive power ought to be in the hands of a monarch, because this branch of government, having need of despatch, is better administered by one than by many: on the other hand, whatever depends on the legislative power is oftentimes better regulated by many than by a single person.

* * * * * * * *

In perusing the admirable treatise of Tacitus "On the Manners of the Germans," we find it is from that nation the English have borrowed the idea of their political government. This beautiful system was invented first in the woods.

As all human things have an end, the state we are speaking of will lose its liberty, will perish. Have not Rome, Sparta, and Carthage perished? It will perish when the legislative power shall be more corrupt than the executive.

It is not my business to examine whether the English actually enjoy this liberty or not. Sufficient it is for my purpose to observe that it is established by their laws; and I inquire no further.

Jean-Jacques Rousseau

The Social Contract

The French thinker Jean-Jacques Rousseau (1712-1778) con-
tinued the tradition of the contract theorists, such as Thomas
Hobbes and John Locke. His solution, set forth in The Social
Contract *(1762), is that an ideal political society should emerge*
from the corporate will of the people. His most difficult task was
in reconciling his belief in individual freedom with his concept of
authority as expressed through the general will.

Man is born free; and everywhere he is in chains. One thinks
himself the master of others, and still remains a greater slave than
they. How did this change come about? I do not know. What
can make it legitimate? That question I think I can answer.

If I took into account only force, and the effects derived from
it, I should say: "As long as a people is compelled to obey, and
obeys, it does well; as soon as it can shake off the yoke, and
shakes it off, it does still better; for, regaining its liberty by the
same right as took it away, either it is justified in resuming it, or
there was no justification for those who took it away." But the
social order is a sacred right which is the basis of all other rights.
Nevertheless, this right does not come from nature, and must
therefore be founded on conventions. Before coming to that, I
have to prove what I have just asserted.

* * * * * * * *

The strongest is never strong enough to be always the master,
unless he transforms strength into right, and obedience into duty.
Hence the right of the strongest, which, though to all seeming
meant ironically, is really laid down as a fundamental principle.

Text: Jean-Jacques Rousseau, The Social Contract, *trans. by G.*
D. H. Cole (London: J. M. Dent, 1913), pp. 5-6, 8-9, 14-19, 22-
23, 90-94.

But are we never to have an explanation of this phrase? Force is a physical power, and I fail to see what moral effect it can have. To yield to force is an act of necessity, not of will -- at the most, an act of prudence. In what sense can it be a duty?

Suppose for a moment that this so-called "right" exists. I maintain that the sole result is a mass of inexplicable nonsense. For, if force creates right, the effect changes with the cause: every force that is greater than the first succeeds to its right. As soon as it is possible to disobey with impunity, disobedience is legitimate; and, the strongest being always in the right, the only thing that matters is to act so as to become the strongest. But what kind of right is that which perishes when force fails? If we must obey perforce, there is no need to obey because we ought; and if we are not forced to obey, we are under no obligation to do so. Clearly, the word "right" adds nothing to force: in this connection, it means absolutely nothing.

Obey the powers that be. If this means yield to force, it is a good precept, but superfluous: I can answer for its never being violated. All power comes from God, I admit; but so does all sickness: does that mean that we are forbidden to call in the doctor? A brigand surprises me at the edge of a wood: must I not merely surrender my purse on compulsion; but, even if I could withhold it, am I in conscience bound to give it up? For certainly the pistol he holds is also a power.

Let us then admit that force does not create right, and that we are obliged to obey only legitimate powers. In that case, my original question recurs.

* * * * * * * *

I suppose men to have reached the point at which the obstacles in the way of their preservation in the state of nature show their power of resistance to be greater than the resources at the disposal of each individual for his maintenance in that state. That primitive condition can then subsist no longer; and the human race would perish unless it changed its manner of existence.

But, as men cannot engender new forces, but only unite and direct existing ones, they have no other means of preserving themselves than the formulation, by aggregation, of a sum of forces great enough to overcome the resistance. These they have to bring into play by means of a single motive power, and cause to act in concert.

This sum of forces can arise only where several persons come together: but, as the force and liberty of each man are the chief instruments of his self-preservation, how can he pledge them without harming his own interests, and neglecting the care he owes to himself? This difficulty, in its bearing on my present subject, may be stated in the following terms:

"The problem is to find a form of association which will defend and protect with the whole common force the person and goods of each associate, and in which each, while uniting himself with all, may still obey himself alone, and remain as free as before." This is the fundamental problem of which the *Social Contract* provides the solution.

The clauses of this contract are so determined by the nature of the act that the slightest modification would make them vain and ineffective; so that, although they have perhaps never been formally set forth, they are everywhere the same and everywhere tacitly admitted and recognised, until, on the violation of the social compact, each regains his original rights and resumes his natural liberty, while losing the conventional liberty in favour of which he renounced it.

These clauses, properly understood, may be reduced to one -- the total alienation of each associate, together with all his rights, to the whole community; for, in the first place, as each gives himself absolutely, the conditions are the same for all; and, this being so, no one has any interest in making them burdensome to others.

Moreover, the alienation being without reserve, the union is as perfect as it can be, and no associate has anything more to demand: for, if the individuals retained certain rights, as there would be no common superior to decide between them and the public, each, being on one point his own judge, would ask to be so on all; the state of nature would thus continue, and the association would necessarily become inoperative or tyrannical.

Finally, each man, in giving himself to all, gives himself to nobody; and as there is no associate over whom he does not acquire the same right as he yields others over himself, he gains an equivalent for everything he loses, and an increase of force for the preservation of what he has.

If then we discard from the social compact what is not of its essence, we shall find that it reduces itself to the following terms: "Each of us puts his person and all his power in common under the supreme direction of the general will, and, in our corporate capacity, we receive each member as an indivisible part of the whole."

At once, in place of the individual personality of each contracting party, this act of association creates a moral and collective body, composed of as many members as the assembly contains votes, and receiving from this act its unity, its common identity, its life and its will. This public person, so formed by the union of all other persons, formerly took the name of *city*, and now takes that of *republic* or *body politic*; it is called by its members *State* when passive, *Sovereign* when active, and *Power* when compared with others like itself. Those who are associated in it take collectively the name of *people*, and severally are called *citizens*, as sharing in the sovereign power and *subjects* as being under the laws of the State. But these terms are often confused and taken one for another: it is enough to know how to distinguish them when they are being used with precision.

This formula shows us that the act of association comprises a mutual undertaking between the public and the individuals, and that each individual, in making a contract, as we may say, with himself, is bound in a double capacity; as a member of the Sovereign he is bound to the individuals; and as a member of the State to the Sovereign. But the maxim of civil right, that no one is bound by undertakings made to himself, does not apply in this case; for there is a great difference between incurring an obligation to yourself and incurring one to a whole of which you form a part.

Attention must further be called to the fact that public deliberation, while competent to bind all the subjects to the

Sovereign, because of the two different capacities in which each of them may be regarded, cannot, for the opposite reason, bind the Sovereign to itself; and that it is consequently against the nature of the body politic for the Sovereign to impose on itself a law which it cannot infringe. Being able to regard itself in only one capacity, it is in the position of an individual who makes a contract with himself; and this makes it clear that there neither is nor can be any kind of fundamental law binding on the body of the people -- not even the social contract itself. This does not mean that the body politic cannot enter into undertakings with others, provided the contract is not infringed by them; for in relation to what is external to it, it becomes a simple being, an individual.

But the body politic or the Sovereign, drawing its being wholly from the sanctity of the contract, can never bind itself, even to an outsider, to do anything derogatory to the original act, for instance, to alienate any part of itself, or to submit to another Sovereign. Violation of the act by which it exists would be self-annihilation; and that which is itself nothing can create nothing.

As soon as this multitude is so united in one body, it is impossible to offend against one of the members without attacking the body, and still more to offend against the body without the members resenting it. Duty and interest therefore equally oblige the two contracting parties to give each other help; and the same men should seek to combine, in their double capacity, all the advantages dependent upon that capacity.

Again, the Sovereign, being formed wholly of the individuals who compose it, neither has nor can have any interest contrary to theirs; and consequently the sovereign power need give no guarantee to its subjects, because it is impossible for the body to wish to hurt all its members. We shall also see later on that it cannot hurt any in particular. The Sovereign, merely by virtue of what it is, is always what it should be.

This, however, is not the case with the relation of the subjects to the Sovereign, which, despite the common interest, would have no security that they would fulfil their undertakings, unless it found means to assure itself of their fidelity.

In fact, each individual, as a man, may have a particular will contrary or dissimilar to the general will which he has as a citizen. His particular interest may speak to him quite differently from the common interest: his absolute and naturally independent existence may make him look upon what he owes to the common cause as a gratuitous contribution, the loss of which will do less harm to others than the payment of it is burdensome to himself; and, regarding the moral person which constitutes the State as a *persona ficta,* because not a man, he may wish to enjoy the rights of citizenship without being ready to fulfil the duties of a subject. The continuance of such an injustice could not but prove the undoing of the body politic.

In order then that the social compact may not be an empty formula, it tacitly includes the undertaking, which alone can give force to the rest, that whoever refuses to obey the general will shall be compelled to do so by the whole body. This means nothing less than that he will be forced to be free; for this is the condition which, by giving each citizen to his country, secures him against all personal dependence. In this lies the key to the working of the political machine; this alone legitimises civil undertakings, which, without it, would be absurd, tyrannical, and liable to the most frightful abuses.

The passage from the state of nature to the civil state produces a very remarkable change in man, by substituting justice for instinct in his conduct, and giving his actions the morality they had formerly lacked. Then only, when the voice of duty takes the place of physical impulses and right of appetite, does man, who so far had considered only himself, find that he is forced to act on different principles, and to consult his reason before listening to his inclinations. Although, in this state he deprives himself of some advantages which he got from nature, he gains in return others so great, his faculties are so stimulated and developed, his ideas so extended, his feelings so ennobled, and his whole soul so uplifted, that, did not the abuses of this new condition often degrade him below that which he left, he would be bound to bless continually the happy moment which took him from it for ever, and, instead of a stupid and unimaginative animal, made him an intelligent being and a man.

Let us draw up the whole account in terms easily commensurable. What man loses by the social contract is his natural liberty and an unlimited right to everything he tries to get and succeeds in getting; what he gains is civil liberty and the proprietorship of all he possesses. If we are to avoid mistake in weighing one against the other, we must clearly distinguish natural liberty, which is bounded only by the strength of the individual, from civil liberty, which is limited by the general will; and possession, which is merely the effect of force or the right of the first occupier, from property, which can be founded only on a positive title.

We might, over and above all this, add, to what man acquires in the civil state, moral liberty, which alone makes him truly master of himself; for the mere impulse of appetite is slavery, while obedience to a law which we prescribe to ourselves is liberty.

* * * * * * * *

The first and most important decision from the principles we have so far laid down is that the general will alone can direct the State according to the object for which it was instituted, i.e. the common good: for if the clashing of particular interests made the establishment of societies necessary, the agreement of these very interests made it possible. The common element in these different interests is what forms the social tie; and, were there no point of agreement between them all, no society could exist. It is solely on the basis of this common interest that every society should be governed.

I hold then that Sovereignty, being nothing less than the exercise of the general will, can never be alienated, and that the Sovereign, who is no less than a collective being, cannot be represented except by himself: the power indeed may be transmitted, but not the will.

In reality, if it is not impossible for a particular will to agree on some point with the general will, it is at least impossible for the agreement to be lasting and constant; for the particular will tends, by its very nature, to partiality, while the general will tends to equality. It is even more impossible to have any guarantee of this agreement; for even if it should always exist, it would be the effect not of art, but of chance. The Sovereign may indeed say: "I now will actually what this man wills, or at least what he says he wills"; but it cannot say: "What he wills tomorrow, I too shall will," because it is absurd for the will to bind itself for the future, nor is it incumbent on any will to consent to anything that is not for the good of the being who wills. If then the people promises simply to obey, by that very act it dissolves itself and loses what makes it a people; the moment a master exists, there is no longer a Sovereign, and from that moment the body politic has ceased to exist.

This does not mean that the commands of the rulers cannot pass for general wills, so long as the Sovereign, being free to oppose them, offers no opposition. In such a case, universal silence is taken to imply the consent of the people.

* * * * * * * *

As long as several men in assembly regard themselves as a single body, they have only a single will which is concerned with their common preservation and general well-being. In this case, all the springs of the State are vigorous and simple and its rules clear and luminous; there are no embroilments or conflicts of interests; the common good is everywhere clearly apparent, and only good sense is needed to perceive it. Peace, unity and equality are the enemies of political subtleties. Men who are upright and simple are difficult to deceive because of their simplicity; lures and ingenious pretexts fail to impose upon them, and they are not even subtle enough to be dupes. When, among the happiest people in the world, bands of peasants are seen regulating affairs of State under an oak, and always acting wisely, can we help scorning the ingenious methods of other nations, which make themselves illustrious and wretched with so much art and mystery?

A State so governed needs very few laws; and, as it becomes necessary to issue new ones, the necessity is universally seen. The first man to propose them merely says what all have already felt, and there is no question of factions or intrigues or eloquence in order to secure the passage into law of what every one has already decided to do, as soon as he is sure that the rest will act with him.

Theorists are led into error because, seeing only States that have been from the beginning wrongly constituted, they are struck by the impossibility of applying such a policy to them. They make great game of all the absurdities a clever rascal or an insinuating speaker might get the people of Paris or London to believe. They do not know that Cromwell would have been put to "the bells" by the people of Berne, and the Duc de Beaufort on the treadmill by the Genevese.

But when the social bond begins to be relaxed and the State to grow weak, when particular interests begin to make themselves felt and the smaller societies to exercise an influence over the larger, the common interest changes and finds opponents: opinion is no longer unanimous; the general will ceases to be the will of all; contradictory views and debates arise; and the best advice is not taken without question.

Finally, when the State, on the eve of ruin, maintains only a vain, illusory and formal existence, when in every heart the social bond is broken, and the meanest interest brazenly lays hold of the sacred name of "public good," the general will becomes mute: all men, guided by secret motives, no more give their views as citizens than if the State had never been; and iniquitous decrees directed solely to private interest get passed under the name of laws.

Does it follow from this that the general will is exterminated or corrupted? Not at all: it is always constant, unalterable and pure; but it is subordinated to other wills which encroach upon its sphere. Each man, in detaching his interest from the common interest, sees clearly that he cannot entirely separate them; but his share in the public mishaps seems to him negligible beside the exclusive good he aims at making his own. Apart from this particular good, he wills the general good in his own interest, as strongly as any one else. Even in selling his vote for money, he does not extinguish in himself the general will, but only eludes it

The fault he commits is that of changing the state of the question, and answering something different from what he is asked. Instead of saying, by his vote, "It is to the advantage of the State," he says, "It is of advantage to this or that man or party that this or that view should prevail." Thus the law of public order in assemblies is not so much to maintain in them the general will as to secure that the question be always put to it, and the answer always given by it.

I could here set down many reflections on the simple right of voting in every act of Sovereignty -- a right which no one can take from the citizens -- and also on the right of stating views, making proposals, dividing and discussing, which the government is always most careful to leave solely to its members; but this important subject would need a treatise to itself, and it is impossible to say everything in a single work.

It may be seen, from the last chapter, that the way in which general business is managed may give a clear enough indication of the actual state of morals and the health of the body politic. The more concert reigns in the assemblies, that is, the nearer opinion approaches unanimity, the greater is the dominance of the general will. On the other hand, long debates, dissensions and tumult proclaim the ascendancy of particular interests and the decline of the State.

This seems less clear when two or more orders enter into the constitution, as patricians and plebeians did at Rome; for quarrels between these two orders often disturbed the comitia, even in the best days of the Republic. But the exception is rather apparent than real; for then, through the defect that is inherent in the body politic, there were, so to speak, two States in one, and what is not true of the two together is true of either separately. Indeed, even in the most stormy times, the plebiscita of the people, when the Senate did not interfere with them, always went through quietly and by large majorities. The citizens having but one interest, the people had but a single will.

At the other extremity of the circle, unanimity recurs; this is the case when the citizens, having fallen into servitude, have lost both liberty and will. Fear and flattery then change votes into acclamation; deliberation ceases, and only worship or malediction is left. Such was the vile manner in which the senate expressed its views under the Emperors. It did so sometimes with absurd precautions Tacitus observes that, under Otho, the senators, while they heaped curses on Vitellius, contrived at the same time to make a deafening noise, in order that, should he ever become their master, he might not know what each of them had said.

On these various considerations depend the rules by which the methods of counting votes and comparing opinions should be regulated, according as the general will is more or less easy to discover, and the State more or less in its decline.

There is but one law which, from its nature, needs unanimous consent. This is the social compact; for civil association is the most voluntary of all acts. Every man being born free and his own master, no-one under any pretext whatsoever, can make any man subject without his consent. To decide that the son of a slave is born a slave is to decide that he is not born a man.

If then there are opponents when the social compact is made, their opposition does not invalidate the contract, but merely prevents them from being included in it. They are foreigners among citizens. When the State is instituted, residence constitutes consent; to dwell within its territory is to submit to the Sovereign.

Apart from this primitive contract, the vote of the majority always binds all the rest. This follows from the contract itself. But it is asked how a man can be both free and forced to conform to wills that are not his own. How are the opponents at once free and subject to laws they have not agreed to?

I retort that the question is wrongly put. The citizen gives his consent to all the laws, including those which are passed in spite of his opposition, and even those which punish him when he dares to break any of them. The constant will of all the members of the State is the general will; by virtue of it they are citizens and free. When in the popular assembly a law is proposed, what the people is asked is not exactly whether it approves or rejects the proposal, but whether it is in conformity with the general will, which is their will. Each man, in giving his vote, states his opinion on that point; and the general will is found by counting votes. When therefore the opinion that is contrary to my own prevails, this proves neither more nor less than that I was mistaken, and that what I thought to be the general will was not so. If my particular opinion had carried the day I should have achieved the opposite of what was my will; and it is in that case that I should not have been free.

This presupposes, indeed, that all the qualities of the general will still reside in the majority: when they cease to do so, whatever side a man may take, liberty is no longer possible.

In my earlier demonstration of how particular wills are substituted for the general will in public deliberation, I have adequately pointed out the practicable methods of avoiding this abuse; and I shall have more to say of them later on. I have also given the principles for determining the proportional number of votes for declaring that will. A difference of one vote destroys equality; a single opponent destroys unanimity; but between equality and unanimity, there are several grades of unequal division, at each of which this proportion may be fixed in accordance with the condition and the needs of the body politic.

There are two general rules that may serve to regulate this relation. First, the more grave and important the questions discussed, the nearer should the opinion that is to prevail approach unanimity. Secondly, the more the matter in hand calls for speed, the smaller the prescribed difference in the numbers of votes may be allowed to become: where an instant decision has to be reached, a majority of one vote should be enough. The first of these two rules seems more in harmony with the laws, and the second with practical affairs. In an case, it is the combination of them that gives the best proportions for etermining the majority necessary.

Adam Smith

The Wealth of Nations

Adam Smith (1723-1790) in his analysis of a country's economic well-being, rejected the traditional theory of mercantilism, which called for a favorable balance of trade through government regulation and state chartered monopolies. In The Wealth of Nations *(1776), Smith advocated free enterprise in trade and manufacturing, contending that government restrictions obstruct the natural laws that otherwise would regulate the economy. His arguments served as a basis of economic liberalism in the nineteenth century.*

That wealth consists in money, or in gold and silver, is a popular notion which naturally arises from the double function of money, as the instrument of commerce, and as the measure of value. In consequence of its being the instrument of commerce, when we have money we can more readily obtain whatever else we have occasion for, than by means of any other commodity. The great affair, we always find, is to get money. When that is obtained, there is no difficulty in making any subsequent purchase. In consequence of its being the measure of value, we estimate that of all other commodities by the quantity of money which they will exchange for. We say of a rich man that he is worth a great deal, and of a poor man that he is worth very little money. A frugal man, or a man eager to be rich, is said to love money; and a careless, a generous, or a profuse man, is said to be indifferent about it. To grow rich is to get money; and wealth and money, in short, are in common language considered as in every respect synonymous.

Text: Adam Smith, An Inquiry into the Nature and Causes of the Wealth of Nations. *(Oxford: Clarendon Press, 1880), I, pp. 90-91; II, pp. 1-2, 23-24, 28-29, 63, 68-69, 90-91, 272-273.*

A rich country, in the same manner as a rich man, is supposed to be a country abounding in money; and to heap up gold and silver in any country is supposed to be the readiest way to enrich it.

* * * * * * * *

Money in common language, as I have already observed, frequently signifies wealth; and this ambiguity of expression has rendered this popular notion so familiar to us, that even they who are convinced of its absurdity are very apt to forget their own principles, and in the course of their reasonings to take it for granted as a certain and undeniable truth.

Some of the best English writers upon commerce set out with observing, that the wealth of a country consists, not in its gold and silver only, but in its lands, houses, and consumable goods of all different kinds. In the course of their reasonings, however, the lands, houses, and consummable goods seem to slip out of their memory, and the strain of their argument frequently supposes that all wealth consists in gold and silver, and that to multiply those metals is the great object of national industry and commerce.

The two principles being established, however, that wealth consisted in gold and silver, and that those metals could be brought into a country which had no mines only by the balance of trade, or by exporting to a greater value than it imported, it necessarily became the great object of political economy to diminish as much as possible the importance of foreign goods for home consumption, and to increase as much as possible the exportation of the produce of domestic industry. Its two great engines for enriching the country, therefore, were restraints upon importation, and encouragements to exportation.

The restraints upon importation were of two kinds. First, restraints upon the importation of such foreign goods for home consumption as could be produced at home, from whatever country they were imported.

Secondly, restraints upon the importation of goods of almost all kinds from those particular countries with which the balance of trade was supposed to be disadvantageous.

Those different restraints consisted sometimes in high duties, and sometimes in absolute prohibitions.

Exportation was encouraged sometimes by drawbacks, sometimes by bounties, sometimes by advantageous treaties of commerce with sovereign states, and sometimes by the establishment of colonies in distant countries.

Drawbacks were given upon two different occasions. When the home manufactures were subject to any duty or excise, either the whole or a part of it was frequently drawn back upon their exportation; and when foreign goods liable to a duty were imported in order to be exported again, either the whole or a part of this duty was sometimes given back upon such exportations.

Bounties were given for the encouragement either of some beginning manufactures, or of such sorts of industry of other kinds as were supposed to deserve particular favour.

By advantageous treaties of commerce, particular privileges were procured in some foreign state for the goods and merchants of the country, beyond what were granted to those of other countries.

By the establishment of colonies in distant countries, not only particular privileges but a monopoly was frequently procured for the goods and merchants of the country which established them.

The two sorts of restraints upon importation above mentioned, together with these four encouragements to exportation, constitute the six principal means by which the commercial system proposes to increase the quantity of gold and silver in any country by turning the balance of trade in its favour.

* * * * * * * *

Nothing, however, can be more absurd than this whole doctrine of the balance of trade, upon which not only these restraints, but almost all the other regulations of commerce are founded. When two places trade with one another, this doctrine supposes that, if the balance be even, neither of them either loses or gains; but if it leans in any degree to one side, that one of them loses and the other gains in proportion to its declension from the exact equilibrium. Both suppositions are false. A trade which is forced by means of bounties and monopolies, may be and commonly is disadvantageous to the country in whose favour it is meant to be established, as I shall endeavour to show hereafter. But that trade which, without force or constraint, is naturally and regularly carried on between any two places, is always advantageous, though not always equally so, to both.

By advantage or gain, I understand not the increase of the quantity of gold and silver, but that of the exchangeable value of the annual produce of the land and labour of the country, or the increase of the annual revenue of its inhabitants.

* * * * * * * *

Each nation has been made to look with an invidious eye upon the prosperity of all the nations with which it trades, and to consider their gain as its own loss. Commerce, which ought naturally to be, among nations, as among individuals, a bond of union and friendship, has become the most fertile source of discord and animosity. The capricious ambition of kings and ministers has not, during the present and the preceding century, been more fatal to the repose of Europe than the impertinent jealousy of merchants and manufacturers. The violence and injustice of the rulers of mankind is an ancient evil, for which, I am afraid, the nature of human affairs can scarce admit of a remedy. But the mean rapacity, the monopolizing spirit of merchants and manufacturers, who neither are nor ought to be the rulers of mankind, though it cannot perhaps be corrected, may very easily be prevented from disturbing the tranquility of anybody but themselves.

That it was the spirit of monopoly which originally both invented and propagated this doctrine, cannot be doubted; and they who first taught it were by no means such fools as they who believed it. In every country it always is and must be the interest of the great body of the people to buy whatever they want of those who sell it cheapest. The proposition is so very manifest, that it seems ridiculous to take any pains to prove it; nor could it ever have been called in question, had not the interested sophistry of merchants and manufacturers confounded the common sense of mankind. Their interest is, in this respect, directly opposite to that of the great body of the people. As it is the interest of the freemen of a corporation to hinder the rest of the inhabitants from employing only workmen but themselves, so it is the interest of the merchants and manufacturers of every country to secure to themselves the monopoly of the home market. Hence in Great Britain, and in most other European countries, the extraordinary duties upon almost all goods imported by alien merchants. Hence the high duties and prohibitions upon all those foreign manufactures which can come into competition with our own. Hence too the extraordinary restraints upon the importation of almost all sorts of goods from those countries with which the balance of trade is supposed to be disadvantageous; that is, from those against whom national animosity happens to be most violently inflamed.

The wealth of a neighbouring nation, however, though dangerous in war and politics, is certainly advantageous in trade. In a state of hostility, it may enable our enemies to maintain fleets and armies superior to our own; but in a state of peace and commerce, it must likewise enable them to exchange with us to a greater value, and to afford a better market, either for the immediate produce of our own industry, or for whatever is purchased with that produce. As a rich man is likely to be a better customer to the industrious people in his neighbourhood than a poor, so is likewise a rich nation. A rich man, indeed, who is himself a manufacturer, is a very dangerous neighbour to all those who deal in the same way. All the rest of the neighbourhood, however, by far the greatest number, profit by the good market which his expense affords them. They even profit by his underselling the poorer workmen who deal in the same way with him. The manufacturers of a rich nation, in the same manner, may no doubt be very dangerous rivals to those of their neighbours. This very competition, however, is advantageous to the great body of the people, who profit greatly besides by the good market which the great expense of such a nation affords them in every other way.

* * * * * * * *

Every individual who employs his capital in the support of domestic industry, necessarily endeavours so to direct that industry, that its produce may be of the greatest possible value.

The produce of industry is what it adds to the subject or materials upon which it is employed. In proportion as the value of this produce is great or small, so will likewise be the profits of the employer. But it is only for the sake of profit that any man employs a capital in the support of industry; and he will always, therefore, endeavour to employ it in the support of that industry of which the produce is likely to be of the greatest value, or to exchange for the greatest quantity either of money or of other goods.

But the annual revenue of every society is always precisely equal to the exchangeable value of the whole annual produce of its industry, or rather is precisely the same thing with that exchangeable value. As every individual, therefore, endeavours as much as he can both to employ his capital in the support of domestic industry, and so to direct that industry that its produce may be of the greatest value, every individual necessarily labours to render the annual revenue of the society as great as he can. He generally, indeed, neither intends to promote the public interest, nor knows how much he is promoting it.

By preferring the support of domestic to that of foreign industry, he intends only his own security; and by directing that industry in such a manner as its produce may be of the greatest value, he intends only his own gain, and he is in this, as in many other cases, led by an invisible hand to promote an end which was no part of his intention. Nor is it always the worse for the society that it was no part of it. By pursuing his own interest he frequently promotes that of the society more effectually than when he really intends to promote it. I have never known much good done by those who affected to trade for the public good. It is an affectation, indeed, not very common among merchants, and very few words need be employed in dissuading them from it. What is the species of domestic industry which his capital can employ, and of which the produce is likely to be of the greatest value, every individual, it is evident, can, in his local situation, judge much better than any statesman or lawgiver can do for him. The statesman, who should attempt to direct private people in what manner they ought to employ their capitals, would not only load himself with a most unnecessary attention, but assume an authority which could safely be trusted, not only to no single person, but to no council or senate whatever, and which would nowhere be so dangerous as in the hands of a man who had folly and presumption enough to fancy himself fit to exercise it.

To give the monopoly of the home market to the produce of domestic industry, in any particular art or manufacture, is in some measure to direct private people in what manner they ought to employ their capital, and must, in almost all cases, be either a useless or a hurtful regulation.

* * * * * * * *

The money price of labour is necessarily regulated by two circumstances; the demand for labour, and the price of the necessaries and conveniences of life. The demand for labour, according as it happens to be increasing, stationary, or declining, or to require an increasing, stationary, or declining population, determines the quantity of the necessaries and conveniences of life which must be given to the labourer; and the money price of labour is determined by what is requisite for purchasing this quantity. Though the money price of labour, therefore, is sometimes high where the price of provisions is low, it would be still higher, the demand continuing the same, if the price of provisions was high.

It is because the demand for labour increases in years of sudden and extraordinary plenty, and diminishes in those of sudden and extraordinary scarcity, that the money price of labour sometimes rises in the one, and sinks in the other.

In a year of sudden and extraordinary plenty, there are funds in the hands of many of the employers of industry, sufficient to maintain and employ a greater number of industrious people than had been employed the year before; and this extraordinary number cannot always be had. Those masters, therefore, who want more workmen, bid against one another in order to get them, which sometimes raises both the real and the money price of their labour.

The contrary of this happens in a year of sudden and extra-ordinary scarcity. The funds destined for employing industry are less than they had been the year before. A considerable number of people are thrown out of employment, who bid against one another, in order to get it, which sometimes lowers both the real and the money price of labour. In 1740, a year of extraordinary scarcity, many people were willing to work for bare subsistence. In the succeeding years of plenty, it was more difficult to get labourers and servants.

The scarcity of a dear year, by diminishing the demand for labour, tends to lower its price, as the high price of provisions tends to raise it. The plenty of a cheap year, on the contrary, by increasing the demand, tends to raise the price of labour, as the cheapness of provisions tends to lower it. In the ordinary varia-tions of the price of provisions, those two opposite causes seem to counterbalance one another; which is probably in part the reason why the wages of labour are everywhere so much more steady and permanent than the price of provisions.

* * * * * * * *

All systems either of preference or of restraint, therefore, be-ing thus completely taken away, the obvious and simple system of natural liberty establishes itself of its own accord. Every man, as long as he does not violate the laws of justice, is left perfectly free to pursue his own interest his own way, and to bring both his industry and capital into competition with those of any other man, or order of men. The sovereign is completely discharged from duty, in the attempting to perform which he must always be exposed to innumerable delusions, and for the proper perform-ance of which no human wisdom or knowledge could ever be sufficient -- the duty of superintending the industry of private people, and of directing it towards the employments most suitable to the interest of the society.

According to the system of natural liberty, the sovereign has only three duties to attend to; three duties of great importance, indeed, but plain and intelligible to common understandings: first, the duty of protecting the society from the violence and passion of other independent societies; secondly, the duty of protecting, as far as possible, every member of the society from the injustice or oppression of every other member of it, or the duty of establishing an exact administration of justice; and, thirdly, the duty of erecting band maintaining certain public works and certain public institutions, which it can never be for the interest of any individual, or small number of individuals, to erect and maintain; because the profit could never repay the expense to any individual or small number of individuals, though it may frequently do much more than repay it to a great society.

Voltaire

Philosophical Dictionary

Francois Marie Arouet (1694-1778), who gained fame under his pen name, Voltaire, was one of the most prolific and outspoken writers of the 18th century Enlightenment. In his attacks on ignorance and superstition, prejudice and dogma, he extolled the principles of reason, toleration and freedom of thought. The following selections are drawn from entries in his multi-volume Philosophical Dictionary, *published in 1764 and later expanded.*

Atheism

We are intelligent beings, and intelligent beings cannot have been formed by a blind, brute, insensible being; there is certainly some difference between a clod and the ideas of Newton. Newton's intelligence, then, came from some other intelligence.

When we see a fine machine, we say there is a good machinist, and that he has an excellent understanding. The world is assuredly an admirable machine; therefore there is in the world, somewhere or other, an admirable intelligence. This argument is old, but is not therefore the worse.

All animated bodies are composed of levers and pulleys, which act according to the laws of mechanics; of liquors, which are kept in perpetual circulation by the laws of hydrostatics; and the reflection that all these beings have sentiment which has no relation to their organization, fills us with wonder.

The motions of the stars, that of our little earth round the sun -- all are operated according to the laws of the profoundest mathematics. How could it be that Plato, who knew not one of

Text: The Works of Voltaire: A Contemporary Version, *trans. William F. Fleming (New York: St. Hubert Guild, 1901), III, pp. 109-112; V, 215-216; VII, 102-107, 111-112.*

these laws -- the eloquent but chimerical Plato, who said that the foundation of the earth was an equilateral triangle, and that of water a right-angled triangle -- the strange Plato, who said there could be but five worlds, because there were but five regular bodies -- how, I say, was it that Plato, who was not even acquainted with spherical trigonometry, had nevertheless so fine a genius, so happy an instinct, as to call God the Eternal Geometrician -- to feel that there exists a forming Intelligence? Spinoza himself confesses it. It is impossible to controvert this truth, which surrounds us and presses us on all sides.

I have, however, known refractory individuals, who have said that there is no forming intelligence, and that motion alone has formed all that we see and all that we are. They say boldly that the combination of this universe was possible because it exists; therefore it was possible for motion of itself to arrange it. Take four planets only -- Mars, Venus, Mercury, and the Earth; let us consider them solely in the situations in which they now are; and let us see how many probabilities we have that motion will bring them again to those respective places. There are but twenty-four chances in this combination; that is, it is only twenty-four to one that these planets will not be found in the same situations with respect to one another. To these four globes add that of Jupiter; and it is then only a hundred and twenty to one that Jupiter, Mars, Venus, Mercury, and our globe will not be placed in the same positions in which we now see them.

Lastly, add Saturn; and there will then be only seven hundred and twenty chances to one against putting these planets in their present arrangement, according to their given distances. It is, then, demonstrated that once, at least, in seven hundred and twenty cases, chance might place these planets in their present order.

Then take all the secondary planets, all their motions, all the beings that vegetate, live, feel, think, act, on all these globes; you have only to increase the number of chances; multiply this number to all eternity -- to what our weakness calls infinity -- there will still be an unit in favor of the formation of the world, such as it is, by motion alone; therefore it is possible that, in all eternity, the motion of matter alone has produced the universe as it exists. Nay, this combination must, in eternity, of necessity happen. Thus, say they, not only it is possible that the world is as it is by motion alone, but it was impossible that it should not be so after infinite combinations.

All this supposition seems to me to be prodigiously chimerical, for two reasons: the first is, that in this universe there are intelligent beings, and you cannot prove it possible for motion alone to produce understanding. The second is, that, by your own confession, the chances are infinity to unity, that an intelligent forming cause produced the universe. Standing alone against infinity, a unit makes but a poor figure.

Again, Spinoza himself admits this intelligence; it is the basis of his system. You have not read him, but you must read him. Why would you go further than he, and, through a foolish pride, plunge into the abyss where Spinoza dared not to descend? Are you not aware of the extreme folly of saying that it is owing to a blind cause that the square of the revolution of one planet is always to the squares of the others as the cube of its distance is to the cubes of the distances of the others from the common centre? Either the planets are great geometricians, or the Eternal Geometrician has arranged the planets.

But where is the Eternal Geometrician? Is He in one place, or in all places, without occupying space? I know not. Has He arranged all things of His own substance? I know not. Is He immense, without quantity and without quality? I know not. All I know is, that we must adore Him and be just.

* * * * * * * *

God

My reason alone proves to me a being who has arranged the matter of the world; but my reason is unable to prove to me that he made this matter -- that he brought it out of nothing. All the sages of antiquity, without exception, believed matter to be eternal, and existing by itself. All then that I can do, without the aid of superior light, is to believe that the God of this world is also eternal, and existing by Himself. God and matter exist by the nature of things. May not other gods exist, as well as other worlds? Whole nations, and very enlightened schools, have clearly admitted two gods in this world -- one the source of good, the other the source of evil. They admitted an eternal war between two equal powers. Assuredly, nature can more easily suffer the existence of several independent beings in the immensity of space, than that of limited and powerless gods in this world, of whom one can do no good, and the other no harm.

If God and matter exist from all eternity, as antiquity believed, here then are two necessary beings; now, if there be two necessary beings, there may be thirty. These doubts alone, which are the germ of an infinity of reflections, serve at least to convince us of the feebleness of our understanding. We must, with Cicero, confess our ignorance of the nature of the Divinity; we shall never know any more of it than he did.

We feel that we are under the hand of an invisible being; this is all; we cannot advance one step farther. It is mad temerity to seek to divine what this being is -- whether he is extended or not, whether he is in one place or not, how he exists, or how he operates.

* * * * * * * *

Toleration

It is clear that every private individual who persecutes a man, his brother, because he is not of the same opinion, is a monster. This admits of no difficulty. But the government, the magistrates, the princes -- how do they conduct themselves towards those who have a faith different from their own? If they are powerful foreigners, it is certain that a prince will form an alliance with them. The Most Christian Francis I will league himself with the Mussulmans against the Most Catholic Charles V. Francis I will give money to the Lutherans in Germany, to support them in their rebellion against their emperor; but he will commence, as usual, by having the Lutherans in his own country burned. He pays them in Saxony from policy; he burns them in Paris from policy. But what follows? Persecutions make proselytes. France will soon be filled with new Protestants. At first they will submit to be hanged; afterwards they will hang in their turn. There will be civil wars; then Saint Bartholomew will come; and this corner of the world will be worse than all that the ancients and moderns have ever said of hell.

Blockheads, who have never been able to render a pure worship to the God who made you! Wretches, whom the example of the Noachides, the Chinese literati, the Parsees, and of all the wise, has not availed to guide! Monsters, who need superstitions, just as the gizzard of a raven needs carrion! We have already told you -- and we have nothing else to say -- if you have two religions among you, they will massacre each other; if you have thirty, they will live in peace. Look at the Grand Turk: he governs Guebers, Banians, Christians of the Greek Church, Nestorians, and Roman Catholics. The first who would excite a tumult is empaled; and all is tranquil.

Of all religions, the Christian ought doubtless to inspire the most toleration, although hitherto the Christians have been the most intolerant of all men. Jesus, having deigned to be born in poverty and lowliness like his brethren, never condescended to practise the art of writing. The Jews had a law written with the greatest minuteness, and we have not a single line from the hand of Jesus. The apostles were divided on many points. St. Peter and St. Barnabas ate forbidden meats with the new stranger Christians, and abstained from them with the Jewish Christians. St. Paul reproached them with this conduct; and this same St. Paul, the Pharisee, the disciple of the Pharisee Gamaliel -- this same St. Paul, who had persecuted the Christians with fury, and who after breaking with Gamaliel became a Christian himself -- nevertheless, went afterwards to sacrifice in the temple of Jerusalem, during his apostolic vacation. For eight days he observed publicly all the ceremonies of the Jewish law which he had renounced; he even added devotions and purifications which were superabundant; he completely Judaized. The greatest apostle of the Christians did, for eight days, the very things for which men are condemned to the stake among a large portion of Christian nations.

Theudas and Judas were called Messiahs, before Jesus: Dositheus, Simon, Menander, called themselves Messiahs, after Jesus. From the first century of the Church, and before even the name of Christian was known, there were a score of sects in Judaea.

The contemplative Gnostics, the Dositheans, the Cerintheins, existed before the disciples of Jesus had taken the name of Christians. There were soon thirty churches, each of which belonged to a different society; and by the close of the first century thirty sects of Christians might be reckoned in Asia Minor, in Syria, in Alexandria, and even in Rome.

All these sects, despised by the Roman government, and concealed in their obscurity, nevertheless persecuted each other in the hiding holes where they lurked; that is to say, they reproached one another. This is all they could do in their abject condition: they were almost wholly composed of the dregs of the people.

When at length some Christians had embraced the dogmas of Plato, and mingled a little philosophy with their religion, which they separated from the Jewish, they insensibly became more considerable, but were always divided into many sects, without there ever having been a time when the Christian church was reunited. It took its origin in the midst of the divisions of the Jews, the Samaritans, the Pharisees, the Sadducees, the Essenians, the Judaites, the disciples of John, and the Therapeutae. It was divided in its infancy; it was divided even amid the persecutions it sometimes endured under the first emperors. The martyr was often regarded by his brethren as an apostate; and the Carpocratian Christian expired under the sword of the Roman executioner, excommunicated by the Ebionite Christian, which Ebionite was anathematized by the Sabellian.

This horrible discord, lasting for so many centuries, is a very striking lesson that we ought mutually to forgive each other's errors: discord is the great evil of the human species, and toleration is its only remedy.

There is nobody who does not assent to this truth, whether meditating coolly in his closet, or examining the truth peaceably with his friends. Why, then, do the same men who in private admit charity, beneficence, and justice, oppose themselves in public so furiously against these virtues? Why? It is because their interest is their god; because they sacrifice all to that monster whom they adore.

I possess dignity and power, which ignorance and credulity have founded. I trample on the heads of men prostrated at my feet; if they should rise and look me in the face, I am lost; they must, therefore, be kept bound down to the earth with chains of iron.

Thus have men reasoned, whom ages of fanaticism have rendered powerful. They have other persons in power under them, and these latter again have underlings, who enrich themselves with the spoils of the poor man, fatten themselves with his blood, and laugh at his imbecility. They detest all toleration, as contractors enriched at the expense of the public are afraid to render their accounts, and as tyrants dread the name of liberty. To crown all, in short, they encourage fanatics who cry aloud: Respect the absurdities of my master; tremble, pay, and be silent.

Such was the practice for a long time in a great part of the world; but now, when so many sects are balanced by their power, what side must we take among them? Every sect, we know, is a mere title of error; while there is no sect of geometricians, of algebraists, of arithmeticians, because all the propositions of geometry, algebra, and arithmetic, are true. In all the other sciences, one may be mistaken.

* * * * * * * *

I would say to my brother the Turk: Let us eat together a good hen with rice, invoking Allah; your religion seems to me very respectable; you adore but one God; you are obliged to give the fortieth part of your revenue every day in alms, and to be reconciled with your enemies on the day of the Bairam. Our bigots, who calumniate the world, have said a hundred times, that your religion succeeded only because it was wholly sensual.

They have lied, poor fellows! Your religion is very austere; it commands prayer five times a day; it imposes the most rigorous fast; it denies you the wine and the liquors which our spiritual directors encourage; and if it permits only four wives to those who can support them -- which are very few -- it condemns by this restriction the Jewish incontinence, which allowed eighteen wives to the homicide David, and seven hundred, without reckoning concubines, to Solomon, the assassin of his brother.

I will say to my brother the Chinese: Let us sup together without ceremony, for I dislike grimaces; but I like your law, the wisest of all, and perhaps the most ancient. I will say nearly as much to my brother the Indian.

But what shall I say to my brother the Jew? Shall I invite him to supper. Yes, on condition that, during the repast, Balaam's ass does not take it into its head to bray; that Ezekiel does not mix his dinner with our supper; that a fish does not swallow up one of the guests, and keep him three days in his belly; that a serpent does not join in the conversation, in order to seduce my wife; that a prophet does not think proper to sleep with her, as the worthy man, Hosea, did for five francs and a bushel of barley; above all, that no Jew parades through my house to the sound of the trumpet, causes the walls to fall down, and cuts the throats of myself, my father, my mother, my wife, my children, my cat and my dog, according to the ancient practice of the Jews. Come, my friends, let us have peace, and say grace at our meal.

Marie Jean de Condorcet

The Progress of the Human Mind

Marie Jean Antoine Nicolas Caritat, Marquis de Condorcet (1743-1794), was by birth a member of the French aristocracy, and by inclination a scholar and social reformer. A capable mathematician, he served for several years as secretary of the Academy of Sciences. Like many European intellectuals of the Enlightenment, Condorcet anticipated an unprecedented future of happiness, peace, and prosperity, based on the exercise of reason. These sentiments of human perfectibility are admirably expressed in his essay, The Progress of the Human Mind, *which was published in 1795, a year after his death.*

Such is the object of the work I have undertaken, the result of which will be to show, from reasoning and from facts, that no bounds have been fixed to the improvement of the human faculties; that the perfectibility of man is absolutely indefinite; that the progress of this perfectibility, henceforth above the control of every power that would impede it, has no other limit than the duration of the globe upon which nature has placed us. The course of this progress may doubtless be more or less rapid, but it can never be retrograde; at least while the earth retains its situation in the system of the universe, and the laws of this system shall neither effect upon the globe a general overthrow, nor introduce such changes as would no longer permit the human race to preserve and exercise therein the same faculties, and find the same resources.

* * * * * * * *

Text: M. de Condorcet, Outlines of An Historical View of the Progress of the Human Mind *(London: J. Johnson, 1795), pp. 4-5, 316-319, 341-344, 366-368, and 370-371.*

If man can predict, almost with certainty, those appearances of which he understands the laws; if, even when the laws are unknown to him, experience of the past enables him to foresee, with considerable probability, future appearances; why should we suppose it a chimerical undertaking to delineate, with some degree of truth, the picture of the future destiny of mankind from the results of its history? The only foundation of faith in the natural sciences is the principle that the general laws, known or unknown, which regulate the phenomena of the universe, are regular and constant; and why should this principle, applicable to the other operations of nature, be less true when applied to the development of the intellectual and moral faculties of man? In short, as opinions formed from experience, relative to the same class of objects, are the only rule by which men of soundest understanding are governed in their conduct, why should the philosopher be proscribed from supporting his conjectures upon a similar basis, provided he attribute to them no greater certainty than the number, the consistency, and the accuracy of actual observations shall authorise?

Our hopes, as to the future condition of the human species, may be reduced to three points: the destruction of inequality between different nations; the progress of equality in one and the same nation; and lastly, the real improvement of man.

Will not every nation one day arrive at the state of civilization attained by those people who are most enlightened, most free, most exempt from prejudices, as the French, for instance, and the Anglo-Americans? Will not the slavery of countries subjected to kings, the barbarity of African tribes, and the ignorance of savages gradually vanish? Is there upon the face of the globe a single spot the inhabitants of which are condemned by nature never to enjoy liberty, never to exercise their reason?

Does the difference of knowledge, of means, and of wealth, observable hitherto in all civilized nations, between the classes into which the people constituting those nations are divided; does that inequality, which the earliest progress of society has augmented, or, to speak more properly, produced, belong to civilization itself or to the imperfections of the social order?

Must it not continually weaken, in order to give place to that actual equality, the chief end of the social art, which, diminishing even the effects of the natural difference of the faculties, leaves no other inequality subsisting but what is useful to the interest of all, because it will favour civilization, instruction, and industry, without drawing after it either dependence, humiliation, or poverty? In a word, will not men be continually verging towards that state, in which all will possess the requisite knowledge for conducting themselves in the common affairs of life by their own reason, and of maintaining that reason uncontaminated by prejudices; in which they will understand their rights, and exercise them according to their opinion and their conscience; in which all will be able, by the development of their faculties, to procure the certain means of providing for their wants; lastly, in which folly and wretchedness will be accidents, happening only now and then, and not the habitual lot of a considerable portion of society?

In fine, may it not be expected that the human race will be meliorated by new discoveries in the sciences and the arts, and, as an unavoidable consequence, in the means of individual and general prosperity; by farther progress in the principles of conduct, and in moral practice; and lastly, by the real improvement of our faculties, moral, intellectual, and physical, which may be the result either of the improvement of the instruments which increase the power and direct the exercise of those faculties, or of the improvement of our natural organization itself?

* * * * * * * *

By applying these general reflections to the different sciences, we might exhibit, respecting each, examples of this progressive improvement, which would remove all possibility of doubt as to the certainty of the further improvement that may be expected. We might indicate particularly in those which prejudice considers as nearest to being exhausted, the marks of an almost certain and early advance. We might illustrate the extent, the precision, the unity which must be added to the system comprehending all human knowledge, by a more general and philosophical application of the science of calculation to the individual branches of which that system is composed. We might show how favourable to our hopes a more universal instruction would prove, by which a greater number of individuals would acquire the elementary knowledge that might inspire them with a taste for a particular kind of study; and how much these hopes would be further heightened if this application to study were to be rendered still more extensive by a more general ease of circumstances. At present, in the most enlightened countries, scarcely do one in fifty of those whom nature has blessed with talents receive the necessary instruction for the development of them: how different would be the proportion in the case we are supposing? And, of consequence, how different the number of men destined to extend the horizon of the sciences?

We might show how much this equality of instruction, joined to the national equality we have supposed to take place, would accelerate those sciences, the advancement of which depends upon observations repeated in a greater number of instances, and extending over a larger portion of territory; how much benefit would be derived therefrom to mineralogy, botany, zoology, and the doctrine of meteors; in short, how infinite the difference between the feeble means hitherto enjoyed by these sciences, and which yet have led to useful and important truths, and the magnitude of those which man would then have it in his power to employ.

Lastly, we might prove that, from the advantage of being cultivated by a greater number of persons, even the progress of those sciences, in which discoveries are the fruit of individual meditation, would also be considerably advanced by means of minuter improvements, not requiring the strength of intellect necessary for inventions, but that present themselves to the reflection of the least profound understandings.

If we pass to the progress of the arts, those arts particularly the theory of which depends on these very same sciences, we shall find that it can have no inferior limits; that their processes are susceptible of the same improvement, the same simplifications, as the scientific methods; that instruments, machines, looms, will add every day to the capabilities and skill of man -- will augment at once the excellence and precision of his works, while they will diminish the time and labour necessary for executing them; and that then will disappear the obstacles that still oppose themselves to the progress in question, accidents which will be foreseen and prevented; and, lastly, the unhealthiness at present attendant upon certain operations, habits and climates.

A smaller portion of ground will then be made to produce a portion of provisions of higher value or greater utility; a greater quantity of enjoyment will be procured at a smaller expence of consumption; the same manufactured or artificial commodity will be produced at a smaller expence of raw materials, or will be stronger and more durable; every soil will be appropriated to productions which will satisfy a greater number of wants with the least labour, and taken in the smallest quantities. Thus the means of health and frugality will be increased, together with the instruments in the arts of production, of curing commodities' and manufacturing their produce, without demanding the sacrifice of one enjoyment by the consumer.

Thus, not only the same species of ground will nourish a greater number of individuals, but each individual, with a less quantity of labour, will labour more successfully, and be surrounded with greater conveniences.

* * * * * * * *

All the causes which contribute to the improvement of the human species, all the means we have enumerated that insure its progress, must, from their very nature, exercise an influence always active, and acquire an extent for ever increasing. The proofs of this have been exhibited, and from their development in the work itself they will derive additional force: accordingly we may already conclude, that the perfectibility of man is indefinite. Meanwhile we have hitherto considered him as possessing only the same natural faculties, as endowed with the same organization. How much greater would be the certainty, how much wider the compass of our hopes, could we prove that these natural faculties themselves, that this very organization, are also susceptible of melioration? And this is the last question we shall examine.

The organic perfectibility or deterioration of the classes of the vegetable, or species of the animal kingdom, may be regarded as one of the general laws of nature.

This law extends itself to the human race; and it cannot be doubted that the progress of the sanative art, that the use of more wholesome food and more comfortable habitations, that a mode of life which shall develop the physical powers by exercise, without at the same time impairing them be excess; in fine, that the destruction of the two most active causes of deterioration, penury and wretchedness on the one hand, and enormous wealth on the other, must necessarily tend to prolong the common duration of man's existence, and secure him a more constant health and a more robust constitution. It is manifest that the improvement of the practice of medicine, become more efficacious in consequence of the progress of reason and the social order, must in the end put a period to transmissible or contagious disorders, as well to those general maladies resulting from climate, ailments and the nature of certain occupations. Nor would it be difficult to prove that this hope might be extended to almost every other malady, of which it is probable we shall hereafter discover the most remote causes. Would it even be absurd to suppose this quality of melioration in the human species as susceptible of an indefinite advancement; to suppose that a period must one day arrive when death will be nothing more than the effect either of extraordinary accidents, or of the flow and gradual decay of the vital powers; and that the duration of the middle space, of the interval between the birth of man and this decay, will itself have no assignable limit?

Certainly man will not become immortal; but may not the distance between the moment in which he draws his first breath, and the common term, when, in the course of nature, without malady, without accident, he finds it impossible any longer to exist, be necessarily protracted?

* * * * * * * *

Lastly, may we not include in the same circle the intellectual and moral faculties? May not our parents, who transmit to us the advantages or defects of their conformation, and from whom we receive our features and shape, as well as our propensities to certain physical affections, transmit to us also that part of organization upon which intellect, strength of understanding, energy of soul or moral sensibility depend? Is it not probable that education, by improving these qualities, will at the same time have an influence upon, will modify and improve this organization itself? Analogy, an investigation of the human faculties, and even some facts, appear to authorise these conjectures, and thereby to enlarge the boundary of our hopes.

Such are the questions with which we shall terminate the last division of our work. And how admirably calculated in this view of the human race, emancipated from its chains, released alike from the dominion of chance, as well as from that of the enemies of its progress, and advancing with a firm and indeviate step in the paths of truth, to console the philosopher lamenting the errors, the flagrant acts of injustice, the crimes with which the earth is still polluted? It is the contemplation of this prospect that rewards him for all his efforts to assist the progress of reason and the establishment of liberty.

Frederick the Great

Essay on Forms of Government

Frederick the Great, who ruled Prussia from 1740 to 1786, was one of the most heralded of the 18th-century monarchs. Along with Catherine the Great of Russia and Joseph II of Austria, he upheld the principle of enlightened absolutism, based on the exercise of reason, justice, and benevolence. Though his actions did not always match his stated intentions, he quite explicitly expressed his views on the responsibilities of a monarch in his Essay on Forms of Government, *first published in 1781.*

I once more repeat, the sovereign represents the state; he and his people form but one body, which can only be happy as far as united by concord. The prince is to the nation he governs what the head is to the man; it is his duty to see, think, and act for the whole community, that he may procure it every advantage of which it is capable. If it be intended that a monarchical should excel a republican government, sentence is pronounced on the sovereign. He must be active, possess integrity, and collect his whole powers, that he may be able to run the career he has commenced. Here follow my ideas concerning his duties.

He ought to procure exact and circumstantial information of the strength and weakness of his country, as well relative to pecuniary resources as to population, finance, trade, laws, and the genius of the nation whom he is appointed to govern. If the laws are good they will be clear in their definitions; otherwise, chicanery will seek to elude their spirit to its advantage, and arbitrarily and irregularly determine on the fortunes of individuals. Lawsuits ought to be as short as possible, to prevent the

---

Text: Posthumous Works of Frederick II, King of Prussia, *trans. by Thomas Holcroft (London: G. G. J. and J. Robinson, 1809), V, pp. 15-18, 20-22, 23-25, 27-29, 31.*

ruin of the appellants, who consume in useless expenses what is justly and duly their right. This branch of government cannot be too carefully watched, that every possible barrier may be opposed to the avidity of judges and counsellors. Every person is kept within the limits of his duty, by occasional visits into the provinces. Whoever imagines himself to be injured will venture to make his complaints to the commission; and those who are found to be prevaricators ought to be severely punished. It is perhaps superfluous to add that the penalty ought never to exceed the crime; that violence never ought to supersede law; and that it were better the sovereign should be too merciful than too severe.

As every person who does not proceed on principle is inconsistent in his conduct, it is still more necessary that the magistrate who watches over the public good should act from a determinate system of politics, war, finance, commerce, and law. Thus, for example, a people of mild manners ought not to have severe laws, but such as are adapted to their character. The basis of such systems ought always to correspond to the greatest good society can receive. Their principles ought to be comformable to the situation of the country, to its ancient customs, if they are good, and to the genius of the nation.

As an instance, it is a known truth, in politics, that the most natural allies, and consequently the best, are those whose interests concur, and who are not such near neighbours as to be engaged in any contest respecting frontiers. It sometimes happens that strange accidents give place to extraordinary alliances. We have seen, in the present times, nations that had always been rivals, and even enemies, united under the same banners. But these are events that rarely take birth, and which never can serve as examples. Such connections can be no more than momentary; whereas the other kind, which are contracted from a unity of interests, are alone capable of exertion. In the present situation of Europe, when all her princes are armed, and among whom predominant powers rise up capable of crushing the feeble, prudence requires alliances should be formed with other powers, as well to secure aid, in case of attack, as to repress the dangerous projects of enemies, and to sustain all just pretensions, by the succour of such allies, in opposition to those by whom they are controverted.

Nor is this sufficient. It is necessary to have among our neighbours, especially among our enemies, eyes and ears which shall be open to receive, and report with fidelity what they have seen and heard. Men are wicked. Care must especially be taken not to suffer surprise, because whatever surprises intimidates and terrifies, which never happens when preparations are made, however vexatious the event may be which there is reason to expect. European politics are so fallacious that the most sage may become dupes, if they are not always alert and on their guard.

The military system ought, in like manner, to rest on good principles, which from experience are known to be certain. The genius of the nation ought to be understood; of what it is capable, and how far its safety may be risked by leading it against the enemy. The warlike customs of the Greeks and Romans are interdicted in these ages. The discovery of gunpowder has entirely changed the mode of making war. A superiority of fire at present decides the day. Discipline, rules, and tactics have all been changed, in order that they may conform to this new custom; and the recent and enormous abuse of numerous trains of artillery, which incumber armies, obliges others, in like manner, to adopt this method; as well to maintain themselves in their posts as to attack the foe in those which they shall occupy, should reasons of importance so require.

* * * * * * * *

The number of troops which a state maintains ought to be in proportion to the troops maintained by its enemies. Their force should be equal, or the weakest is in danger of being oppressed. It perhaps may be objected that a king ought to depend on the aid of his allies. The reasoning would be good were allies what they ought to be; but their zeal is only lukewarm; and he who shall depend upon another as upon himself will most certainly be deceived. If frontiers permit them to be defended by fortress, there must be no neglect in building, nor any expense spared to bring them to perfection. Of this France has given an example, and she has found the advantage of it on different occasions.

But neither politics nor the army can prosper if the finances are not kept in the greatest order, and if the prince himself be not a prudent economist. Money is like the wand of the necromancer, for by its aid miracles are performed. Grand political views, the maintenance of the military, and the best conceived plans for the ease of the people will all remain in a lethargic state, if not animated by money. The economy of the sovereign is the more useful to the public good, because if he have not sufficient funds in reserve, either to supply the expenses of war, without loading his people with extraordinary taxes, or to succour citizens in times of public calamity, all these burdens will fall on the subject, who will be without the resource in such unhappy times, of which they will then stand in the most need.

No government can exist without taxation, which is equally necessary to the republic and to the monarchy. The sovereign who labours in the public cause must be paid by the public; the judge the same, that he may have no need to prevaricate. The soldier must be supported that he may commit no violence, for want of having whereon to subsist. In like manner, it is necessary that those persons who are employed in collecting the finances should receive such salaries as may not lay them under any temptation to rob the public. These various expenses demand very considerable sums, and to these must still be added money that should only be laid apart to serve for extraordinary exigencies. This money must all be necessarily levied on the people; and the grand art consists in levying so as not to oppress. That taxes may be equally and not arbitrarily laid on, surveys and registers should be made, by which, if the people are properly classed, the money will be proportionate to the income of the persons paying.

This is a thing so necessary that it would be an unpardonable fault, in finance, if ill-imposed taxes should disgust the husbandman with his labours. Having performed his duties, it is afterward necessary he and his family should live in a certain degree of ease. Far from oppressing the nursing fathers of the state, they ought to be encouraged in the cultivation of the lands, for in this cultivation the true riches of a country consist.

* * * * * * * *

Excise is another species of taxes, levied on cities, and this must be managed by able persons; otherwise, those provisions which are most necessary to life, such as bread, small beer, meat, etc., will be overloaded; and the weight will fall on the soldier, the labourer, and the artisan. The result will be, unhappily to the people, that the price of labour will be raised; consequently merchandise will become so dear as not to be saleable in foreign markets. Such is at present the case in Holland and in England. These two nations, having contracted immensely heavy debts in the last wars, have imposed new taxes to pay the interest; but, having very unadvisedly taxed labour, they have almost ruined their manufacture. Hence, all things having become dearer in Holland the Dutch are obliged to purchase their cloths from Verviers and Liege; and England has lost a very considerable sale of her woollens in Germany. To obviate such inconveniences, the sovereign ought frequently to remember the condition of the poor. . . .

* * * * * * * *

In most of the kingdoms of Europe there are provinces in which the peasants are attached to the soil, or are serfs to their lords. This, of all conditions, is the most unhappy, and that at which humanity most revolts. No man certainly was born to be the slave of his equal. We reasonably detest such an abuse; and it is supposed that nothing more than will is wanting to abolish so barbarous a custom. But this is not true; it is held on ancient tenures, and contracts made between the landholders and the colonists. Tillage is regulated according to the service performed by the peasantry; and whoever should suddenly desire to abolish this abominable administration would entirely overthrow the mode of managing estates and must be obliged, in part, to indemnify the nobility for the losses which their rents must suffer.

The state of manufactures and of trade . . . next presents itself. For the country to be preserved in prosperity, it is indubitably necessary that the balance of trade should be in its favour. If it pay more for importation than it gains by exportation, the result will be that it will be annually impoverished.

* * * * * * * *

Three things are to be considered in respect to commerce: first the surplus of native products which are exported; next the products of foreign states, which enrich those by whom they are carried; and third foreign merchandise, which home consumption obliges the state to import. The trade of any kingdom must be regulated according to these three articles, for of these only is it susceptible, according to the nature of things. England, Holland, France, Spain and Portugal, have possessions in the two Indies, and more extensive resources for their merchant ships than other kingdoms. To profit by such advantages as we are in possession of, and to undertake nothing beyond our strength, is the advice of wisdom.

* * * * * * * *

We shall now speak of another article, which perhaps is equally interesting. There are few countries in which the people are all of one religious opinion; they often totally differ. . . . The question then is asked: Is it requisite that the people should all think alike, or may each one be allowed to think as he pleases? Gloomy politicians will tell us everybody ought to be of the same opinion, that there may be no division among the citizens. The priest will add whoever does not think like me is damned; and it is by no means proper that my king should be the king of the damned. The inevitable deduction is they must be destroyed in this world, that they may be the more prosperous in the next.

To this is answered that all the members of one society never thought alike . . . . Tolerance is itself so advantageous, to the people among whom it is established, that it constitutes the happiness of the state. As soon as there is that perfect freedom of opinion, the people are all at peace; whereas persecution has given birth to the most bloody civil wars, and such as have been the most inveterate and the most destructive. The least evil that results from persecution is to occasion the persecuted to emigrate. The population of France has suffered in certain provinces, and those provinces still are sensible of the revocation of the edict of Nantes.

Such are in general the duties imposed upon a prince, from which, in order that he may never depart, he ought often to re-collect he himself is but a man, like the least of his subjects. If he be the first general, the first minister of the realm, it is not that he should remain the shadow of authority, but that he should fulfil the duties of such titles. He is only the first servant of the state, who is obliged to act with probity and prudence and to remain as totally disinterested as if he were each moment liable to render an account of his administration to his fellow citizens.

* * * * * * * *

As the sovereign is properly the head of a family of citizens, the father of his people, he ought on all occasions to be the last refuge of the unfortunate; to be the parent of the orphan, and the husband of the widow; to have as much pity for the lowest wretch as for the greatest courtier, and to shed his benefactions over those who, deprived of all other aid, can only find succour in his benevolence.

Declaration of the Rights
of Man and Citizen

If any document epitomizes the ideals of the French Revolution, it is the Declaration of the Rights of Man and Citizen. *Passed by the revolutionary French National Assembly on August 26, 1789, it is in a sense a continuation of the ideas of Locke and Rousseau and other natural rights theorists. It also brings into focus (as does the American Constitution) the idea that liberty, equality, and fraternity are not to be determined by specific individuals, but by laws emerging from the people.*

The representatives of the French people, organized in National Assembly, considering that ignorance, forgetfulness or contempt of the rights of man are the sole causes of the public miseries and of the corruption of governments, have resolved to set forth in a solemn declaration the natural, inalienable, and sacred rights of man, in order that this declaration, being ever present to all the members of the social body, may unceasingly remind them of their rights and their duties: in order that the acts of the legislative power and those of the executive power may be each moment compared with the aim of every political institution and thereby may be more respected; and in order that the demands of the citizens, grounded henceforth upon simple and incontestable principles, may always take the direction of maintaining the constitution and the welfare of all.

In consequence, the National Assembly recognizes and declares, in the presence and under the auspices of the Supreme Being, the following rights of man and citizen.

1. Men are born and remain free and equal in rights. Social distinctions can be based only upon public utility.

Text: Frank Maloy Anderson, ed., The Constitutions and Other Select Documents Illustrative of the History of France, 1709-1901 *(Minneapolis: H. W. Wilson Company, 1904), pp. 58-60.*

2. The aim of every political association is the preservation of the natural and imprescriptible rights of man. These rights are liberty, property, security, and resistance to oppression.

3. The source of all sovereignty is essentially in the nation; no body, no individual can exercise authority that does not proceed from it in plain terms.

4. Liberty consists in the power to do anything that does not injure others; accordingly, the exercise of the natural rights of each man has for its only limits those that secure to the other members of society the enjoyment of these same rights. These limits can be determined only by law.

5. The law has the right to forbid only such actions as are injurious to society. Nothing can be forbidden that is not interdicted by the law and no one can be constrained to do that which it does not order.

6. Law is the expression of the general will. All citizens have the right to take part personally or by their representatives in its formation. It must be the same for all, whether it protects or punishes. All citizens being equal in its eyes, are equally eligible to all public dignities, places and employments, according to their capacities, and without other distinction than that of their virtues and their talents.

7. No man can be accused, arrested, or detained except in the cases determined by the law and according to the forms that it has prescribed. Those who procure, expedite, execute, or cause to be executed arbitrary orders ought to be punished: but every citizen summoned or seized in virtue of the law ought to render instant obedience; he makes himself guilty by resistance.

8. The law ought to establish only penalties that are strictly and obviously necessary and no one can be punished except in virtue of a law established and promulgated prior to the offence and legally applied.

9. Every man being presumed innocent until he has been pronounced guilty, if it is thought indispensable to arrest him, all severity that may not be necessary to secure his person ought to be strictly suppressed by law.

10. No one ought to be disturbed on account of his opinions,

even religious, provided their manifestation does not derange the public order established by law.

11. The free communication of ideas and opinions is one of the most precious of the rights of man; every citizen then can freely speak, write and print, subject to responsibility for the abuse of his freedom in the cases determined by law.

12. The guarantee of the rights of man and citizen requires a public force; this force then is instituted for the advantage of all and not for the personal benefit of those to whom it is entrusted.

13. For the maintenance of the public force and for the expenses of administration a general tax is indispensable; it ought to be equally apportioned among all the citizens according to their means.

14. All the citizens have the right to ascertain, by themselves or by their representatives, the necessity of the public tax, to consent to it freely, to follow the employment of it, and to determine the quota, the assessment, the collection, and the duration of it.

15. Society has the right to call for an account from every public agent of its administration.

16. Any society in which the guarantee of the rights is not secured or the separation of powers not determined has no constitution at all.

17. Property being a sacred and inviolable right, no one can be deprived of it unless a legally established public necessity evidently demands it, under the condition of a just and prior indemnity.

Edmund Burke

Reflections on the Revolution in France

Even though the English politician and publicist Edmund Burke (1729-1797) had sympathized with aspects of the American Revolution, he became deeply suspicious of the political upheaval in France. In 1790, he published his Reflections on the Revolution in France *to show his disapproval. Written in the form of a letter to a young Frenchman, it has become famous not only as a thoroughgoing attack on the revolution and the natural rights theory, but also as a statement setting forth the principles of modern conservative thought.*

Dear Sir:

You are pleased to call again, and with some earnestness, for my thoughts on the late proceedings in France. I will not give you reason to imagine that I think my sentiments of such value as to wish myself to be solicited about them. They are of too little consequence to be very anxiously either communicated or withheld. It was from attention to you, and to you only, that I hesitated at the time when you first desired to receive them. In the first letter I had the honor to write to you, and which at length I sent, I wrote neither for nor from any description of men; nor shall I in this. My errors, if any, are my own. My reputation alone is to answer for them.

You see, Sir, by the long letter I have transmitted to you, that, though I do most heartily wish that France may be animated by a spirit of rational liberty, and that I think you bound, in all

Text: Edmund Burke, The Works of the Right Honorable Edmund Burke *(Boston: Little, Brown and Company, 1899), III, pp. 235, 241-242, 274-275, 276-280, 310-312, 396-398, 562.*

honest policy, to provide a permanent body in which that spirit may reside, and an effectual organ by which it may act, it is my misfortune to entertain great doubts concerning several material points in your late transactions.

* * * * * * * *

When I see the spirit of liberty in action, I see a strong principle at work; and this, for a while, is all I can possibly know of it. The wild gas, the fixed air, is plainly broke loose: but we ought to suspend our judgment until the first effervescence is a little subsided, till the liquor is cleared, and until we see something deeper than the agitation of a troubled and frothy surface. I must be tolerably sure, before I venture publicly to congratulate men upon a blessing, that they have really received one. Flattery corrupts both the receiver and the giver; and adulation is not of more service to the people than to kings. I should therefore suspend my congratulations on the new liberty of France, until I was informed how it had been combined with government, with public force, with the discipline and obedience of armies, with the collection of an effective and well-distributed revenue, with morality and religion, with solidity and property, with peace and order, with civil and social manners. All these (in their way) are good things, too; and without them, liberty is not a benefit whilst it lasts, and is not likely to continue long. The effect of liberty to individuals is, that they may do what they please: we ought to see what it will please them to do, before we risk congratulations, which may be soon turned into complaints. Prudence would dictate this in the case of separate, insulated, private men. But liberty, when men act in bodies, is *power.* Considerate people, before they declare themselves, will observe the use which is made of *power* -- and particularly of so trying a thing as *new* power in *new* persons, of whose principles, tempers, and dispositions they have little or no experience, and in situations where those who appear the most stirring in the scene may possibly not be the real movers.

* * * * * * * *

You will observe that, from Magna Carta to the Declaration of Right, it has been the uniform policy of our Constitution to claim and assert our liberties as an entailed inheritance derived to us from our forefathers, and to be transmitted to our posterity -- as an estate specially belonging to the people of this kingdom, without any reference whatever to any other more general or prior right. By this means our Constitution preserves an unity in so great a diversity of its parts. We have an inheritable crown, an inheritable peerage, and a House of Commons and a people inheriting privileges, franchises, and liberties from a long line of ancestors.

This policy appears to me to be the result of profound reflection -- or rather the happy effect of following Nature, which is wisdom without reflection, and above it. A spirit of innovation is generally the result of a selfish temper and confined views. People will not look forward to posterity, who never look backward to their ancestors. Besides, the people of England well know that the idea of inheritance furnishes a sure principle of conservation, and a sure principle of transmission, without at all excluding a principle of improvement. It leaves acquisition free: but it secures what it acquires. Whatever advantages are obtained by a state proceeding on these maxims are locked fast as in a sort of family settlement, grasped as in a kind of mortmain forever. By a constitutional policy working after the pattern of Nature, we receive, we hold, we transmit our government and our privileges, in the same manner in which we enjoy and transmit our property and our lives. The institutions of policy, the goods of fortune, the gifts of Providence, are handed down to us, and from us, in the same course and order. Our political system is placed in a just correspondence and symmetry with the order of the world, and with the mode of existence decreed to a permanent body composed of transitory parts -- wherein, by the disposition of a stupendous wisdom, moulding together the great mysterious incorporation of the human race, the whole, at one time, is never old or middle-aged or young, but, in a condition of unchangeable constancy, moves on through the varied tenor of perpetual decay, fall, renovation, and progression. Thus, by preserving the method of Nature in the conduct of the state, in what we improve we are never wholly new, in what we retain we are never wholly obsolete. By adhering in this manner and on those principles to our forefathers, we are guided, not by the superstition of antiquarians, but by the spirit of philosophic analogy. In this choice of inheritance we have given to our frame of polity the image of a relation in blood: binding up the Constitution of our country with our dearest domestic ties; adopting our fundamental laws into the bosom of our family affections; keeping inseparable, and cherishing with the warmth of all their combined and mutually reflected charities, our state, our hearths, our sepulchres, and our altars.

* * * * * * * *

You might, if you pleased, have profited of our example, and have given to your recovered freedom a correspondent dignity. Your privileges, though discontinued, were not lost to memory. Your Constitution, it is true, whilst you were out of possession, suffered waste and dilapidation; but you possessed in some parts the walls, and in all the foundations, of a noble and venerable castle. You might have repaired those walls; you might have built on those old foundations. Your Constitution was suspended before it was perfected; but you had the elements of a Constitution very nearly as good as could be wished. In your old estates you possessed that variety of parts corresponding with the various descriptions of which your community was happily composed; you had all that combination and all that opposition of interests, you had that action and counteraction, which, in the natural and in the political world, from the reciprocal struggle of discordant powers draws out the harmony of the universe. These opposed and conflicting interests, which you considered as so great a blemish in your old and in our present Constitution, interpose a salutary check to all precipitate resolutions. They render deliberation a matter, not of choice, but of necessity; they make all change a subject of compromise, which naturally begets moderation; they produce temperaments, preventing the sore evil of harsh, crude, unqualified reformations, and rendering all the headlong exertions of arbitrary power, in the few or in the many, forever impracticable. Through that diversity of members and interests, general liberty had as many securities as there were separate views in the several orders; whilst by pressing down the whole by the weight of a real monarchy, the separate parts would have been prevented from warping and starting from their allotted places.

You had all these advantages in your ancient estates; but you chose to act as if you had never been moulded into civil society, and had everything to begin anew. You began ill, because you began by despising everything that belonged to you. You set up your trade without a capital. If the last generations of your country appeared without much lustre in your eyes, you might have passed them by, and derived your claims from a more early race of ancestors. Under a pious predilection for those ancestors, your imaginations would have realized in them a standard of virtue and wisdom beyond the vulgar practice of the hour; and you would have risen with the example to whose imitation you aspired. Respecting your forefathers, you would have been taught to respect yourselves. You would not have chosen to consider the French as a people of yesterday, as a nation of low-born, servile wretches until the emancipating year of 1789. In order to furnish, at the expense of your honor, an excuse to your apologists here for several enormities of yours, you would not have been content to be represented as a gang of Maroon slaves, suddenly broke loose from the house of bondage, and therefore to be pardoned for your abuse of the liberty to which you were not accustomed, and were ill fitted.

Would it not, my worthy friend, have been wiser to have you thought, what I for one always thought you, a generous and gal-lant nation, long misled to your disadvantage by your high and romantic sentiments of fidelity, honor, and loyalty; that events had been unfavorable to you, but that you were not enslaved through any illiberal or servile disposition; that, in your most devoted submission, you were actuated by a principle of public spirit; and that it was your country you worshipped, in the person of your king? Had you made it to be understood, that, in the delusion of this amiable error, you had gone further than your wise ancestors -- that you were resolved to resume your ancient privileges, whilst you preserved the spirit of your ancient and your recent loyalty and honor; or if, diffident of yourselves, and not clearly discerning the almost obliterated Constitution of your ancestors, you had looked to your neighbours in this land, who had kept alive the ancient principles and models of the old common law of Europe, meliorated and adapted to its present state -- by following wise examples you would have given new examples of wisdom to the world. You would have rendered the cause of liberty vulnerable in the eyes of every worthy mind in every nation. You would have shamed despotism from the earth, by showing that freedom was not only reconcilable, but, as, when well disciplined, it is, auxiliary to law. You would have had an unoppressive, but a productive revenue. You would have had a flourishing commerce to feed it. You would have had a free Constitution, a potent monarchy, a disciplined army, a reformed and venerated clergy -- a mitigated, but spirited nobility, to lead your virtue, not to overlay it; you would have had a liberal order of commons, to emulate and to recruit that nobility; you would have had a protected, satisfied, laborious, and obedient people, taught to seek and to recognize the happiness that is to be found by virtue in all conditions -- in which consists the true moral equality of mankind, and not in that monstrous fiction which, by inspiring false ideas and vain expectations into men destined to travel in the obscure walk of laborious life, serves only to aggravate and embitter that real inequality which it never can remove, and which the order of civil life establishes as much for the benefit of those whom it must leave in an humble state as those whom it is able to exalt to a condition more splendid, but not more happy. You had a smooth and easy career of felicity and glory laid open to you, beyond anything recorded in the history of the world; but you have shown that difficulty is good for man.

Compute your gains; see what is got by those extravagant and presumptuous speculations which have taught your leaders to despise all their predecessors, and all their contemporaries, and even to despise themselves, until the moment in which they became truly despicable.

* * * * * * * *

Government is not made in virtue of natural rights, which may and do exist in total independence of it -- and exist in much greater clearness, and in a much greater degree of abstract perfection: but their abstract perfection is their practical defect. By having a right to everything they want everything. Government is a contrivance of human wisdom to provide for human wants. Men have a right that these wants should be provided for by this wisdom. Among these wants is to be reckoned the want, out of civil society, of a sufficient restraint upon their passions. Society requires not only that the passions of individuals should be subjected, but that even in the mass and body, as well as in the individuals, the inclinations of men should frequently be thwarted, their will controlled, and their passions brought into subjection. This can only be done by a power out of themselves, and not, in the exercise of its function, subject to that will and to those passions which it is its office to bridle and subdue. In this sense the restraints on men, as well as their liberties, are to be reckoned among their rights. But as the liberties and the restrictions vary with times and circumstances, and admit of infinite modifications, they cannot be settled upon any abstract rule; and nothing is so foolish as to discuss them upon that principle.

The moment you abate anything from the full rights of men each to govern himself, and suffer any artificial, positive limitation upon those rights, from that moment the whole organization of government becomes a consideration of convenience. This it is which makes the constitution of a state, and the due distribution of its powers, a matter of the most delicate and complicated skill. It requires a deep knowledge of human nature and human necessities, and of the things which facilitate or obstruct the various ends which are to be pursued by the mechanism of civil institutions. The state is to have recruits to its strength and remedies to its distempers. What is the use of discussing a man's abstract right to food or medicine? The question is upon the method of procuring and administering them. In that deliberation I shall always advise to call in the aid of the farmer and the physician, rather than the professor of metaphysics.

The science of constructing a commonwealth, or renovating it, or reforming it, is, like every other experimental science, not to be taught a priori. Nor is it a short experience that can instruct us in that practical science; because the real effects of moral causes are not always immediate, but that which in the first instance is prejudicial may be excellent in its remoter operation, and its excellence may arise even from the ill effects it produces in the beginning. The reverse also happens; and very plausible schemes, with very pleasing commencements, have often shameful and lamentable conclusions. In states there are often some obscure and almost latent causes, things which appear at first view of little moment, on which a very great part of its prosperity or adversity may most essentially depend. The science of government being, therefore, so practical in itself, and intended for such practical purposes, a matter which requires experience, and even more experience than any person can gain in his whole life, however sagacious and observing he may be, it is with infinite caution that any man ought to venture upon pulling down an edifice which has answered in any tolerable degree for ages the common purposes of society, or on building it up again without having models and patterns of approved utility before his eyes.

* * * * * * * *

I do not know under what description to class the present ruling authority in France. It affects to be a pure democracy, though I think it in a direct train of becoming shortly a mischievous and ignoble oligarchy. But for the present I admit it to be a contrivance of the nature and effect of what it pretends to. I reprobate no form of government merely upon abstract principles. There may be situations in which the purely democratic form will become necessary. There may be some (very few, and very particularly circumstanced) where it would be clearly desirable. This I do not take to be the case of France, or of any other great country. Until now, we have seen no examples of considerable democracies. The ancients were better acquainted with them. Not being wholly unread in the authors who had seen the most of those constitutions, and who best understood them, I

cannot help concurring with their opinion, that an absolute democracy no more than absolute monarchy is to be reckoned
among the legitimate forms of government. They think it rather
the corruption and degeneracy than the sound constitution of a
republic. If I recollect rightly, Aristotle observes, that a democracy has many striking points of resemblance with a tyranny. Of
this I am certain, that in a democracy the majority of the citizens
is capable of exercising the most cruel oppressions upon the minority, whenever strong divisions prevail in that kind of polity, as
they often must -- and that oppression of the minority will extend
to far greater numbers, and will be carried on with much greater
fury, than can almost ever be apprehended from the dominion of
a single sceptre. In such a popular persecution, individual sufferers are in a much more deplorable condition than in any other.
Under a cruel prince they have the balmy compassion of mankind
to assuage the smart of their wounds, they have the plaudits of
the people to animate their generous constancy under their sufferings: but those who are subjected to wrong under multitudes
are deprived of all external consolation; they seem deserted by
mankind, overpowered by a conspiracy of their whole species.

* * * * * * * *

I have told you candidly my sentiments. I think they are not
likely to alter yours. I do not know that they ought. You are
young; you cannot guide, but must follow, the fortune of your
country. But hereafter they may be of some use to you, in some
future form which your commonwealth may take. In the present
it can hardly remain; but before its final settlement, it may be
obliged to pass, as one of our poets says, "through great varieties
of untried being," and in all its transmigrations to be purified by
fire and blood.

Napoleon Bonaparte

Journal

Napoleon Bonaparte (1769-1821) was one of the most dynamic leaders in modern history. However, his overweening ambition and his desire to spread the ideas of the French Revolution throughout Europe brought him into conflict with the other Great Powers, which eventually defeated his armies and had him exiled to the island of St. Helena in 1815. Before his death there, he dictated his recollections to Count de las Cases and others, thus perpetuating "the Napoleonic legend." The following excerpts are from 1816.

April 9th-10th. On the 9th a ship arrived from England, bringing papers to the 21st of January. The Emperor continued his morning rides on horseback, and passed the rest of the day in examining the newspapers in his own chamber. The contents of these late papers were no less interesting than those which we had already examined. The agitation in France continued to increase; the King of Prussia had issued proclamations respecting secret societies; a misunderstanding had arisen between Austria and Bavaria; in England the persecution of the French Protestants, and the violence of the party which was gaining the ascendency, agitated the public mind, and gave arms to the opposition. Europe never presented a more violent fermentation.

On hearing of the deluge of evils and sanguinary events which overwhelmed all the French departments, the Emperor rose from his couch, and stamping his foot violently on the ground, he exclaimed, "How unfortunate was I in not proceeding to America!

Text: Count de las Cases, Journal of the Private Life and Conversations of the Emperor Napoleon *(New York: E. Bliss and E. White, 1823), II, pt. III, pp. 20-21, 102-103; III, pt. IV, pp. 57, 62-64.*

From the other hemisphere I might have protected France against reaction! The dread of my reappearance would have been a check on their violence and folly. My name would have sufficed to bridle their excess, and to fill them with terror!"

Then continuing the same subject, he said with a degree of warmth, bordering on inspiration, "The counter-revolution even had it been suffered to proceed, must inevitably have been lost in the grand revolution. The atmosphere of modern ideas is sufficient to stifle the old feudalists; for hence-forth nothing can destroy or efface the grand principles of our revolution. Those great and excellent truths can never cease to exist, so completely are they blended with our fame, our monuments, and our prodigies. We have washed away their first stains in the flood of glory, and they will henceforth be immortal! Created in the French tribune, cemented with the blood of battles, adorned with the laurels of victory, saluted with the acclamations of the people, sanctioned by the treaties and alliances of Sovereigns, and having become familiar to the ears as well as in the mouths of Kings, these principles can never again retrograde!"

"Liberal ideas flourish in Great Britain, they enlighten America, and they are nationalized in France; and this may be called the tripod whence issues the light of the world! Liberal opinions will rule the universe. They will become the faith, the religion, the morality of all nations; and in spite of all that may be advanced to the contrary, this memorable era will be inseparably connected with my name; for, after all, it cannot be denied that I kindled the torch and consecrated the principle, and now persecution renders me the Messiah. Friends and enemies, all must acknowledge me to be the first soldier, the grand representative of the age. Thus I shall for ever remain the leading star."

* * * * * * * *

May 1st. The Emperor kept his room today as he had done yesterday. I felt ill from the fatigue of my ride from the Briars; I had a slight degree of fever, accompanied by great lassitude. The Emperor sent for me about 7 o'clock in the evening. I went to his chamber, and found him reading Rollin, whom he accused, as usual, of being too indulgent a historian. He did not appear to have been indisposed, and even said he was very well; but this only rendered me the more uneasy at his seclusion and his calmness of manner. He put off dinner to a later hour than usual, and detained me with him. He called for a glass of Constancia some time before dinner; this he generally does when he feels the want of excitation.

After dinner he looked over a few of the addresses, proclamations, or acts in Goldsmith's imperfect collection. The perusal of some of these documents seemed to interest him; then laying down the book, he began to walk about, and said, "After all, let them abridge, suppress, and mutilate as much as they please, they will find it very difficult to throw me entirely into the shade. The historian of France cannot pass over the Empire, and, if he have any honesty, he will not fail to render me my share of justice. His task will be easy; for the facts speak of themselves; they shine like the sun."

"I closed the gulf of anarchy and cleared the chaos. I purified the Revolution, dignified Nations, and established Kings. I excited every kind of emulation, rewarded every kind of merit, and extended the limits of glory! This is at least something! And on what point can I be assailed on which a historian could not defend me? Can it be for my intentions? But even here I can find absolution. Can it be for my despotism? It may be demonstrated that the Dictatorship was absolutely necessary. Will it be said that I restrained liberty? It can be proved that licentiousness, anarchy, and the greatest irregularities, still haunted the threshold of freedom. Shall I be accused of having been too fond of war? It can be shown that I always received the first attack. Will it be said that I aimed at universal monarchy? It can be proved that this was merely the result of fortuitous circumstances, and that our enemies themselves led me step by step to this determination. Lastly, shall I be blamed for my ambition? This passion I must doubtless be allowed to have possessed, and that in no small degree; but, at the same time, my ambition was of the highest and noblest kind that ever, perhaps, existed -- that of establishing and of consecrating the Empire of reason, and the full exercise and complete enjoyment of all the human faculties! And here the historian will probably feel compelled to regret that such ambition should not have been fulfilled and gratified!" Then, after a few moments of silent reflection: "This," said the Emperor, "is my whole history in a few words."

* * * * * * * *

September 8th. The Emperor some time ago analyzed to us a subject which he said he intended to dictate in fourteen chapters, and which had forcibly struck me by its truth, its force, its just reasoning, and its dignity. I frequently alluded to it, when I happened to be alone with him; and he laughed more than once at the perseverance I evinced, which, he said, was not usual with me. Today he informed me that he had at length produced something, though not in fourteen chapters, nor on the promised subject; but that I must be content with it. I have read it; and it is certainly a very remarkable fragment. I do not believe that the revolution has produced any thing more comprehensive and energetic on the governments of the last twenty-five years in France, namely, the Republic, the Consulate, and the Empire.

The French Revolution was not produced by the jarring interests of two families disputing the possession of the throne; it was a general rising of the mass of the nation against the privileged classes. The French nobility, like that of every country in Europe, dates its origin from the incursion of the barbarians, who divided among themselves the possession of the Roman Empire. In France the nobles represented the Franks and the Burgundians, and the rest of the nation the Gauls. The feudal system that was introduced established the principle that all land should have a lord.

All political privileges were exercised by the priests and nobles; the peasants were slaves, and in part attached to the glebe. The progress of civilization and knowledge emancipated the people. This new state of things promoted industry and trade. The chief portion of the land, wealth, and information, fell to the share of the people in the eighteenth century. The nobles, however, still continued to be a privileged class: they were empowered to administer justice, and they possessed feudal rights under various denominations and forms: they were exempt from contributing to support any of the burthens of the state, and enjoyed exclusive possession of the most honourable posts.

These abuses roused the indignation of the citizens. The principal object of the revolution was to destroy all privileges; to abolish signiorial jurisdictions, justice being an inseparable attribute of sovereign authority; to suppress feudal rights, as being a remnant of the old slavery of the people; to oblige all citizens and all property, equally and without distinction, to contribute to maintain the burthens of the state. In short, the Revolution proclaimed equality of rights. A citizen might attain any public employment, according to his talent and the chances of fortune. The kingdom was composed of provinces which had been united to the crown at various periods; they had no natural limits, and were differently divided, unequal in extent and in population. They possessed many laws of their own, civil as well as criminal; they were more or less privileged and very unequally taxed, both with respect to the amount and the nature of the contributions, which rendered it necessary to detach them from each other by lines of customhouses.

France was not a state, but a combination of several states, connected together without amalgamation. The whole had been determined by chance and by the events of past ages. The Revolution, guided by the principle of equality both with respect to the citizens and the different portions of the territory, destroyed all these small nations: there was no longer a Brittany, a Normandy, a Burgundy, a Champaign, a Provence, or a Lorraine; but the whole formed a France. A division of homogeneous territory, prescribed by local circumstances, confounded the limits of all the provinces. They possessed the same judiciary and administrative organization, the same civil and criminal laws, and the same system of taxation. The dreams of the upright men of all ages were realized. The opposition which the court, the clergy, and the nobility, set up against the Revolution, occasioned the war of foreign powers, and produced the law of emigration and the sequestration of emigrant property, which subsequently it was found necessary to sell, to assist in supporting the charges of the war. A great portion of the French nobility enrolled themselves under the banner of the princes of the Bourbon family, and formed an army which marched in junction with the Austrian, Prussian, and English forces. Gentlemen who had been brought up in the enjoyment of competency served as private soldiers: numbers were cut off by fatigue and the sword; others perished of want in foreign countries; and the wars of La Vendee and of the Chouans, and the revolutionary tribunals, swept away thousands. Three-fourths of the French nobility were thus destroyed; and all posts, civil, judicial, or military, were filled by citizens who had risen from the common mass of the people. The change produced in persons and property, by the events of the Revolution, was no less remarkable than that which was effected by the principles of the Revolution. A new church was created; the dioceses of Vienna, Narbonne, Frejus, Sisteron, Rheims, etc. were superseded by sixty new dioceses, the boundaries of which were circumscribed, in the Concordate, by new Bulls applicable to the present state of the French territory. The suppression of religious orders, the sale of convents and of all ecclesiastical property, were sanctioned, and the clergy were pensioned by the state. Every thing that was the result of the events which had succeeded since the time of Clovis, ceased to exist.

All these changes were so advantageous to the people, that they were effected with the utmost facility, and in 1800, there no longer remained any recollection of the old privileges and sovereigns of the provinces, the old parliaments and bailiwicks, or the old dioceses; and to trace back the origin of all that existed, it was sufficient to refer to the new law by which it had been established. One half of the land had changed its proprietors; the peasantry and the citizens were enriched. The advancement of agriculture and manufactures exceeded the most sanguine hopes. France presented the imposing spectacle of upwards of thirty millions of inhabitants, circumscribed within their natural limits, and composing only a single class of citizens, governed by one law, one rule, and one order. All these changes were conformable with the welfare and rights of the nation, and with the justice and intelligence of the age.

Thomas Malthus

An Essay on the Principle of Population

In 1798, Thomas Malthus (1766-1834), an English clergyman and lecturer in history and political economy at Haileybury College, published a striking counter-argument to Condorcet and others who predicted an era of unbounded human progress. In subsequent editions, Malthus accumulated additional evidence to support his arguments, but his central thesis remained the same as that presented in his original publication, excerpts of which are included here.

The great and unlooked for discoveries that have taken place of late years in natural philosophy; the increasing diffusion of general knowledge from the extension of the art of printing; the ardent and unshackled spirit of inquiry that prevails throughout the lettered, and even unlettered world; the new and extra-ordinary lights that have been thrown on political subjects, which dazzle, and astonish the understanding; and particularly that tremendous phenomenon in the political horizon, the French revolution, which, like a blazing comet, seems destined either to inspire with fresh life and vigour, or to scorch up and destroy the shrinking inhabitants of the earth, have all concurred to lead many able men into the opinion that we are touching on a period big with the most important changes -- changes that would in some measure be decisive of the future fate of mankind.

It has been said that the great question is now at issue whether man shall henceforth start forwards with accelerated

Text: Thomas Robert Malthus, An Essay on the Principle of Population, as It Affects the Future Improvement of Society *(London: J. Johnson, 1798), pp. 1-3, 7-17.*

velocity towards illimitable, and hitherto unconceived improvement; or be condemned to a perpetual oscillation between happiness and misery, and after every effort remain still at an immeasurable distance from the wished-for goal.

* * * * * * * *

I have read some of the speculations on the perfectibility of man and of society with great pleasure. I have been warmed and delighted with the enchanting picture which they hold forth. I ardently wish for such happy improvements. But I see great and, to my understanding, unconquerable difficulties in the way to them. These difficulties it is my present purpose to state; declaring, at the same time, that so far from exulting in them, as a cause of triumph over the friends of innovation, nothing would give me greater pleasure than to see them completely removed.

The most important argument that I shall adduce is certainly not new. The principles on which it depends have been explained in part by Hume, and more at large by Dr. Adam Smith. It has been advanced and applied to the present subject, though not with its proper weight, or in the most forcible point of view, by Mr. Wallace; and it may probably have been stated by many writers that I have never met with. I should certainly therefore not think of advancing it again, though I mean to place it in a point of view in some degree different from any that I have hitherto seen, if it had ever been fairly and satisfactorily answered.

The cause of this neglect on the part of the advocates for the perfectibility of mankind is not easily accounted for. I cannot doubt the talents of such men as Godwin and Condorcet. I am unwilling to doubt their candour. To my understanding, and probably to that of most others, the difficulty appears insurmountable. Yet these men of acknowledged ability and penetration scarcely deign to notice it, and hold on their course in such speculations with unabated ardour and undiminished confidence. I have certainly no right to say that they purposely shut their eyes to such arguments. I ought rather to doubt the validity of them, when neglected by such men, however forcibly their truth may strike on my own mind. Yet in this respect it must be acknowledged that we are all of us too prone to err. If

I saw a glass of wine repeatedly presented to a man, and he took no notice of it, I should be apt to think that he was blind or uncivil. A juster philosophy might teach me rather to think that my eyes deceived me, and that the offer was not really what I conceived it to be.

In entering upon the argument I must premise that I put out of the question, at present, all mere conjectures; that is, all suppositions, the probable realization of which cannot be inferred upon any just philosophical grounds. A writer may tell me that he thinks man will ultimately become an ostrich. I cannot properly contradict him. But before he can expect to bring any reasonable person over to his opinion, he ought to show that the necks of mankind have been gradually elongating; that the lips have grown harder, and more prominent; that the legs and feet are daily altering their shape; and that the hair is beginning to change into stubs of feathers. And till the probability of so wonderful a conversion can be shown, it is surely lost time and lost eloquence to expatiate on the happiness of man in such a state; to describe his powers, both of running and flying; to paint him in a condition where all narrow luxuries would be condemned; where he would be employed only in collecting the necessaries of life; and where, consequently, each man's share of labour would be light and his portion of leisure ample.

I think I may fairly make two postulata.

Firstly, that food is necessary to the existence of man.

Secondly, that the passion between the sexes is necessary, and will remain nearly in its present state.

These two laws ever since we have had any knowledge of mankind, appear to have been fixed laws of our nature; and, as we have not hitherto seen any alteration in them, we have no right to conclude that they will ever cease to be what they now are, without an immediate act of power in that Being who first arranged the system of the universe; and for the advantage of his creatures, still executes, according to fixed laws, all its various operations.

I do not know that any writer has supposed that on this earth man will ultimately be able to live without food. But Mr. Godwin has conjectured that the passion between the sexes may in time be extinguished. As, however, he calls this part of his work, a deviation into the land of conjecture, I will not dwell longer upon it at present, than to say, that the best arguments for the perfectibility of man, are drawn from a contemplation of the great progress that he has already made from the savage state, and the difficulty of saying where he is to stop. But towards the extinction of the passion between the sexes, no progress whatever has hitherto been made. It appears to exist in as much force at present as it did two thousand, or four thousand years ago. There are individual exceptions now as there always have been. But, as these exceptions do not appear to increase in number, it would surely be a very unphilosophical mode of arguing to infer merely from the existence of an exception that the exception would, in time, become the rule, and the rule the exception.

Assuming then, my postulata as granted, I say that the power of population is indefinitely greater than the power in the earth to produce subsistence for man.

Population, when unchecked, increases in a geometrical ratio. Subsistence increases only in an arithmetical ratio. A slight acquaintance with numbers will show the immensity of the first power in comparison of the second.

By that law of our nature which makes food necessary to the life of man, the effects of these two unequal powers must be kept equal.

This implies a strong and constantly operating check on population from the difficulty of subsistence. This difficulty must fall some where; and must necessarily be severely felt by a large portion of mankind.

Through the animal and vegetable kingdoms, nature has scattered the seeds of life abroad with the most profuse and liberal hand. She has been comparatively sparing in the room and the nourishment necessary to rear them. The germs of existence contained in this spot of earth, with ample food and ample room to expand in, would fill millions of worlds in the course of a few thousand years. Necessity, that imperious, all pervading law of nature, restrains them within the prescribed bounds. The race of plants, and the race of animals shrink under this great restrictive law. And the race of man cannot, by any efforts of reason, escape from it. Among plants and animals its effects are waste of seed, sickness, and premature death; among mankind, misery and vice. The former, misery, is an absolutely necessary consequence of it. Vice is a highly probable consequence, and we therefore see it abundantly prevail; but it ought not, perhaps, to be called an absolutely necessary consequence. The ordeal of virtue is to resist all temptation to evil.

This natural inequality of the two powers of population and of production in the earth, and that great law of our nature which must constantly keep their effects equal, form the great difficulty that to me appears insurmountable in the way to the perfectibility of society. All other arguments are of slight and subordinate consideration in comparison of this. I see no way by which man can escape from the weight of this law which pervades all animated nature. No fancied equality, no agrarian regulations in their utmost extent, could remove the pressure of it even for a single century. And it appears, therefore, to be decisive against the possible existence of a society, all the members of which should live in ease, happiness, and comparative leisure; and feel no anxiety about providing the means of subsistence for themselves and families.

Consequently, if the premises are just, the argument is conclusive against the perfectibility of the mass of mankind.

Clemens von Metternich

Memoirs of Prince Metternich

Prince Metternich (1773-1859) served as first minister, or chancellor, for the Habsburg monarchy from 1809 to 1849. During this time he became one of Europe's leading statesmen and the chief architect of the Congress of Vienna, which met to restore order and stability to Europe following the Napoleonic Wars. Metternich's distaste for the ideas fostered by the French Revolution and spread by Napoleon, together with his support of monarchy, are apparent in the following passage.

Union between the monarchs is the basis of the policy which must now be followed to save society from total ruin.

What is the particular object towards which this policy should be directed? The more important this question is, the more necessary it is to solve it. A principle is something, but it acquires real value only in its application.

The first sources of the evil which is crushing the world have been indicated by us in a paper which has no pretension to be anything more than a mere sketch. Its further causes have also there been pointed out if, with respect to individuals, it may be defined by the word presumption, in applying it to society, taken as a whole, we believe we can best describe the existing evil as the confusion of ideas, to which too much generalization constantly leads. This is what now troubles society. Everything which up to this time has been considered as fixed in principle is attacked and overthrown.

If the same elements of destruction which are now throwing society into convulsion have existed in all ages -- for every age

Text: Clemens von Metternich, Memoirs of Prince Metternich, *trans. Mrs. Alexander Napier (London: Charles Scribner's Sons, 1881), pp. 555, 470-476.*

has seen immoral and ambitious men, hypocrites, men of heated imaginations, wrong motives, and wild projects -- yet ours, by the single fact of the liberty of the press, possesses more than any preceding age the means of contact, seduction, and attraction whereby to act on these different classes of men.

We are certainly not alone in questioning if society can exist with the liberty of the press, a scourge unknown to the world before the latter half of the seventeenth century, and restrained until the end of the eighteenth, with scarcely any exceptions but England -- a part of Europe separated from the continent by the sea, as well as by her language and by her peculiar manners.

The first principle to be followed by the monarchs, united as they are by the coincidence of their desires and opinions, should be that of maintaining the stability of political institutions against the disorganised excitement which has taken possession of men's minds; the immutability of principles against the madness of their interpretation; and respect for laws actually in force against a desire for their destruction.

The first and greatest concern for the immense majority of every nation is the stability of the laws, and their uninterrupted action -- never their change. Therefore let the Governments govern, let them maintain the groundwork of their institutions, both ancient and modern; for if it is at all times dangerous to touch them, it certainly would not now, in the general confusion, be wise to do so.

Let them announce this determination to their people, and demonstrate it by facts. Let them reduce the Doctrinaires to silence within their States, and show their contempt for them abroad. Let them not encourage by their attitude or actions the suspicion of being favourable or indifferent to error: let them not allow it to be believed that experience has lost all its rights to make way for experiments which at the least are dangerous. Let them be precise and clear in all their words, and not seek by concessions to gain over those parties who aim at the destruction of all power but their own, whom concessions will never gain over, but only further embolden in their pretensions to power.

Let them in these troublous times be more than usually cautious in attempting real ameliorations, not imperatively claimed by the needs of the moment, to the end that good itself may not turn against them -- which is the case whenever a Government measure seems to be inspired by fear.

Let them not confound concessions made to parties with the good they ought to do for their people, in modifying, according to their recognised needs, such branches of the administration as require it.

Let them give minute attention to the financial state of their kingdoms, so that their people may enjoy, by the reduction of public burdens, the real, not imaginary, benefits of a state of peace.

Let them be just, but strong; beneficent, but strict. Let them maintain religious principles in all their purity, and not allow the faith to be attacked and morality interpreted according to the social contract or the visions of foolish sectarians.

In short, let the great monarchs strengthen their union, and prove to the world that if it exists, it is beneficent, and ensures the political peace of Europe: that it is powerful only for the maintenance of tranquility at a time when so many attacks are directed against it; that the principles which they profess are paternal and protective, menacing only the disturbers of public tranquillity.

The Governments of the second order will see in such a union the anchor of their salvation, and they will be anxious to connect themselves with it. The people will take confidence and courage, and the most profound and salutary peace which the history of any time can show will have been effected. This peace will first act on countries still in a good state, but will not be without a very decided influence on the fate of those threatened with destruction, and even assist the restoration of those which have already passed under the scourge of revolution.

To every great State determined to survive the storm there still remain many chances of salvation, and a strong union between the States on the principles we have announced will overcome the storm itself.

John Stuart Mill

On liberty

John Stuart Mill was a distinguished political philosopher in nineteenth-century England. His essay, On Liberty, *published in 1859, has often been called the classic statement of liberalism. Although Mill later moved toward a position favoring moderate state intervention, his argument for individual rights and the limitation of state sovereignty has a familiar ring even today.*

The subject of this essay is not the so-called Liberty of the Will, so unfortunately opposed to the misnamed doctrine of Philosophical Necessity; but Civil, or Social, Liberty: the nature and limits of the power which can be legitimately exercised by society over the individual -- a question seldom stated, and hardly ever discussed, in general terms, but which profoundly influences the practical controversies of the age by its latent presence, and is likely soon to make itself recognised as the vital question of the future . . . .

What, then, is the rightful limit to the sovereignty of the individual over himself? Where does the authority of society begin? How much of human life should be assigned to individuality, and how much to society?

Each will receive its proper share, if each has that which more particularly concerns it. To individuality should belong the part of life in which it is chiefly the individual that is interested; to society, the part which chiefly interests society.

Though society is not founded on a contract, and though no good purpose is answered by inventing a contract in order to deduce social obligations from it, every one who receives the

---

Text: John Stuart Mill, On Liberty, *4th ed. (London: Longmans, Green, Reader and Dyer, 1869), pp. 4, 134-135, 140-141, 195-199, 206-207.*

protection of society owes a return for the benefit, and the fact of living in society renders it in dispensable that each should be bound to observe a certain line of conduct towards the rest. This conduct consists first, in not injuring the interests of one another; or rather certain interests, which, either by express legal provision or by tacit understanding, ought to be considered as rights; and secondly, in each person's bearing his share (to be fixed on some equitable principle) of the labours and sacrifices incurred for defending the society or its members from injury and molestation. These conditions society is justified in enforcing at all costs to those who endeavor to withhold fulfillment.

Nor is this all that society may do. The acts of an individual may be hurtful to others or wanting in due consideration for their welfare, without going the length of violating any of their constituted rights. The offender may then be justly punished by opinion, though not by law. As soon as any part of a person's conduct affects prejudicially the interests of others, society has jurisdiction over it, and the question whether the general welfare will or will not be promoted by interfering with it, becomes open to discussion. But there is no room for entertaining any such question when a person's conduct affects the interests of no persons besides himself, or needs not affect them unless they like (all the persons concerned being of full age, and the ordinary amount of understanding). In all such cases there should be perfect freedom, legal and social, to do the action and stand the consequences . . . .

What I contend for is that the inconveniences which are strictly inseparable from the unfavourable judgment of others, are the only ones to which a person should ever be subjected for that portion of his conduct and character which concerns his own good, but which does not affect the interests of others in their relations with him. Acts injurious to others require a totally different treatment. Encroachment on their rights; infliction on them of any loss or damage not justified by his own rights; falsehood or duplicity in dealing with them; unfair or ungenerous use of advantages over them; even selfish abstinence from defending them against injury -- these are fit objects of moral reprobation, and, in grave cases, of moral retribution and punishment. And not only these acts, but the dispositions which lead to them, are properly immoral, and fit subjects of disapprobation which may rise to abhorrence. Cruelty of disposition; malice and ill-nature; that most anti-social and odious of all passions, envy; dissimulation and insincerity; irascibility on insufficient cause, and resentment disproportioned to the provocation; the love of domineering over others; the desire to engross more than one's share of advantages; the pride which derives gratification from the abasement of others; the egotism which thinks self and its concerns more important than everything else, and decides all doubtful questions in its own favour; these are moral vices, and constitute a bad and odious moral character: unlike the self-regarding faults previously mentioned, which are not properly immoralities, and to whatever pitch they may be carried, do not constitute wickedness. They may be proofs of any amount of folly, or want of personal dignity and self-respect; but they are only a subject of moral reprobation when they involve a breach of duty to others, for whose sake the individual is bound to have care for himself. What are called duties to ourselves are not socially obligatory, unless circumstances render them at the same time duties to others. The term duty to oneself, when it means anything more than prudence, means self-respect or self development; and for none of these is any one accountable to his fellow creatures, because for none of them is it for the good of mankind that he be held accountable to them.

* * * * * * * *

I have reserved for the last place a large class of questions respecting the limits of government interference, which, though closely connected with the subject of this essay, do not, in strictness, belong to it. These are cases in which the reasons against interference do not turn upon the principle of liberty: the question is not about restraining the actions of individuals, but about helping them: it is asked whether the government should do, or cause to be done, something for their benefit, instead of leaving it to be done by themselves, individually or in voluntary combination.

The objections to government interference, when it is not such as to involve infringement of liberty, may be of three kinds.

The first is when the thing to be done is likely to be better done by individuals than by the government. Speaking generally, there is no one so fit to conduct any business, or to determine how or by whom it shall be conducted, as those who are personally interested in it. This principle condemns the interferences, once so common, of the legislature or the officers of government with the ordinary processes of industry. But this part of the subject has been sufficiently enlarged upon by political economists, and is not particularly related to the principles of this essay.

The second objection is more nearly allied to our subject. In many cases, though individuals may not do the particular thing so well, on the average, as the officers of the government, it is nevertheless desirable that it should be done by them, rather than by the government, as a means to their own mental education -- a mode of strengthening their active faculties, exercising their judgment, and giving them a familiar knowledge of the subjects with which they are thus left to deal. This is a principal, though not the sole, recommendation of jury trial (in cases not political); of free and popular local and municipal institutions; of the conduct of industrial and philanthropic enterprises by voluntary associations. These are not questions of liberty and are connected with that subject only by remote tendencies; but they are questions of development. It belongs to a different occasion from the present to dwell on these things as parts of national education; as being, in truth, the peculiar training of a citizen, the practical part of the political education of a free people, taking them out of the narrow circle of personal and family selfishness, and accustoming them to the comprehension of joint interests, the management of joint concerns -- habituating them to act from public or semi-public motives, and guide their conduct by aims which unite instead of isolating them from one another. Without these habits and powers, a free constitution can neither be worked nor preserved; as is exemplified by the too often transitory nature of political freedom in countries where it does not rest upon a sufficient basis of local liberties. The management of purely local business by the localities, and of the great enterprises of industry by the union of those who voluntarily supply the pecuniary means, is further recommended by all the advantages which have been set forth in this essay as belonging to individuality of development, and diversity of modes of action. Government operations tend to be everywhere alike. With individuals and voluntary associations, on the contrary, there are varied experiments, and endless diversity of experience. What the State can usefully do is to make itself a central depository and active circulator and diffuser of the experience resulting from many trials. Its business is to enable each experimentalist to benefit by the experiments of others; instead of tolerating no experiments but its own.

The third, and most cogent, reason for restricting the interference of government is the great evil of adding unnecessarily to its power. Every function superadded to those already exercised by the government causes its influence over hopes and fears to be more widely diffused, and converts, more and more, the active and ambitious part of the public into hangers-on of the government, or of some party which aims at becoming the government. If the roads, the railways, the banks, the insurance offices, the great joint-stock companies, the universities, and the public charities were all of them branches of the government; if, in addition, the municipal corporations and local boards, with all that now devolves on them, became departments of the central administration; if the employees of all these different enterprises were appointed and paid by the government, and looked to the government for every rise in life -- not all the freedom of the press and popular constitution of the legislature would make this or any other country free otherwise than in name. And the evil would be greater, the more efficiently and scientifically the administrative machinery was constructed -- the more skillful the arrangements for obtaining the best qualified hands and heads with which to work it . . . .

A government cannot have too much of the kind of activity which does not impede, but aids and stimulates, individual exertion and development. The mischief begins when, instead of calling forth the activity and powers of individuals and bodies, it substitutes its own activity for theirs; when, instead of informing, advising, and, upon occasion, denouncing, it makes them work in fetters, or bids them stand aside and does their work instead of them. The worth of a State, in the long run, is the worth of the individuals composing it; and a State which postpones the interests of their mental expansion and elevation, to a little more of administrative skill, or of that semblance of it which practice gives, in the details of business; a State which dwarfs its men, in order that they may be more docile instruments in its hands even for beneficial purposes -- will find that with small men no great thing can really be accomplished; and that the perfection of machinery to which it has sacrificed everything will in the end avail it nothing for want of the vital power which, in order that the machine might work more smoothly, it has preferred to banish.

Andrew Ure

The Philosophy of Manufactures

The process of industrialization created a new social stratum of factory workers in early nineteenth century Britain, as it did later in the century on the Continent. The plight of the working class during this difficult period of transformation from rural to urban life drew varied responses from the upper levels of society. In the following selection from The Philosophy of Manufactures, *first published in 1835, Andrew Ure, a successful Scottish druggist, extols the achievements of industrialization and its benefits for the workers, including the children who labored in the factories.*

In its precise acceptation, the Factory system is of recent origin, and may claim England for its birthplace. The mills for throwing silk, or making organzine, which were mounted centuries ago in several of the Italian states, and furtively transferred to this country by Sir Thomas Lombe in 1718, contained indeed certain elements of a factory, and probably suggested some hints of those grander and more complex combinations of self-acting machines, which were first embodied half a century later in our cotton manufacture by Richard Arkwright, assisted by gentlemen of Derby, well acquainted with its celebrated silk establishment.

But the spinning of an entangled flock of fibres into a smooth thread, which constitutes the main operation with cotton, is in silk superfluous, being already performed by the unerring instinct of a worm, which leaves to human art the simple task of doubling and twisting its regular filaments. The apparatus requisite for this purpose is more elementary, and calls for few of those

---

Text: Andrew Ure, The Philosophy of Manufactures *(London: Frank Cass and Co., Ltd., 1967), pp. 14-19, 300. Reprint of 1839 edition.*

gradations of machinery which are needed in the carding, drawing, roving, and spinning processes of a cotton-mill.

When the first water-frames for spinning cotton were erected at Cromford, in the romantic valley of the Derwent, about sixty years ago, mankind were little aware of the mighty revolution which the new system of labour was destined by Providence to achieve, not only in the structure of British society, but in the fortunes of the world at large. Arkwright alone had the sagacity to discern, and the boldness to predict in glowing language, how vastly productive human industry would become, when no longer proportioned in its results to muscular effort, which is by its nature fitful and capricious, but when made to consist in the task of guiding the work of mechanical fingers and arms, regularly impelled with great velocity by some indefatigable physical power. What his judgment so clearly led him to perceive, his energy of will enabled him to realize with such rapidity and success, as would have done honour to the most influential individuals, but were truly wonderful in that obscure and indigent artisan.

The main difficulty did not, to my apprehension, lie so much in the invention of a proper self-acting mechanism for drawing out and twisting cotton into a continuous thread, as in the distribution of the different members of the apparatus into one cooperative body, in impelling each organ with its appropriate delicacy and speed, and above all, in training human beings to renounce their desultory habits of work, and to identify themselves with the unvarying regularity of the complex automation. To devise and administer a successful code of factory discipline, suited to the necessities of factory diligence, was the Herculean enterprise, the noble achievement of Arkwright. Even at the present day, when the system is perfectly organized, and its labour lightened to the utmost, it is found nearly impossible to convert persons past the age of puberty, whether drawn from rural or from handicraft occupations, into useful factory hands. After struggling for a while to conquer their listless or restive habits, they either renounce the employment spontaneously, or are dismissed by the overlookers on account of inattention.

* * * * * * * *

In my recent tour, continued during several months, through the manufacturing districts, I have seen tens of thousands of old, young, and middle-aged of both sexes, many of them too feeble to get their daily bread by any of the former modes of industry, earning abundant food, raiment, and domestic accommodation, without perspiring at a single pore, screened meanwhile from the summer's sun and the winter's frost, in apartments more airy and salubrious than those of the metropolis, in which our legislative and fashionable aristocracies assemble. In those spacious halls the benignant power of steam summons around him his myriads of willing menials, and assigns to each the regulated task, substituting for painful muscular effort on their part, the energies of his own gigantic arm, and demanding in return only attention and dexterity to correct such little aberrations as casually occur in his workmanship.

The gentle docility of this moving force qualifies it for impelling the tiny bobbins of the lace-machine with a precision and speed inimitable by the most dexterous hands, directed by the sharpest eyes. Hence, under its auspices, and in obedience to Arkwright's polity, magnificent edifices, surpassing far in number, value, usefulness, and ingenuity of construction, the boasted monuments of Asiatic, Egyptian, and Roman despotism, have, within the short period of fifty years, risen up in this kingdom, to show to what extent, capital, industry, and science may augment the resources of a state, while they meliorate the condition of its citizens. Such is the factory system, replete with prodigies in mechanics and political economy, which promises, in its future growth, to become the great minister of civilization to the terraqueous globe, enabling this country, as its heart, to diffuse along with its commerce, the life-blood of science and religion to myriads of people still lying "in the region and shadow of death."

* * * * * * * *

No master would wish to have any wayward children to work within the walls of his factory, who do not mind their business without beating, and he therefore usually fines or turns away any spinners who are known to maltreat their assistants. Hence, ill-usage of any kind is a very rare occurrence. I have visited many factories, both in Manchester and in the surrounding districts, during a period of several months, entering the spinning rooms, unexpectedly, and often alone, at different times of the day, and I never saw a single instance of corporal chastisement inflicted on a child, nor indeed did I ever see children in ill-humour. They seemed to be always cheerful and alert, taking pleasure in the light play of their muscles -- enjoying the mobility natural to their age. The scene of industry, so far from exciting sad emotions in my mind, was always exhilarating. It was delightful to observe the nimbleness with which they pieced the broken ends, as the mule-carriage began to recede from the fixed roller beam, and to see them at leisure, after a few seconds' exercise of their tiny fingers, to amuse themselves in any attitude they chose, till the stretch and winding-on were once more completed. The work of these lively elves seemed to resemble a sport, in which habit gave them a pleasing dexterity. Conscious of their skill, they were delighted to show it off to any stranger. As to exhaustion by the day's work, they evinced no trace of it on emerging from the mill in the evening; for they immediately began to skip about any neighbouring playground, and to commence their little amusements with the same alacrity as boys issuing from a school. It is moreover my firm conviction, that if children are not ill-used by bad parents or guardians, but receive in food and raiment the full benefit of what they earn, they would thrive better when employed in our modern factories, than if left at home in apartments too often ill-aired, damp, and cold.

British Parliament Papers

The Sadler Report

In contrast to Andrew Ure's glowing description of industrial working conditions is the Sadler Report. In 1831, Michael Sadler, one of a group of social reformers in England, introduced a bill into Parliament to regulate labor practices in the textile mills. Parliament referred the bill to a committee, headed by Sadler, which collected evidence of child labor abuses. The investigation resulted in the Factory Act of 1833, restricting the working hours of children and creating an inspection system to enforce regulations.

Mr. Matthew Crabtree, called in; and Examined.

What age are you? -- Twenty-two.

What is your occupation? -- A blanket manufacturer.

Have you ever been employed in a factory? -- Yes.

At what age did you first go to work in one? -- Eight.

How long did you continue in that occupation? -- Four years.

Will you state the hours of labour at the period when you first went to the factory, in ordinary times? -- From 6 in the morning to 8 at night.

Fourteen hours? -- Yes.

With what intervals for refreshment and rest? -- An hour at noon.

Then you had no resting time allowed in which to take your breakfast, or what is in Yorkshire called your "drinking?" -- No.

Text: British Parliamentary Papers Industrial Revolution. Children's Employment. *II, pp. 95-104.*

When trade was brisk what were your hours? -- From 5 in the morning to 9 in the evening.

Sixteen hours? -- Yes.

With what intervals at dinner? -- An hour.

How far did you live from the mill? -- About two miles.

Was there any time allowed for you to get your breakfast in the mill? -- No.

Did you take it before you left your home? -- Generally.

During those long hours of labour could you be punctual; how did you awake? -- I seldom did awake spontaneously; I was most generally awoke or lifted out of bed, sometimes asleep, by my parents.

Were you always in time? -- No.

What was the consequence if you had been too late? -- I was most commonly beaten.

Severely? -- Very severely, I thought.

In whose factory was this? -- Messrs. Hague & Cook's, of Dewsbury.

Will you state the effect that those long hours had upon the state of your health and feelings? -- I was, when working those long hours, commonly very much fatigued at night, when I left my work; so much so that I sometimes should have slept as I walked if I had not stumbled and started awake again; and so sick often that I could not eat, and what I did eat I vomited.

Did this labour destroy your appetite? -- It did.

In what situation were you in that mill? -- I was a piecener.

Will you state to this Committee whether piecening is a very laborious employment for children, or not? -- It is a very laborious employment. Pieceners are continually running to and fro, and on their feet the whole day.

The duty of the piecener is to take the cardings from one part of the machinery, and to place them on another? -- Yes.

So that the labour is not only continual, but it is unabated to the last? -- It is unabated to the last.

Do you not think, from your own experience, that the speed of the machinery is so calculated as to demand the utmost exertions of a child, supposing the hours were moderate? -- It is as much as they could do at the best; they are always upon the stretch, and it is commonly very difficult to keep up with their work.

State the condition of the children towards the latter part of the day, who have thus to keep up with the machinery? -- It is as much as they can do when they are not very much fatigued to keep up with their work, and towards the close of the day, when they come to be more fatigued, they cannot keep up with it very well, and the consequence is that they are beaten to spur them on.

Were you beaten under those circumstances? -- Yes.

Frequently? -- Very frequently.

And principally at the latter end of the day? -- Yes.

And is it your belief that if you had not been so beaten you should not have got through the work? -- I should not if I had not been kept up to it by some means.

Does beating then principally occur at the latter end of the day, when the children are exceedingly fatigued? -- It does at the latter end of the day, and in the morning sometimes, when they are very drowsy, and have not got rid of the fatigue of the day before.

What were you beaten with principally? -- A strap.

Any thing else? -- Yes, a stick sometimes; and there is a kind of roller which runs on the top of the machine called a billy, perhaps two or three yards in length, and perhaps an inch and a half, or more, in diameter; the circumference would be four or five inches; I cannot speak exactly.

Were you beaten with that instrument? -- Yes.

Have you yourself been beaten, and have you seen other children struck severely with that roller? -- I have been struck very severely with it myself, so much so as to knock me down, and I have seen other children have their heads broken with it.

You think that it is a general practice to beat the children with the roller? -- It is.

You do not think then that you were worse treated than other children in the mill? -- No, I was not, perhaps not so bad as some were.

In those mills is chastisement towards the latter part of the day going on perpetually? -- Perpetually.

So that you can hardly be in a mill without hearing constant crying? -- Never an hour, I believe.

Do you think that if the overlooker were naturally a humane person it would be still found necessary for him to beat the children, in order to keep up their attention and vigilance at the termination of those extraordinary days of labour? -- Yes; the machine turns off a regular quantity of cardings, and of course they must keep as regularly to their work the whole of the day; they must keep up with the machine, and therefore however humane the slubber may be, as he must keep up with the machine or be found fault with, he spurs the children to keep up also by various means but that which he commonly resorts to is to strap them when they become drowsy.

At the time you were beaten for not keeping up with your work, were you anxious to have done it if you possibly could? -- Yes; the dread of being beaten if we could not keep up with our work was a sufficient impulse to keep us to it if we could.

When you got home at night after this labour, did you feel much fatigued? -- Very much so.

Had you any time to be with your parents, and to receive instruction from them? -- No.

What did you do? -- All that we did when we got home was to get the little bit of supper that was provided for us and go to bed immediately. If the supper had not been ready directly, we should have gone to sleep while it was preparing.

Did you not, as a child, feel it a very grievous hardship to be roused so soon in the morning? -- I did.

Were the rest of the children similarly circumstanced? -- Yes, all of them; but they were not all of them so far from their work as I was.

And if you had been too late you were under the apprehension of being cruelly beaten? -- I generally was beaten when I happened to be too late; and when I got up in the morning the apprehension of that was so great, that I used to run, and cry all the way as I went to the mill.

That was the way by which your punctual attendance was secured? -- Yes.

And you do not think it could have been secured by any other means? -- No.

Then it is your impression from what you have seen, and from your own experience, that those long hours of labour have the effect of rendering young persons who are subject to them exceedingly unhappy? -- Yes.

You have already said it had a considerable effect upon your health? -- Yes.

Do you conceive that it diminished your growth? -- I did not pay much attention to that; but I have been examined by some persons who said they thought I was rather stunted, and that I should have been taller if I had not worked at the mill.

What were your wages at that time? -- Three shillings.

And how much a day had you for over-work when you were worked so exceedingly long? -- A halfpenny a day.

Did you frequently forfeit that if you were not always there to a moment? -- Yes; I most frequently forfeited what was allowed for those long hours.

You took your food to the mill; was it in your mill, as is the case in cotton mills, much spoiled by being laid aside? -- It was very frequently covered by flues from the wool; and in that case they had to be blown off with the mouth, and picked off with the fingers before it could be eaten.

So that not giving you a little leisure for eating your food, but obliging you to take it at the mill, spoiled your food when you did get it? -- Yes, very commonly.

And that at the same time that this over-labour injured your appetite? -- Yes.

Could you eat when you got home? -- Not always.

What is the effect of this piecening upon the hands? -- It makes them bleed; the skin is completely rubbed off, and in that case they bleed in perhaps a dozen parts.

The prominent parts of the hand? -- Yes, all the prominent parts of the hand are rubbed down till they bleed; every day they are rubbed in that way.

All the time you continue at work? -- All the time we are working. The hands never can be hardened in that work, for the grease keeps them soft in the first instance, and long and continual rubbing is always wearing them down, so that if they were hard they would be sure to bleed.

Is it attended with much pain? -- Very much.

Do they allow you to make use of the back of the hand? -- No; the work cannot be so well done with the back of the hand, or I should have made use of that.

Is the work done as well when you are so many hours engaged in it, as it would be if you were at it a less time? -- I believe it is not done so well in those long hours; towards the latter end of the day the children become completely bewildered, and know not what they are doing, so that they spoil their work without knowing.

Then you do not think that the masters gain much by the continuance of the work to so great a length of time? I believe not.

Were there girls as well as boys employed in this manner? -- Yes.

Were they more tenderly treated by the overlookers, or were they worked and beaten in the same manner? -- There was no difference in their treatment.

Were they beaten by the overlookers, or by the slubber? -- By the slubber.

But the overlooker must have been perfectly aware of the treatment that the children endured at the mill? -- Yes; and sometimes the overlooker beat them himself; but the man that they wrought under had generally the management of them.

Did he pay them their wages? -- No; their wages were paid by the master.

But the overlooker of the mill was perfectly well aware that they could not have performed the duty exacted from them in the mill without being thus beaten? -- I believe he was.

You seem to say that this beating is absolutely necessary, in order to keep the children up to their work; is it universal throughout all factories? -- I have been in several other factories, and I have witnessed the same cruelty in them all.

Did you say that you were beaten for being too late? -- Yes.

Is it not the custom in many of the factories to impose fines upon children for being too late, instead of beating them?-- It was not in that factory.

What then were the fines by which you lost the money you gained by your long hours? -- The spinner could not get so fast with his work when we happened to be too late; he could not begin his work so soon, and therefore it was taken by him.

Did the slubber pay you your wages? -- No, the master paid our wages.

And the slubber took your fines from you? -- Yes.

Then you were fined as well as beaten? -- There was nothing deducted from the ordinary scale of wages, but only from that received for over-hours, and I had only that taken when I was too late, so that the fine was not regular.

When you were not working over-hours, were you so often late as when you were working over-hours? -- Yes.

You were not very often late whilst you were not working over-hours? -- Yes, I was often late when I was not working over-hours; I had to go at six o'clock in the morning, and consequently had to get up at five to eat my breakfast and go to the mill, and if I failed to get up by five I was too late; and it was nine o'clock before we could get home, and then we went to bed; in the best times I could not be much above eight hours at home, reckoning dressing and eating my meals, and everything.

Was it a blanket-mill in which you worked? -- Yes.

Did you ever know that the beatings to which you allude inflicted a serious injury upon the children? -- I do not recollect any very serious injury, more than that they had their heads broken, if that may be called a serious injury; that has often happened; I, myself, had no more serious injury than that.

You say that the girls as well as the boys were employed as you have described, and you observed no difference in treatment? -- No difference.

The girls were beat in this unmerciful manner? -- They were.

They were subject, of course, to the same bad effects from this over-working? -- Yes.

Could you attend an evening school during the time you were employed in the mill? -- No, that was completely impossible.

Did you attend the Sunday-school? -- Not very frequently when I worked at the mill.

How then were you engaged during the Sunday? -- I very often slept till it was too late for school time or for divine worship, and the rest of the day I spend in walking out and taking a little fresh air.

Did your parents think that it was necessary for you to enjoy a little fresh air? -- I believe they did; they never said anything against it; before I went to the mill I used to go to the Sunday-school.

Did you frequently sleep nearly the whole of the day on Sunday? -- Very often.

At what age did you leave that employment? -- I was about 12 years old.

Why did you leave that place? -- I went very late one morning, about seven o'clock, and I got severely beaten by the spinner, and he turned me out of the mill, and I went home, and never went any more.

Was your attendance as good as the other children? -- Being at rather a greater distance than some of them, I was generally one of the latest.

Where was your next work? -- I worked as bobbin-winder in another part of the works of the same firm.

How long were you a bobbin-winder? -- About two years, I believe.

What did you become after that? -- A weaver.

How long were you a weaver? -- I was a weaver till March in last year.

A weaver of what? -- A blanket-weaver.

With the same firm? -- With the same firm.

Did you leave them? -- No; I was dismissed from my work for a reason which I am willing and anxious to explain.

Have you had opportunities of observing the way in which the children are treated in factories up to a late period? -- Yes.

You conceive that their treatment still remains as you first found it, and that the system is in great want of regulation? -- It does.

Children you still observe to be very much fatigued and injured by the hours of labour? -- Yes.

From your own experience, what is your opinion as to the utmost labour that a child in piecening could safely undergo? -- If I were appealed to from my own feelings to fix a limit, I should fix it at ten hours, or less.

And you attribute to longer hours all the cruelties that you describe? -- A good deal of them.

Are the children sleepy in mills? -- Very.

Are they more liable to accidents in the latter part of the day than in the other part? -- I believe they are; I believe a greater number of accidents happen in the latter part of the day than in any other. I have known them so sleepy that in the short interval while the others have been going out, some of them have fallen asleep, and have been left there.

Is it an uncommon case for children to fall asleep in the mill, and remain there all night? -- Not to remain there all night; but I have known a case the other day, of a child whom the overlooker found when he went to lock the door, that had been left there.

So that you think there has been no change for the better in the treatment of those children; is it your opinion that there will be none, except Parliament interfere in their behalf? -- It is my decided conviction.

Have you recently seen any cruelties in mills? -- Yes; not long since I was in a mill, and I saw a girl severely beaten; at a mill called Hick-lane Mill, in Batley; I happened to be in at the other end of the room talking; and I heard the blows, and I looked that way, and saw the spinner beating one of the girls severely with a large stick. Hearing the sound, led me to look round, and to ask what was the matter, and they said it was "Nothing but _____ paying (beating) his ligger-on."

What age was the girl? -- About 12 years.

Was she very violently beaten? -- She was.

Was this when she was over-fatigued? -- It was in the afternoon.

Can you speak as to the effect of this labour in the mills and factories on the morals of the children, as far as you have observed? -- As far as I have observed with regard to morals in the mills, there is every thing about them that is disgusting to every one conscious of correct morality.

Do you find that the children, the females especially, early demoralized in them? -- They are.

Is their language indecent? -- Very indecent; and both sexes take great familiarities with each other in the mills, without at all being ashamed of their conduct.

Do you connect their immorality of language and conduct with their excessive labour? -- It may be somewhat connected with it, for it is to be observed that most of that goes on towards night, when they begin to be drowsy; it is a kind of stimulus which they use to keep them awake; they say some pert thing or other to keep themselves from drowsiness, and it generally happens to be some obscene language.

Have not a considerable number of the females employed in mills illegitimate children very early in life? -- I believe there are; I have known some of them have illegitimate children when they were between 16 and 17 years of age.

How many grown-up females had you in the mill? -- I cannot speak to the exact number that were grown up; perhaps there might be thirty-four or so that worked in the mill at that time.

How many of those had illegitimate children? -- A great many of them; eighteen or nineteen of them, I think.

Did they generally marry the men by whom they had the children? -- No; it sometimes happens that young women have children by married men, and I have known an instance, a few weeks since, where one of the young women had a child by a married man.

Is it your opinion that those who have the charge of mills very often avail themselves of the opportunity they have to debauch the young women? -- No, not generally; most of the improper conduct takes place among the younger part of those that work in the mill.

Do you find that the children and young persons in those mills are moral in other respects, or does their want of education tend to encourage them in a breach of the law? -- I believe it does, for there are very few of them that can know anything about it; few of them can either read or write.

Are criminal offenses then very frequent? -- Yes, theft is very common; it is practised a great deal in the mills, stealing their bits of dinner, or something of that sort. Some of them have not so much to eat as they ought to have, and if they can fall in with the dinner of some of their partners they steal it. The first day my brother and I went to the mill we had our dinner stolen, because we were not up to the tricks; we were more careful in future, but still we did not always escape.

Was there any correction going on at the mills for indecent language or improper conduct? -- No, I never knew of any.

From what you have seen and known of those mills, would you prefer that the hours of labour should be so long with larger wages, or that they should be shortened with a diminution of wages? -- If I were working at the mill now, I would rather have less labour and receive a trifle less, than so much labour and receive a trifle more.

Is that the general impression of individuals engaged in mills with whom you are acquainted? -- I believe it is.

What is the impression in the country from which you come with respect to the effect of this Bill upon wages? -- They do not anticipate that it will affect wages at all.

They think it will not lower wages? -- They do.

Do you mean that it will not lower wages by the hour, or that you will receive the same wages per day? -- They anticipate that it may perhaps lower their wages at a certain time of the year when they are working hard, but not at other times, so that they will have their wages more regular.

Does not their wish for this Bill mainly rest upon their anxiety to protect their children from the consequences of this excessive labour, and to have some opportunity of affording them a decent education? -- Yes; such are the wishes of every humane father that I have heard speak about the thing.

Have they not some feeling of having the labour equalized? -- That is the feeling of some that I have heard speak of it.

Did your parents work in the same factories? -- No.

Were any of the slubbers' children working there? -- Yes.

Under what slubber did you work in that mill? -- Under a person of the name of Thomas Bennett, in the first place; and I was changed from him to another of the name of James Webster.

Did the treatment depend very much upon the slubber under whom you were? -- No, it did not depend directly upon him, for he was obliged to do a certain quantity of work, and therefore to make us keep up with that.

Were the children of the slubbers strapped in the same way? -- Yes, except that it is very natural for a father to spare his own child.

Did it depend upon the feelings of a slubber towards his children? -- Very little.

Did the slubbers find their own spinners? -- I believe not.

You said that the piecening was very hard labour; what labour is there besides moving about; have you anything heavy to carry or to lift? -- We have nothing heavy to carry, but we are kept upon our feet in brisk times from 5 o'clock in the morning to 9 at night.

How soon does the hand get sore in piecening? -- How soon mine became sore I cannot speak to exactly; but they get a little hard on the Sunday, when we are not working, and they will get sore again very soon on the Monday.

Is it always the case in piecening that the hand bleeds, whether you work short or long hours? -- They bleed more when we work more.

Do they always bleed when you are working? -- Yes.

Do you think that the children would not be more competent to this task, and their hands far less hurt, if the hours were fewer every day, especially when their hands had become seasoned to the labour? -- I believe it would have an effect, for the longer they are worked the more their hands are worn, and the longer it takes to heal them, and they do not get hard enough after a day's rest to be long without bleeding again; if they were not so much worn down, they might heal sooner, and not bleed so often or so soon.

After a short day's work, have you found your hands hard the next morning? -- They do not bleed much after we have ceased work; they then get hard; they will bleed soon in the morning when in regular work.

Do you think if the work of the children were confined to about ten hours a day, that after they were accustomed to it, they would not be able to perform this piecening without making their hands bleed? -- I believe they would.

So that it is your opinion, from your experience, that if the hours were mitigated, their hands would not be so much worn, and would not bleed by the business of piecening? -- Yes.

Do you mean to say that their hands would not bleed at all? -- I cannot say exactly, for I always wrought long hours, and therefore my hands always did bleed.

Have you any experience of mills where they only work ten hours? -- I have never wrought at such mills, and in most of the mills I have seen their hands bleed.

At a slack time, when you were working only a few hours, did your hands bleed? -- No, they did not for three or four days, after we had been standing still for a week; the mill stood still sometimes for a week together, but when we did work we worked the common number of hours.

Were all the mills in the neighbourhood working the same number of hours in brisk times? -- Yes.

So that if any parent found it necessary to send his children to the mill for the sake of being able to maintain them, and wished to take them from any mill where they were excessively worked, he could not have found any other place where they would have been less worked? -- No, he could not; for myself, I had no desire to change, because I thought I was as well off as I could be at any other mill.

And if the parent, to save his child, had taken him from the mill, and had applied to the parish for relief, would the parish, knowing that he had withdrawn his child from its work, have relieved him? -- No.

So that the long labour which you have described, or actual starvation, was, practically, the only alternative that was presented to the parent under such circumstances? -- It was; they must either work at the mill they were at or some other, and there was no choice in the mills in that respect.

What, in your opinion, would be the effect of limiting the hours of labour upon the happiness, and the health, and the intelligence of the rising generation? -- If the hours are shortened, the children may, perhaps, have a chance of attending some evening-school, and learning to read and to write; and those that I know who have been to school and learned to read and write, have much more comfort than those who have not. For myself, I went to a school when I was 6 years old, and I learned to read and write a little then.

At a free-school? -- Yes, at a free-school in Dewsbury; but I left school when I was 6 years old. The fact is, that my father was a small manufacturer, and in comfortable circumstances; and he got into debt with Mr. Cook for a wool bill, and as he had no other means of paying him, he came and agreed with my father, that my brother and I should go to work at his mill till that debt was paid; so that the whole of the time that we wrought at the mill we had no wages.

Thomas Bennett, called in; and Examined.

Where do you reside? -- At Dewsbury.

What is your business? -- A slubber.

What age are you? -- About 48.

Have you had much experience regarding the working of children in factories? -- Yes, about twenty-seven years.

Have you a family? -- Yes, eight children.

Have any of them gone to factories? -- All.

At what age? -- The first went at 6 years of age.

To whose mill? -- To Mr. Halliley's, to piece for myself.

What hours did you work at that mill? -- We have wrought from 4 to 9, from 4 to 10, and from 5 to 9, and from 5 to 10.

What sort of a mill was it? -- It was a blanket-mill; we sometimes altered the time, according as the days increased and decreased.

What were your regular hours? -- Our regular hours, when we were not so throng, was from 6 to 7.

And when you were the throngest, what were your hours then? -- From 5 to 9, and from 5 to 10, and from 4 to 9.

Seventeen hours? -- Yes.

What intervals for meals had the children at that period? -- Two hours; an hour for breakfast and an hour for dinner.

Did they always allow two hours for meals at Mr. Halliley's? -- Yes, it was allowed, but the children did not get it, for they had business to do at that time, such as fettling and cleaning the machinery?

But they did not all stop in at that time, did they? -- They all had their share of the cleaning and other work to do.

That is, they were cleaning the machinery? -- Cleaning the machinery at the time of dinner.

How long a time together have you known those excessive hours to continue? -- I have wrought so myself very nearly two years together.

Were your children working under you then? -- Yes, two of them.

State the effect upon your children? -- Of a morning when they had to get up, they have been so fast asleep that I have had to go up stairs and lift them out of bed, and have heard their crying with the feelings of a parent; I have been much affected by it.

Were not they much fatigued at the termination of such a day's labour as that? -- Yes, many a time I have seen their hands moving while they have been nodding, almost asleep; they have been doing their business almost mechanically.

While they have been almost asleep, they have attempted to work? -- Yes; and they have missed the carding and spoiled the thread, when we have had to beat them for it.

Could they have done their work towards the termination of such a long day's labour, if they had not been chastised to it? -- No.

You do not think that they could have kept awake or up to their work till the seventeenth hour, without being chastised? -- No.

Will you state what effect it had upon your children at the end of their day's work? -- At the end of their day's work, when they have come home, instead of taking their victuals, they have dropped asleep with the victuals in their hands; and sometimes when we have sent them to bed with a little bread or something to eat in their hand, I have found it in their bed the next morning.

Has it affected their health? -- I cannot say much of that; they were very hearty children.

Do you live at a distance from the mill? -- Half a mile.

Did your children feel a difficulty in getting home? -- Yes, I have had to carry the lesser child on my back, and it has been asleep when I got home.

Did these hours of labour fatigue you? -- Yes; they fatigued me to that excess, that in divine worship I have not been able to stand according to order; I have sat to worship.

So that even during the Sunday you have felt fatigue from your labour in the week? -- Yes, we felt it, and always took as much rest as we could.

Were you compelled to beat your own children, in order to make them keep up with the machine? -- Yes, that was forced upon us, or we could not have done the work; I have struck them often, though I felt as a parent.

If the children had not been your own, you would have chastised them still more severely? -- Yes.

What did you beat them with? -- A strap sometimes; and when I have seem my work spoiled, with the roller.

Was the work always worst done at the end of the day? -- That was the greatest danger.

Do you conceive it possible that the children could do their work well at the end of such a day's labour as that?-- No.

Matthew Crabtree, the last Witness examined by this Committee, I think mentioned you as one of the slubbers under whom he worked? -- Yes.

He states that he was chastised and beaten at the mill? -- Yes, I have had to chastise him.

You can confirm then what he has stated as to the length of time he had to work as a child, and the cruel treatment that he received? -- Yes, I have had to chastise him in the evening, and often in the morning, for being too late; when I had one out of the three wanting I could not keep up with the machine; and I was getting behind-hand compared with what another man was doing; and therefore I should have been called to account on Saturday night if the work was not done.

Was he worse than others? -- No.

Was it the constant practice to chastise the children? -- Yes.

It was necessary in order to keep up your work? -- Yes.

And you would have lost your place if you had not done so? -- Yes; when I was working at Mr. Wood's mill, at Dews-bury, which at present is burnt down, but where I slubbed for him until it was, while we were taking our meals he used to come up' and put the machine agoing; and I used to say, "You do not give us time to eat"; he used to reply, "Chew it at your work"; and I often replied to him, "I have not yet become debased like a brute, I do not chew my cud." Often has that man done that, and then gone below to see if a strap were off, which would have shown the machinery was not working, and then he would come up again.

Was this at the drinking time? -- Yes, at breakfast and at drinking.

Was this where the children were working? -- Yes, my own children and others.

Were your own children obliged to employ most of their time at breakfast and at the drinking in cleansing the machine, and in fettling the spindles? -- I have seen at that mill, and I have experienced and mentioned it with grief, that the English children were enslaved worse than the Africans. Once when Mr. Wood was saying to the carrier who brought his work in and out, "How long has that horse of mine been at work?" and the carrier told him the time, and he said, "Loose him directly, he has been in too long," I made this reply to him, "You have more mercy and pity for your horse than you have for your men."

Did not this beating go on principally at the latter part of the day? -- Yes.

Was it not also dangerous for the children to move about those mills when they became so drowsy and fatigued? -- Yes, especially by lamp-light.

Do the accidents principally occur at the latter end of those long days of labour? -- Yes, I believe mostly so.

Do you know of any that have happened? -- I know of one; it was at Mr. Wood's mill; part of the machine caught a lass who had been drowsy and asleep, and the strap which ran close by her catched her at about her middle, and bore her to the ceiling, and down she came, and her neck appeared broken, and the slubber ran up to her and pulled her neck, and I carried her to the doctor.

Did she get well? -- Yes, she came about again.

What time was that? -- In the evening.

You say that you have eight children who have gone to the factories? -- Yes.

There has been no opportunity for you to send them to a day-school? -- No; one boy had about twelve months' schooling.

Have they gone to Sunday-schools? -- Yes.

Can any of them write? -- Not one.

They do not teach writing at Sunday-schools? -- No; it is objected to, I believe.

So that none of your children can write? -- No.

What would be the effect of a proper limitation of the hours of labour upon the conduct of the rising generation? -- I believe it would have a very happy effect in regard to cor- recting their morals; for I believe there is a deal of evil that takes place in one way or other in consequence of those long hours.

Is it your opinion that they would then have an opportunity of attending night-schools? -- Yes; I have often regretted, while working those long hours, that I could not get my children there.

Is it your belief that if they were better instructed, they would be happier and better members of society? -- Yes, I believe so.

If you had your choice, would you rather that the hours of the labour of your children were diminished, even though their wages were proportionably reduced? -- Yes, I would with regard both to their health and their morals; I would rather they should work five days than seven in the week.

The wages being reduced to the like extent? -- It would only be about a halfpenny a day, for when they work those long hours, they give a halfpenny a day to the pieceners.

Are the mills working those long hours now? -- No, not at present; the country is very slack about us.

How long is it since they ceased to work those long hours? -- I believe last July.

Did they begin to work short hours last July? -- Yes, they have not wrought three days in a week, one week with another, since last July; the work has been very slack; and with regard to long hours, when one factory is working long hours, another is not working legal hours, so that if there was a press for time, it would only cause people to put out work to those factories which are not now fully employed, and the work would get more equalized; but the weavers of some factories have to work night and day, while others have not sufficient work for the day-time.

What did you and your children earn a week? -- Thirty shillings a week, myself and children, working those long hours.

Did you engage your own children? -- Yes.

Had you several children besides those who slubbed with you? -- Yes.

Could you not have got other children to supply the place of your children occasionally? -- No, it was forbidden; and if one neighbour wished to take another neighbour's children, without they were out of work, they would not come.

When there was a child out of work, could you not get help? -- Yes, but there were not many children out of employ; they do not call it being out of employ when they have a place to work.

When work is again obtained, do they pay those children which are thus engaged their weekly wages when the mill is not working more than two or three days a week? -- No.

Are there many children out of employ now? -- Yes, the work is so slack.

What effect do you suppose the passing a Bill regulating the labour to ten hours would have upon wages? -- I believe it would have very little effect, when we look at it in this manner, it would cause merchants to put out their orders in time to get them done; and it has been proved that merchants have kept their orders back almost to the last moment, and then the master that has taken the orders had been urgent upon their hands, and wrought them night and day; and so if the time was regulated they would know it, and put out their orders in time for them to be completed.

Did you prefer to work those long hours? -- I preferred to work the legal hours.

When you were working in the mill, were you bound, when required, to work those long hours? -- Yes, if I had not done it, by master would have got somebody else that would.

And the parish officers would not have relieved you, if you had left? -- No, they would have said, "You refused to work."

You would then have been left to starve? -- Yes.

Karl Marx and Friedrich Engels

The Communist Manifesto

The collaboration between Karl Marx (1818-1883) and Friedrich Engels (1820-1895) resulted in some of the most influential social analysis of the nineteenth century. Both men were German, Marx being the son of a lawyer and himself educated in philosophy, Engels coming from a family of wealthy industrialists. However, they allied themselves with the grievances of the working class, and during their years of exile in London developed their theory of the class struggle. Their central arguments and their call to action are summarized in the Communist Manifesto, *published in 1848.*

A spectre is haunting Europe -- the spectre of communism. All the powers of old Europe have entered into a holy alliance to exorcise this spectre: Pope and tsar, Metternich and Guizot, French Radicals and German police-spies.

Where is the party in opposition that has not been decried as communistic by its opponents in power? Where is the opposition that has not hurled back the branding reproach of communism, against the more advanced opposition parties, as well as against its reactionary adversaries?

Two things result from this fact:

I. Communism is already acknowledged by all European powers to be itself a power.

II. It is high time that Communists should openly, in the face of the whole world, publish their views, their aims, their tendencies, and meet this nursery tale of the spectre of communism with a manifesto of the party itself.

To this end, Communists of various nationalities have assem-

Text: Karl Marx, Selected Works *(New York: International Publishers, 1936), I, pp. 204-207, 212-220, 225, 240-241.*

bled in London, and sketched the following manifesto, to be published in the English, French, German, Italian, Flemish and Danish languages.

The history of all hitherto existing society is the history of class struggles.

Freeman and slave, patrician and plebeian, lord and serf, guild-master and journeyman, in a word, oppressor and oppressed stood in constant opposition to one another, carried on an uninterrupted, now hidden, now open fight, a fight that each time ended either in a revolutionary reconstitution of society at large, or in the common ruin of the contending classes.

In the earlier epochs of history, we find almost everywhere a complicated arrangement of society into various orders, a manifold gradation of social rank. In ancient Rome we have patricians, knights, plebeians, slaves; in the Middle Ages, feudal lords, vassals, guild-masters, journeymen, apprentices, serfs; in almost all of these classes, again, subordinate gradations.

The modern bourgeois society that has sprouted from the ruins of feudal society has not done away with class antagonisms. It has but established new classes, new conditions of oppression, new forms of struggle in place of the old ones.

Our epoch, the epoch of the bourgeoisie, possesses, however, this distinctive feature: It has simplified the class antagonisms. Society as a whole is more and more splitting up into two great hostile camps, into two great classes directly facing each other -- bourgeoisie and proletariat.

From the serfs of the Middle Ages sprang the chartered burghers of the earliest towns. From these burgesses the first elements of the bourgeoisie were developed.

The discovery of America, the rounding of the Cape, opened up fresh ground for the rising bourgeoisie. The East-Indian and Chinese markets, the colonisation of America, trade with the colonies, the increase in the means of exchange and in commodities generally, gave to commerce, to navigation, to industry, an impulse never before known, and thereby, to the revolutionary element in the tottering feudal society, a rapid development.

The feudal system of industry, in which industrial production was monopolised by closed guilds, now no longer sufficed for the growing wants of the new markets. The manufacturing system took its place. The guild-masters were pushed aside by the manufacturing middle class; division of labour between the different corporate guilds vanished in the face of division of labour in each single workshop.

Meantime the markets kept ever growing, the demand ever rising. Even manufacture no longer sufficed. Thereupon, steam and machinery revolutionised industrial production. The place of manufacture was taken by the giant, modern industry, the place of the industrial middle class by industrial millionaires, the leaders of whole industrial armies, the modern bourgeois.

Modern industry has established the world market, for which the discovery of America paved the way. This market has given an immense development to commerce, to navigation, to communication by land. This development has, in its turn, reacted on the extension of industry; and in proportion as industry, commerce, navigation, railways extended in the same proportion the bourgeoisie developed, increased its capital, and pushed into the background every class handed down from the Middle Ages.

We see, therefore, how the modern bourgeoisie is itself the product of a long course of development, of a series of revolutions in the modes of production and of exchange.

Each step in the development of the bourgeoisie was accompanied by a corresponding political advance of that class. An oppressed class under the sway of the feudal nobility, an armed and self-governing association in the mediaeval commune; here independent urban republic (as in Italy and Germany), there taxable "third estate" of the monarchy (as in France); afterwards, in the period of manufacture proper, serving either the semi-feudal or the absolute monarchy as a counterpoise against the nobility, and, in fact, corner-stone of the great monarchies in general -- the bourgeoisie has at last, since the establishment of modern industry and of the world market, conquered for itself, in the modern representative state, exclusive political sway. The executive of the modern state is but a committee for managing the common affairs of the whole bourgeoisie.

The bourgeoisie, historically, has played a most revolutionary part.

The bourgeoisie, wherever it has got the upper hand, has put an end to all feudal, patriarchal, idyllic relations. It has pitilessly torn asunder the motley feudal ties that bound man to his "natural superiors," and has left no other nexus between man and man than naked self-interest, than callous "cash payment." It has drowned the most heavenly ecstasies of religious fervour, of chivalrous enthusiasm, of phllistine sentimentalism, in the icy water of egotistical calculation. It has resolved personal worth into exchange value, and in place of the numberless indefeasible chartered freedoms, has set up that single, unconscionable freedom -- Free Trade. In one word, for exploitation, veiled by religious and political illusions, it has substituted naked, shameless, direct, brutal exploitation.

The bourgeoisie has stripped of its halo every occupation hitherto honoured and looked up to with reverent awe. It has converted the physician, the lawyer, the priest, the poet, the man of science, into its paid wage labourers . . . .

In proportion as the bourgeoisie, i.e., capital, is developed, in the same proportion is the proletariat, the modern working class, developed -- a class of labourers, who live only so long as they find work, and who find work only so long as their labour increases capital. These labourers, who must sell themselves piecemeal, are a commodity, like every other article of commerce, and are consequently exposed to all the vicissitudes of competition, to all the fluctuations of the market.

Owing to the extensive use of machinery and to division of labour, the work of the proletarians has lost all individual character, and, consequently, all charm for the workman. He becomes an appendage of the machine, and it is only the most simple, most monotonous, and most easily acquired knack that is required of him. Hence, the cost of production of a workman is restricted, almost entirely, to the means of subsistence that he requires for his maintenance, and for the propagation of his race.

But the price of commodity, and therefore also of labour, is equal to its cost of production. In proportion, therefore, as the repulsiveness of the work increases, the wage decreases. Nay more, in proportion as the use of machinery and division of labour increases, in the same proportion the burden of toil also increases, whether by prolongation of the working hours, by increase of the work exacted in a given time, or by increased speed of the machinery, etc.

Modern industry has converted the little workshop of the patriarchal master into the great factory of the industrial capitalist. Masses of labourers, crowded into the factory, are organised like soldiers. As privates of the industrial army they are placed under the command of a perfect hierarchy of officers and sergeants. Not only are they slaves of the bourgeois class, and of the bourgeois state; they are daily and hourly enslaved by the machine, by the overlooker, and, above all, by the individual bourgeois manufacturer himself. The more openly this despotism proclaims gain to be its end and aim, the more petty, the more hateful, and the more embittering it is.

The less the skill and exertion of strength implied in manual labour, in other words, the more modern industry becomes developed, the more is the labour of men superseded by that of women. Differences of age and sex have no longer any distinctive social validity for the working class. All are instruments of labour, more or less expensive to use, according to their age and sex.

No sooner is the exploitation of the labourer by the manufacturer, so far at an end, that he receives his wages in cash, than he is set upon by the other portions of the bourgeoisie, the landlord, the shopkeeper, the pawnbroker, etc.

The lower strata of the middle class -- the small tradespeople, shopkeepers and retired tradesmen, generally, the handicraftsmen and peasants -- all these sink gradually into the proletariat, partly because their diminutive capital does not suffice for the scale on which modern industry is carried on and is swamped in the competition with the large capitalists, partly because their specialised skill is rendered worthless by new methods of production. Thus the proletariat is recruited from all classes of the population . . . .

Altogether, collisions between the classes of the old society further in many ways the course of development of the proletariat. The bourgeoisie finds itself involved in a constant battle. At first with the aristocracy; later on, with those portions of the bourgeoisie itself, whose interests have become antagonistic to the progress of industry; at all times with the bourgeoisie of foreign countries. In all these battles it sees itself compelled to appeal to the proletariat, to ask for its help, and thus to drag it into the political arena. The bourgeoisie itself, therefore, supplies the proletariat with its own elements of political and general education; in other words, it furnishes the proletariat with weapons for fighting the bourgeoisie.

Further, as we have already seen, entire sections of the ruling classes are, by the advance of industry, precipitated into the proletariat, or are at least threatened in their conditions of existence. These also supply the proletariat with fresh elements of enlightenment and progress.

Finally, in times when the class struggle nears the decisive hour, the process of dissolution going on within the ruling class, in fact within the whole range of old society, assumes such a violent, glaring character that a small section of the ruling class cuts itself adrift, and joins the revolutionary class, the class that holds the future in its hands. Just as, therefore, at an earlier period, a section of the nobility went over to the bourgeoisie, so now a portion of the bourgeoisie goes over to the proletariat, and in particular, a portion of the bourgeois ideologists, who have raised themselves to the level of comprehending theoretically the historical movement as a whole.

Of all the classes that stand face to face with the bourgeoisie today, the proletariat alone is a really revolutionary class. The other classes decay and finally disappear in the face of modern industry; the proletariat is its special and essential product.

* * * * * * * *

In what relation do the Communists stand to the proletarians as a whole?

The Communists do not form a separate party opposed to other working class parties. They have no interests separate and apart from those of the proletariat as a whole. They do not set up any sectarian principles of their own, by which to shape and mould the proletarian movement.

The Communists are distinguished from the other working class parties by this only: 1. In the national struggles of the proletarians of the different countries, they point out and bring to the front the common interests of the entire proletariat, independently of all nationality. 2. In the various stages of development which the struggle of the working class against the bourgeoisie has to pass through, they always and everywhere represent the interests of the movement as a whole.

The Communists, therefore, are on the one hand, practically, the most advanced and resolute section of the working class parties of every country, that section which pushes forward all others; on the other hand, theoretically, they have over the great mass of the proletariat the advantage of clearly understanding the line of march, the conditions, and the ultimate general results of the proletarian movement.

The immediate aim of the Communists is the same as that of all the other proletarian parties: Formation of the proletariat into a class, overthrow of the bourgeois supremacy, conquest of political power by the proletariat.

The theoretical conclusions of the Communists are in no way based on ideas or principles that have been invented, or discovered, by this or that would-be universal reformer.

They merely express, in general terms, actual relations springing from an existing class struggle, from a historical movement going on under our very eyes. The abolition of existing property relations is not at all a distinctive feature of communism.

All property relations in the past have continually been subject to historical change consequent upon the change in historical conditions. The French Revolution, for example, abolished feudal property in favour of bourgeois property.

The distinguishing feature of communism is not the abolition of property generally, but the abolition of bourgeois property. But modern bourgeois private property is the final and most complete expression of the system of producing and appropriating products that is based on class antagonisms, on the exploitation of the many by the few.

In this sense, the theory of the Communists may be summed up in the single sentence: Abolition of private property.

We Communists have been reproached with the desire of abolishing the right of personally acquiring property as the fruit of a man's own labour, which property is alleged to be the groundwork of all personal freedom, activity and independence.

Hard-won, self-acquired, self-earned property! Do you mean the property of the petty artisan and of the small peasant, a form of property that preceded the bourgeois form? There is no need to abolish that; the development of industry has to a great extent already destroyed it, and is still destroying it daily.

Or do you mean modern bourgeois private property? But does wage labour create any property for the labourer?

Not a bit. It creates capital, i.e., that kind of property which exploits wage labour, and which cannot increase except upon condition of begetting a new supply of wage labour for fresh exploitation. Property, in its present form, is based on the antagonism of capital and wage labour. Let us examine both sides of this antagonism.

To be a capitalist is to have not only a purely personal, but a social, *status* in production. Capital is a collective product, and only by the united action of many members, nay, in the last resort, only by the united action of all members of society, can it be set in motion.

Capital is therefore not a personal, it is a social power.

When, therefore, capital is converted into common property, into the property of all members of society, personal property is not thereby transformed into social property. It is only the social character of the property that is changed. It loses its class character . . . .

You are horrified at our intending to do away with private property. But in your existing society, private property is already done away with for nine-tenths of the population; its existence for the few is solely due to its non-existence in the hands of those nine-tenths. You reproach us, therefore, with intending to do away with a form of property, the necessary condition for whose existence is the non-existence of any property for the immense majority of society.

In one word, you reproach us with intending to do away with your property. Precisely so; that is just what we intend . . . .

The Communists are further reproached with desiring to abolish countries and nationality.

The workingmen have no country. We cannot take from them what they have not got. Since the proletariat must first of all acquire political supremacy, must rise to be the leading class of the nation, must constitute itself the nation, it is, so far, itself national, though not in the bourgeois sense of the word.

National differences and antagonisms between peoples are daily more and more vanishing, owing to the development of the bourgeoisie, to freedom of commerce, to the world market, to uniformity in the mode of production and in the conditions of life corresponding thereto.

The supremacy of the proletariat will cause them to vanish still faster. United action of the leading civilised countries at least is one of the first conditions for the emancipation of the proletariat.

In proportion as the exploitation of one individual by another is put an end to, the exploitation of one nation by another will also be put an end to. In proportion as the antagonism between classes within the nation vanishes, the hostility of one nation to another will come to an end . . . .

When, in the course of development, class distinctions have disappeared, and all production has been concentrated in the hands of a vast association of the whole nation, the public power will lose its political character. Political power, properly so called, is merely the organised power of one class for oppressing another. If the proletariat during its contest with the bourgeoisie

is compelled, by the force of circumstances, to organise itself as
a class; if, by means of a revolution, it makes itself the ruling
class, and, as such, sweeps away by force the old conditions of
production, then it will, along with these conditions, have swept
away the conditions for the existence of class antagonisms and of
classes generally, and will thereby have abolished its own
supremacy as a class.

In place of the old bourgeois society, with its classes and
class antagonisms, we shall have an association, in which the free
development of each is the condition for the free development of
all.

* * * * * * * *

The Communists fight for the attainment of the immediate
aims, for the enforcement of the momentary interests of the
working class; but in the movement of the present, they also
represent and take care of the future of that movement. In
France the Communists ally themselves with the Social
Democrats, against the conservative and radical bourgeoisie,
reserving, however, the right to take up a critical position in
regard to phrases and illusions traditionally handed down from
the Great Revolution.

In Switzerland they support the Radicals, without losing sight
of the fact that this party consists of antagonistic elements, partly
of Democratic Socialists, in the French sense, partly of radical
bourgeois.

In Poland they support the party that insists on an agrarian
revolution as the prime condition for national emancipation, that
party which fomented the insurrection of Cracow in 1846.

In Germany they fight with the bourgeoisie whenever it acts
in a revolutionary way against the absolute monarchy, the feudal
squirearchy, and the petty-bourgeoisie.

But they never cease, for a single instant, to instill into the
working class the clearest possible recognition of the hostile
antagonism between bourgeoisie and proletariat, in order that the
German workers may straightway use, as so many weapons
against the bourgeoisie, the social and political conditions that the
bourgeoisie must necessarily introduce along with its supremacy,

and in order that, after the fall of the reactionary classes in Germany, the fight against the bourgeoisie itself may immediately begin.

The Communists turn their attention chiefly to Germany, because that country is on the eve of a bourgeois revolution that is bound to be carried out under more advanced conditions of European civilisation and with a much more developed proletariat than that of England was in the seventeenth and of France in the eighteenth century, and because the bourgeois revolution in Germany will be but the prelude to an immediately following proletarian revolution.

In short, the Communists everywhere support every revolutionary movement against the existing social and political order of things.

In all these movements they bring to the front, as the leading question in each, the property question, no matter what its degree of development at the time.

Finally, they labour everywhere for the union and agreement of the democratic parties of all countries.

The Communists disdain to conceal their views and aims. They openly declare that their ends can be attained only by the forcible overthrow of all existing social conditions. Let the ruling classes tremble at a communist revolution. The proletarians have nothing to lose but their chains. They have a world to win.

Workingmen of all countries, unite!

Joseph Mazzini

The Duties of Man

Although the premises of nationalism have been seriously questioned in the twentieth century, the great nineteenth-century Italian patriot, Joseph Mazzini (1805-1872), was convinced of the need to arouse nationalistic sentiments. The following essay, directed to the working men of Italy in 1860, expresses what Mazzini regards as the positive, intangible, even ethereal qualities that can be derived from the love of one's native land.

Oh my brothers, love your Country! Our Country is our Home, the House that God has given us, placing therein a numerous family that loves us, and whom we love; a family with whom we sympathize more readily, and whom we understand more quickly than we do others; and which, from its being centred round a given spot, and from the homogeneous nature of its elements, is adapted to a special branch of activity.

Our Country is our common workshop, whence the products of our activity are sent forth for the benefit of the whole world; wherein the tools and implements of labour we can most usefully employ are gathered together; nor may we reject them without disobeying the plan of the Almighty and diminishing our own strength.

In labouring for our own Country on the right principle, we labour for Humanity. Our Country is the fulcrum of the lever we have to wield for the common good. In abandoning that fulcrum, we run the risk of rendering ourselves useless not only to Humanity but to our Country itself.

Before men can *associate* with the nations of which Humanity is composed, they must have a National existence. There is no

Text: Joseph Mazzini, The Duties of Man *(London: Chapman & Hall, 1862), pp. 88-94.*

true association except among equals. It is only through our Country that we can have a recognized *collective* existence.

Humanity is a vast army, advancing to the conquest of lands unknown, against enemies both powerful and astute. The peoples are the different corps, the divisions of that army. Each of them has its post assigned to it, and its special operation to execute; and the common victory depends upon the exactitude with which those distinct operations shall be fulfilled. Disturb not the order of battle. Forsake not the banner given to you by God. Wheresoever you may be, in the centre of whatsoever people circumstances may have placed you, be ever ready to combat for the liberty of that people should it be necessary, but combat in such wise that the blood you shed may reflect glory, not on yourselves alone, but on your Country. Say not *I*, but *we*. Let each man among you strive to incarnate his Country in himself. Let each man among you regard himself as a guarantee, responsible for his fellow Countrymen, and learn so to govern his actions as to cause his Country to be loved and respected through him.

Your Country is the sign of the mission God has given you to fulfill towards Humanity. The faculties and forces of *all* her sons should be associated in the accomplishment of that mission.

The true Country is a Community of free men and equals, bound together in fraternal concord to labour towards a common aim. You are bound to make it, and to maintain it such.

The Country is not an *aggregation,* but an *association.*

There is therefore no true Country without an uniform Right. There is no true Country where the uniformity of that Right is violated by the existence of Castes, privilege, and inequality.

Where the activity of a portion of the powers and faculties of the individual is either cancel led or dormant; where there is not a common Principle, recognized, accepted, and developed by all, there is no true Nation, no People, but only a multitude, a fortuitous agglomeration of men whom circumstances have called together, and whom circumstances may again divide.

In the name of the love you bear your Country you must peacefully, but untiringly combat the existence of privilege and inequality in the land that gave you life.

There is but one sole legitimate privilege, the privilege of Genius when it reveals itself united with virtue. But this is a privilege given by God, and when you acknowledge it and follow its inspiration, you do so freely, exercising your own reason and your own choice.

Whatever privilege demands submission from you in virtue of power, inheritance, or any other right than the Right common to all is an usurpation and a tyranny, which you are bound to resist and destroy.

Be your Country your Temple. God at the Summit; a people of equals at the base.

Accept no other formula, no other moral Law, if you would not dishonour alike your Country and yourselves. Let all secondary laws be but the gradual regulation of your existence by the progressive application of this Supreme Law.

And in order that they may be such, it is necessary that *all* of you should aid in framing them. Laws framed only by a single fraction of the citizens can never, in the very nature of things, be other than the mere expression of the thoughts, aspirations, and desires of that fraction; the representation, not of the Country, but of a third or fourth part, of a class or zone of the Country.

The Laws should be the expression of the *universal* aspiration, and promote the universal good. They should be a pulsation of the heart of the Nation. The entire Nation should, either directly or indirectly legislate . . . .

Country is not a mere zone of territory. The true Country is the Idea to which it gives birth; it is the Thought of Love, the sense of communion which united in one all the sons of that territory.

So long as a single one amongst your brothers has no vote to represent him in the development of the National life -- so long as there be one left to vegetate in ignorance where others are educated: so long as a single man, able and willing to work, languishes in poverty through want of work to do, you have no Country in the sense in which Country ought to exist, the Country of all and for all.

Education, labour, and the franchise are the three main pillars of the Nation. Rest not until you have built them strongly up with your own labour and exertions.

Never deny your sister Nations. Be it yours to evolve the Life of your Country in loveliness and strength; free from all servile fears or sceptical doubts; maintaining as its basis the People, as its Guide the consequence of the Principles of its Religious Faith, logically and energetically applied; its strength, the united strength of all; its aim, the fulfillment of the mission given to it by God.

And so long as you are ready to die for Humanity, the Life of your Country will be immortal.

Otto von Bismarck

Memoirs

Prince Otto von Bismarck (1815-1898) become minister-president of the Prussian monarchy in 1862 and chancellor of the newly united Germany in 1871. In his Memoirs, *written after his retirement from these offices in 1890, he reflects on the principle of monarchy in Germany and his role in bringing about the unification of the German state.*

The Teutonic stocks of the north, the Swedes and the Danes, have shown themselves pretty free from dynastic sentiment; and in England, though external respect for the Crown is demanded by good society, and the formal maintenance of monarchy is held expedient by all parties that have hitherto had any share in government, I do not anticipate the disruption of the nation, or that such sentiments as were common in the time of the Jacobites would attain to any practical form, if in the course of its historical development the British people should come to deem a change of dynasty or the transition to a republican form of government necessary or expedient. The preponderance of dynastic attachment, and the use of a dynasty as the indispensable cement to hold together a definite portion of the nation calling itself by the name of the dynasty is a specific peculiarity of the German Empire. The particular nationalities, which among us have shaped themselves on the bases of dynastic family and possession, include in most cases heterogeneous elements, whose cohesion rests neither on identity of stock nor on similarity of historical development, but exclusively on the fact of some (in

Text: Otto von Bismarck, The Memoirs, *trans. under the supervision of A. J. Butler (New York: Howard Fertig, 1966), I, pp. 323-325; II, pp. 57-59, 65, 92, 96-97, 100-102. Reprint of 1899 edition.*

most cases questionable) acquisition by the dynasty whether by the right of the strong, or hereditary succession by affinity or compact of inheritance, or by some reversionary grant obtained from the imperial Court as the price of a vote.

Whatever may be the origin of this factitious union of particularist elements, its result is that the individual German readily obeys the command of a dynasty to harry with fire and sword, and with his own hands to slaughter his German neighbours and kinsfolk as a result of quarrels unintelligible to himself. To examine whether this characteristic be capable of rational justification is not the problem of a German statesman, so long as it is strongly enough pronounced for him to reckon upon it. The difficulty of either abolishing or ignoring it, or making any advance in theory towards unity without regard to this practical limitation, has often proved fatal to the champions of unity; conspicuously so in the advantage taken of the favourable circumstances in the national movements of 1848-50 . . . .

Dynastic interests are justified in Germany so far as they fit in with the common national imperial interests: the two may very well go hand in hand; and a duke loyal to the Empire in the old sense is in certain circumstances more serviceable to the community than would be direct relations between the Emperor and the duke's vassals. So far, however, as dynastic interests threaten us once more with national disintegration and impotence, they must be reduced to their proper measure . . . .

At Berlin I was ostensibly occupied with Prussia's relations to the newly acquired provinces and the other North German states, but in reality with the humour of the foreign Powers and in pondering upon their probable attitude. To me, and perhaps to every one, our internal affairs had a provisional and immature aspect. The reaction of the aggrandisement of Prussia, of the impending negotiations concerning the North German Confederation and its constitution, made our internal development appear to be carried along by the current as much as our relations to foreign states, whether in or outside Germany, in consequence of the European situation prevailing when the war had been interrupted. I took it as assured that war with France could necessarily have to be waged on the road to our further national development, for our development at home as well as the extension beyond the Main, and that we must keep this eventuality in sight in all our domestic as well as in our foreign relations.

In some aggrandisement of Prussia in North Germany Louis Napoleon saw not only no danger to France but a means against the unification and national development of Germany; he believed that the non-Prussian portions of Germany would then feel a greater need of French support. He cherished reminiscences of the confederation of the Rhine and wished to hinder development in the direction of a United Germany. He believed that he could do this because he did not realise the national drift of the time, and judged the situation in accordance with his schoolboy reminiscenses of South Germany, and from diplomatic reports which were only based on ministerial moods and sporadic dynastic feeling.

I was convinced that their importance would vanish. I assumed that a United Germany was only a question of time, that the North German Confederation was only the first step in its solution; but that the enmity of France and perhaps of Russia, Austria's need of revenge of 1866, and the King's Prussian and dynastic particularism must not be called too soon into the lists. I did not doubt that a Franco-German war must take place before the construction of a United Germany could be realised. I was at that time preoccupied with the idea of delaying the outbreak of this war until our fighting strength should be increased by the application of the Prussian military legislation not only to Hanover, Hesse, and Holstein, but, as I could hope even at that time from the observation I had made, to the South Germans. I considered a war with France, having regard to the success of the French in the Crimean war and in Italy, as a danger which I at that time overestimated; inasmuch as I imagined the attainable number of troops in France, their order and organisation, and the tactical skill to be higher and better than proved to be the case in 1870. The courage of the French soldiers, the high pitch of national sentiment and of injured vanity, were verified to the full extent, as I had estimated them in the eventuality of a German invasion in France.

I at no time regarded a war with France as a simple matter, considered quite apart from the possible allies that France might find in Austria's thirst for revenge, or in Russia's desire for a balance of power. My strenuous efforts to postpone the outbreak of war until the effect of our military legislation and our military training could be thoroughly developed in all portions of the country which had been newly joined to Prussia, were therefore quite reasonable . . . .

Looking to the necessity, in a fight against an overwhelming foreign Power, of being able, in extreme need, to use even revolutionary means, I had had no hesitation whatever in throwing into the frying-pan, by means of the circular dispatch of June 10, 1866, the most powerful ingredient known at that time to liberty-mongers, namely, universal suffrage, so as to frighten off foreign monarchies from trying to stick a finger into our national omelette. I never doubted that the German people would be strong and clever enough to free themselves from the existing suffrage as soon as they realised that it was a harmful institution. If it cannot, then my saying that Germany can ride when once it has got into the saddle was erroneous. The acceptance of universal suffrage was a weapon in the war against Austria and other foreign countries, in the war for German Unity, as well as a threat to use the last weapons in a struggle against coalitions. In a war of this sort, when it becomes a matter of life and death, one does not look at the weapons that one seizes, nor the value of what one destroys in using them: one is guided at the moment by no other thought than the issue of the war and the preservation of one's external independence; the settling of affairs and reparation of the damage has to take place after the peace. Moreover, I still hold that the principle of universal suffrage is a just one, not only in theory but also in practice, provided always that voting be not secret, for secrecy is a quality that is indeed incompatible with the best characteristics of German blood . . . .

In France, however, a *casus belli* was being sought against Prussia which should be as free as possible from German national colouring; and it was thought one had been discovered in the dynastic sphere by the accession to the Spanish throne of a candidate bearing the name of Hohenzollern. In this the overrating of the military superiority of France and the underrating of the national feeling in Germany was clearly the chief reason why the tenability of this pretext was not examined either with honesty or judgment. The German national outburst which followed the French declaration, and resembled a stream bursting its sluices, was a surprise to French politicians . . . .

Having decided to resign, in spite of the remonstrances which Roon made against it, I invited him and Moltke to dine with me alone on the 13th, and communicated to them at table my views and projects for doing so . . . .

During our conversation I was informed that a telegram from Ems, in cipher, if I recollect rightly, of about 200 "groups" was being deciphered. When the copy was handed to me it showed that Abeken had drawn up and signed the telegram at his Majesty's command, and I read it out to my guests, whose dejection was so great that they turned away from food and drink . . . .

I made use of the royal authorisation communicated to me through Abeken to publish the contents of the telegram; and in the presence of my two guests I reduced the telegram by striking out words, but without adding or altering, to the following form: "After the news of the renunciation of the hereditary Prince of Hohenzollern had been officially communicated to the imperial government of France by the royal government of Spain, the French ambassador at Ems further demanded of his Majesty the King that he would authorise him to telegraph to Paris that his Majesty the King bound himself for all future time never again to give his consent if the Hohenzollerns should renew their candidature. His Majesty the King thereupon decided not to receive the French ambassador again and sent to tell him through the aide-de-camp on duty that his Majesty had nothing further to communicate to the ambassador." The difference in the effect of the abbreviated text of the Ems telegram as compared with that produced by the original was not the result of stronger words but of the form, which made this announcement appear decisive, while Abeken's version would only have been regarded as a fragment of a negotiation still pending and to be continued at Berlin.

After I had read out the concentrated edition to my two guests, Moltke remarked: "Now it has a different ring; it sounded before like a parley; now it is like a flourish in answer to a challenge." I went on to explain: "If in execution of his Majesty's order I at once communicate this text, which contains no alteration in or addition to the telegram, not only to the newspapers but also by telegraph to all our embassies, it will be known in Paris before midnight, and not only on account of its contents but also on account of the manner of its distribution will have the effect of a red rag upon the Gallic bull. Fight we must if we do not want to act the part of the vanquished without a battle. Success, however, essentially depends upon the impression which the origination of the war makes upon us and others; it is important that we should be the party attacked, and this Gallic overweening and touchiness will make us if we announce in the face of Europe, so far as we can without the speaking-tube of the Reichstag, that we fearlessly meet the public threats of France."

This explanation brought about in the two generals a revulsion to a more joyous mood, the liveliness of which surprised me. They had suddenly recovered their pleasure in eating and drinking and spoke in a more cheerful vein. Roon said: "Our God of old lives still and will not let us perish in disgrace." Moltke so far relinquished his passive equanimity that, glancing up joyously towards the ceiling and abandoning his usual punctiliousness of speech, he smote his hand upon his breast and said: "If I may but live to lead our armies in such a war, then the devil may come directly afterwards and fetch away the 'old carcass'."

Charles Darwin

Origin of Species

In his Origin of Species *(1859), Charles Darwin sets forth the hypothesis that evolution operates by "natural selection" through a "struggle for existence" and the "survival of the fittest." While the fusion of these ideas soon gained general acceptance in scientific circles, their social implications resulted in a great deal of controversy. In particular, Darwin's theory caused a storm of indignation among theologians, because it seemed to conflict with the biblical account of creation.*

A struggle for existence inevitably follows from the high rate at which all organic beings tend to increase. Every being, which during its natural lifetime produces several eggs or seeds, must suffer destruction during some period of its life, and during some season or occasional year, otherwise, on the principle of geometrical increase, its numbers would quickly become so inordinately great that no country could support the product. Hence, as more individuals are produced than can possibly survive, there must in every case be a struggle for existence, either one individual with another of the same species, or with the individuals of distinct species, or with the physical conditions of life. It is the doctrine of Malthus applied with manifold force to the whole animal and vegetable kingdoms; for in this case there can be no artificial increase of food, and no prudential restraint from marriage. Although some species may be now increasing, more or less rapidly, in numbers, all cannot do so, for the world would not hold them.

Text: Charles Darwin, The Origin of Species by Means of Natural Selection, or The Preservation of the Favoured Races in the Struggle for Life, *6th ed. (New York: D. Appleton and Company, 1897), I, pp. 79, 83, 91-92, 96, 159-162; II, pp. 293-295, 305-306.*

The causes which check the natural tendency of each species to increase are most obscure. Look at the most vigorous species; by as much as it swarms in numbers, by so much will it tend to increase still further. We know not exactly what the checks are even in a single instance . . . .

In the case of every species, many different checks, acting at different periods of life, and during different seasons or years, probably come into play, some one check or some few being generally the most potent; but all will concur in determining the average number or even the existence of the species. In some cases it can be shown that widely-different checks act on the same species in different districts. When we look at the plants and bushes clothing an entangled bank, we are tempted to attribute their proportional numbers and kinds to what we call chance.

But how false a view is this! Every one has heard that when an American forest is cut down, a very different vegetation springs up; but it has been observed that ancient Indian ruins in the Southern United States, which must formerly have been cleared of trees, now display the same beautiful diversity and proportion of kinds as in the surrounding virgin forest. What a struggle must have gone on during long centuries between the several kinds of trees, each annually scattering its seeds by the thousand; what war between insect and insect -- between insects, snails, and other animals with birds and beasts of prey -- all striving to increase, all feeding on each other, or on the trees, their seeds and seedlings, or on the other plants which first clothed the ground and thus checked the growth of the trees! Throw up a handful of feathers, and all fall to the ground according to definite laws; but how simple is the problem where each shall fall compared to that of the action and reaction of the innumerable plants and animals which have determined, in the course of centuries, the proportional numbers and kinds of trees now growing on the old Indian ruins!

* * * * * * * *

It is good thus to try in imagination to give to any one species an advantage over another. Probably in no single instance should we know what to do. This ought to convince us of our ignorance on the mutual relations of all organic beings; a conviction as necessary, as it is difficult to acquire. All that we can do, is to keep steadily in mind that each organic being is striving to increase in a geometrical ratio; that each at some period of its life, during some season of the year, during each generation or at intervals, has to struggle for life and to suffer great destruction. When we reflect on this struggle, we may console ourselves with the full belief that the war of nature is not incessant, that no fear is felt, that death is generally prompt, and that the vigorous, the healthy, and the happy survive and multiply . . . .

If under changing conditions of life organic beings present individual differences in almost every part of their structure, and this cannot be disputed; if there be, owing to their geometrical rate of increase, a severe struggle for life at some age, season, or year, and this certainly cannot be disputed; then, considering the infinite complexity of the relations of all organic beings to each other and to their conditions of life, causing an infinite diversity in structure, constitution, and habits, to be advantageous to them, it would be a most extraordinary fact if no variations had ever occurred useful to each being's own welfare, in the same manner as so many variations have occurred useful to man. But if variations useful to any organic being ever do occur, assuredly individuals thus characterised will have the best chance of being preserved in the struggle for life; and from the strong principle of inheritance, these will tend to produce offspring similarly characterised. This principle of preservation, or the survival of the fittest, I have called Natural Selection. It leads to the improvement of each creature in relation to its organic and inorganic conditions of life; and consequently, in most cases, to what must be regarded as an advance in organisation. Nevertheless, low and simple forms will long endure if well fitted for their simple conditions of life . . . .

I have now recapitulated the facts and considerations which have thoroughly convinced me that species have been modified, during a long course of descent. This has been effected chiefly through the natural selection of numerous successive, slight, favourable variations, aided in an important manner by the inherited effects of the use and disuse of parts; and in an unimportant manner, that is in relation to adaptive structures, whether past or present, by the direct action of external conditions, and by variations which seem to us in our ignorance to arise spontaneously . . . .

I see no good reason why the views given in this volume should shock the religious feelings of any one. It is satisfactory, as showing how transient such impressions are, to remember that the greatest discovery ever made by man, namely, the law of the attraction of gravity, was also attacked by Leibnitz "as subversive of natural, and inferentially of revealed, religion." A celebrated author and divine has written to me that "he has gradually learnt to see that it is just as noble a conception of the Deity to believe that He created a few original forms capable of self-development into other and needful forms, as to believe that He required a fresh act of creation to supply the voids caused by the action of His laws."

Why, it may be asked, until recently did nearly all the most eminent living naturalists and geologists disbelieve in the mutability of species. It cannot be asserted that organic beings in a state of nature are subject to no variation; it cannot be proved that the amount of variation in the course of long ages is a limited quantity; no clear distinction has been, or can be, drawn between species and well-marked varieties. It cannot be maintained that species when intercrossed are invariably sterile, and varieties invariably fertile; or that sterility is a special endowment and sign of creation.

The belief that species were immutable productions was almost unavoidable as long as the history of the world was thought to be of short duration; and now that we have acquired some idea of the lapse of time, we are too apt to assume, without proof, that the geological record is so perfect that it would have afforded us plain evidence of the mutation of species, if they had undergone mutation.

But the chief cause of our natural unwillingness to admit that one species has given birth to clear and distinct species is that we

are always slow in admitting great changes of which we do not
see the steps . . . .

It is interesting to contemplate a tangled bank, clothed with
many plants of many kinds, with birds singing on the bushes,
with various insects flitting about, and with worms crawling
through the damp earth, and to reflect that these elaborately
constructed forms, so different from each other, and dependent
upon each other in so complex a manner, have all been produced
by laws acting around us. These laws, taken in the largest sense,
being Growth with Reproduction; Inheritance which is almost
implied by reproduction; Variability from the indirect and direct
action of the conditions of life, and from use and disuse: a Ratio
of Increase so high as to lead to a Struggle for Life, and as a
consequence to Natural Selection, entailing Divergence of
Character and the Extinction of less-improved forms. Thus,
from the war of nature, from famine and death, the most exalted
object which we are capable of conceiving, namely, the
production of the higher animals, directly follows. There is
grandeur in this view of life with its several powers, having been
originally breathed by the Creator into a few forms or into one;
and that, whilst this planet has gone cycling on according to the
fixed law of gravity, from so simple a beginning endless forms
most beautiful and most wonderful have been and are being
evolved.

Andrew Carnegie

The Gospel of Wealth

The concept of Darwinism had important ramifications for the rising business community in the late nineteenth century. One of the best known exemplars of "Social Darwinism" was Andrew Carnegie (1835-1919). Carnegie, who emigrated from Scotland to America in 1848, soon rose to prominence in the business world and by 1900 virtually controlled the steel industry in the United States. His essay, The Gospel of Wealth, *written in 1889, summarizes his views on the acquisition and utilization of personal riches.*

The problem of our age is the proper administration of wealth, that the ties of brotherhood may still bind together the rich and poor in harmonious relationship. The conditions of human life have not only been changed, but revolutionized, within the past few hundred years. In former days there was little difference between the dwelling, dress, food, and environment of the chief and those of his retainers. The Indians are today where civilized man then was. When visiting the Sioux, I was led to the wigwam of the chief. It was like the others in external appearance, and even within the difference was trifling between it and those of the poorest of his braves. The contrast between the palace of the millionaire and the cottage of the laborer with us today measures the change which has come with civilization. This change, however, is not to be deplored, but welcomed as highly beneficial. It is well, nay, essential, for the progress of the race that the houses of some should be homes for all that is highest and best in literature and the arts, and for all the refinements of civilization, rather than that none should

Text: Andrew Carnegie, The Gospel of Wealth and Other Timely Essays *(New York: The Century Co., 1900), pp. 1-5, 7-13, 15.*

be so. Much better this great irregularity than universal squalor. Without wealth there can be no Maecenas. The "good old times" were not good old times. Neither master nor servant was as well situated then as today. A relapse to old conditions would be disastrous to both -- not the least so to him who serves -- and would sweep away civilization with it. But whether the change be for good or ill, it is upon us, beyond our power to alter, and, therefore, to be accepted and made the best of. It is a waste of time to criticize the inevitable.

It is easy to see how the change has come. One illustration will serve for almost every phase of the cause. In the manufacture of products we have the whole story. It applies to all combinations of human industry, as stimulated and enlarged by the inventions of this scientific age. Formerly, articles were manufactured at the domestic hearth, or in small shops which formed part of the household. The master and his apprentices worked side by side, the latter living with the master, and therefore subject to the same conditions. When these apprentices rose to be masters, there was little or no change in their mode of life, and they, in turn, educated succeeding apprentices in the same routine. There was, substantially, social equality, and even political equality, for those engaged in industrial pursuits had then little or no voice in the State.

The inevitable result of such a mode of manufacture was crude articles at high prices. Today the world obtains commodities of excellent quality at prices which even the preceding generation would have deemed incredible. In the commercial world similar causes have produced similar results, and the race is benefited thereby. The poor enjoy what the rich could not before afford. What were the luxuries have become the necessaries of life. The laborer has now more comforts than the farmer had a few generations ago. The farmer has more luxuries than the landlord had, and is more richly clad and better housed. The landlord has books and pictures rarer and appointments more artistic than the king could then obtain.

The price we pay for this salutary change is, no doubt, great. We assemble thousands of operatives in the factory, and in the mine, of whom the employer can know little or nothing, and to whom he is little better than a myth. All intercourse between them is at an end. Rigid castes are formed, and, as usual, mutual ignorance breeds mutual distrust. Each caste is without sympathy with the other, and ready to credit anything disparaging in regard to it. Under the law of competition, the employer of thousands is forced into the strictest economies, among which the rates paid to labor figure prominently, and often there is friction between capital and labor, between rich and poor. Human society loses homogeneity.

The price which society pays for the law of competition, like the price it pays for cheap comforts and luxuries, is also great; but the advantages of this law are also greater still than its cost-- for it is to this law that we owe our wonderful material development, which brings improved conditions in its train. But, whether the law be benign or not, we must say of the change in the conditions of men to which we have referred: It is here; we cannot evade it; no substitutes for it have been found; and while the law may be sometimes hard for the individual, it is best for the race, because it insures the survival of the fittest in every department. We accept and welcome, therefore, as conditions to which we must accommodate ourselves, great inequality of environment; the concentration of business, industrial and commercial, in the hands of a few; and the law of competition between these, as being not only beneficial, but essential to the future progress of the race. Having accepted these, it follows that there must be great scope for the exercise of special ability in the merchant and in the manufacturer who has to conduct affairs upon a great scale. That this talent for organization and management is rare among men is proved by the fact that it invariably secures enormous rewards for its possessor, no matter where or under what laws or conditions. The experienced in affairs always rate the man whose services can be obtained as a partner as not only the first consideration, but such as render the question of his capital scarcely worth considering: for able men soon create capital; in the hands of those without the special talent required, capital soon takes wings. Such men become interested in firms or corporations using millions; and, estimating only simple interest to be made upon the capital invested, it is inevitable that their income must exceed their expenditure and that they must, therefore, accumulate wealth. Nor is there any middle ground which such men can occupy, because the great manufacturing or commercial concern which does not earn at least interest upon its capital soon becomes bankrupt. It must either go forward or fall behind; to stand still is impossible. It is a condition essential to its successful operation that it should be thus far profitable, and even that, in addition to interest on capital, it should make profit. It is a law, as certain as any of the others named, that men possessed of this peculiar talent for affairs, under the free play of economic forces must, of necessity, soon be in receipt of more revenue than can be judiciously expended upon themselves; and this law is as beneficial for the race as the others . . . .

We start, then, with a condition of affairs under which the best interests of the race are promoted, but which inevitably gives wealth to the few. Thus far, accepting conditions as they exist, the situation can be surveyed and pronounced good. The question then arises -- and if the foregoing be correct, it is the only question with which we have to deal: What is the proper mode of administering wealth after the laws upon which civilization is founded have thrown it into the hands of the few? And it is of this great question that I believe I offer the true solution. It will be understood that fortunes are here spoken of, not moderate sums saved by many years of effort, the returns from which are required for the comfortable maintenance and education of families. This is not wealth, but only competence, which it should be the aim of all to acquire, and which it is for the best interests of society should be acquired.

There are but three modes in which surplus wealth can be disposed of. It can be left to the families of the decedents; or it can be bequeathed for public purposes; or, finally, it can be administered by its possessors during their lives. Under the first and second modes most of the wealth of the world that has reached the few has hitherto been applied. Let us in turn consider each of these modes. The first is the most injudicious. In monarchical countries, the estates and the greatest portion of the wealth are left to the first son, that the vanity of the parent may be gratified by the thought that his name and title are to descend unimpaired to succeeding generations. The condition of this class in Europe today teaches the failure of such hopes or ambitions. The successors have become impoverished through their follies, or from the fall in the value of land. Even in Great Britain the strict law of entail has been found inadequate to maintain an hereditary class. Its soil is rapidly passing into the hands of the stranger. Under republican institutions the division of property among the children is much fairer; but the question which forces itself upon thoughtful men in all lands is: Why should men leave great fortunes to their children? If this is done from affection, is it not misguided affection? Observation teaches that, generally speaking, it is not well for the children that they should be so burdened. Neither is it well for the State. Beyond providing for the wife and daughters moderate sources of income, and very moderate allowances indeed, if any, for the sons, men may well hesitate; for it is no longer questionable that great sums bequeathed often work more for the injury than for the good of the recipients. Wise men will soon conclude that, for the best interests of the members of their families, and of the State, such bequests are an improper use of their means.

It is not suggested that men who have failed to educate their sons to earn a livelihood shall cast them adrift in poverty. If any man has seen fit to rear his sons with a view to their living idle lives, or, what is highly commendable, has instilled in them the sentiment that they are in a position to labor for public ends without reference to pecuniary considerations, then, of course, the duty of the parent is to see that such are provided for in moderation. There are instances of millionaires' sons unspoiled by wealth who, being rich, still perform great services to the community. Such are the very salt of the earth, as valuable as, unfortunately, they are rare. It is not the exception, however, but the rule, that men must regard; and, looking at the usual result of enormous sums conferred upon legatees, the thoughtful man must shortly say, "I would as soon leave to my son a curse as the almighty dollar," and admit to himself that it is not the welfare of the children, but family pride, which inspires these legacies.

As to the second mode, that of leaving wealth at death for public uses, it may be said that this is only a means for the disposal of wealth, provided a man is content to wait until he is dead before he becomes of much good in the world. Knowledge of the results of legacies bequeathed is not calculated to inspire the brightest hopes of much posthumous good being accomplished by them. The cases are not few in which the real object sought by the testator is not attained, nor are they few in which his real wishes are thwarted. In many cases the bequests are so used as to become only monuments of his folly. It is well to remember that it requires the exercise of not less ability than that which acquires it, to use wealth so as to be really beneficial to the community. Besides this, it may fairly be said that no man is to be extolled for doing what he cannot help doing, nor is he to be thanked by the community to which he only leaves wealth at death. Men who leave vast sums in this way may fairly be thought men who would not have left it at all had they been able to take it with them. The memories of such cannot be held in grateful remembrance, for there is no grace in their gifts. It is not to be wondered at that such bequests seem so generally to lack the blessing . . . .

There remains, then, only one mode of using great fortunes; but in this we have the true antidote for the temporary unequal distribution of wealth, the reconciliation of the rich and the poor -- a reign of harmony, another ideal, differing, indeed, from that of the Communist in requiring only the further evolution of existing conditions, not the total overthrow of our civilization. It is founded upon the present most intense Individualism, and the race is prepared to put it in practice by degrees whenever it pleases. Under its sway we shall have an ideal State, in which the surplus wealth of the few will become, in the best sense, the property of the many, because administered for the common good; and this wealth, passing through the hands of the few, can

be made a much more potent force for the elevation of our race
than if distributed in small sums to the people themselves. Even
the poorest can be made to see this, and to agree that great sums
gathered by some of their fellow citizens and spent for public
purposes, from which the masses reap the principal benefit, are
more valuable to them than if scattered among themselves in
trifling amounts through the course of many years . . . .

This, then, is held to be the duty of the man of wealth: To set
an example of modest, unostentatious living, shunning display or
extravagance; to provide moderately for the legitimate wants of
those dependent upon him; and, after doing so, to consider all
surplus revenues which come to him simply as trust funds, which
he is called upon to administer in the manner which, in his judgment, is best calculated to produce the most beneficial results for
the community -- the man of wealth thus becoming the mere
trustee and agent for his poorer brethren, bringing to their service
his superior wisdom, experience, and ability to administer, doing
for them better than they would or could do for themselves.

The following three selections represent prevailing attitudes toward imperialism in late nineteenth-century Europe. The speech by Joseph Chamberlain, British Colonial Secretary from 1895 to 1903, shifts the rationale for colonies from the traditional argument of economic benefits for the mother country to that of cultural mission. Another Britisher, Rudyard Kipling, in his poem, "The White Man's Burden," amplifies this theme. Kipling, who grew up in India, Britain's colonial "Jewel of the East," not only conveyed through his many poems and stories the allure of living among colonial peoples, but he also emphasized the responsibility of carrying European civilization to them. The speeches of Wilhelm II, who became German emperor in 1888, reflect the feeling of many Germans that their recently united country must become a colonial power if it was to take its rightful place among the major European states.

Joseph Chamberlain

The True Conception of Empire

I have now the honour to propose to you the toast of "Prosperity to the Royal Colonial Institute." The institute was founded in 1868, almost exactly a generation ago, and I confess that I admire the faith of its promoters, who, in a time not altogether favourable to their opinions, sowed the seed of Imperial patriotism, although they must have known that few of them could live to gather the fruit and to reap the harvest. But their faith has been justified by the result of their labours, and their foresight must be recognised in the light of our present experience.

It seems to me that there are three distinct stages in our

Text: Charles W. Boyd, ed., Mr. Chamberlain's Speeches *(London: Constable and Company, Ltd., 1914), II, pp. 1-4.*

Imperial history. We began to be, and we ultimately became a great Imperial power in the eighteenth century, but, during the greater part of that time, the colonies were regarded, not only by us, but by every European power that possessed them, as possessions valuable in proportion to the pecuniary advantage which they brought to the mother country, which, under that order of ideas, was not truly a mother at all, but appeared rather in the light of a grasping and absentee landlord desiring to take from his tenants the utmost rents he could exact. The colonies were valued and maintained because it was thought that they would be a source of profit -- of direct profit -- to the mother country.

That was the first stage, and when we were rudely awakened by the War of Independence in America from this dream that the colonies could be held for our profit alone, the second chapter was entered upon, and public opinion seems then to have drifted to the opposite extreme; and, because the colonies were no longer a source of revenue, it seems to have been believed and argued by many people that their separation from us was only a matter of time, and that that separation should be desired and encouraged lest haply they might prove an encumbrance and a source of weakness.

It was while those views were still entertained, while the little Englanders were in their full career, that this institute was founded to protest against doctrines so injurious to our interests and so derogatory to our honour; and I rejoice that what was then, as it were, "a voice crying in the wilderness" is now the expressed and determined will of the overwhelming majority of the British people. Partly by the efforts of this institute and similar organisations, partly by the writings of such men as Froude and Seeley, but mainly by the instinctive good sense and patriotism of the people at large, we have now reached the third stage in our history, and the true conception of our Empire.

What is that conception? As regards the self-governing colonies we no longer talk of them as dependencies. The sense of possession has given place to the sentiment of kinship. We think and speak of them as part of ourselves, as part of the British Empire, united to us, although they may be dispersed throughout the world, by ties of kindred, of religion, of history, and of language, and joined to us by the seas that formerly seemed to divide us.

But the British Empire is not confined to the self-governing colonies and the United Kingdom. It includes a much greater area, a much more numerous population in tropical climes, where no considerable European settlement is possible, and where the native population must always vastly outnumber the white inhabitants; and in these cases also the same change has come over the Imperial idea. Here also the sense of possession has given place to a different sentiment -- the sense of obligation. We feel now that our rule over these territories can only be justified if we can show that it adds to the happiness and prosperity of the people, and I maintain that our rule does, and has, brought security and peace and comparative prosperity to countries that never knew these blessings before.

In carrying out this work of civilisation we are fulfilling what I believe to be our national mission, and we are finding scope for the exercise of those faculties and qualities which have made of us a great governing race. I do not say that our success has been perfect in every case, I do not say that all our methods have been beyond reproach; but I do say that in almost every instance in which the rule of the Queen has been established and the great *Pax Britannica* has been enforced, there has come with it greater security to life and property, and a material improvement in the condition of the bulk of the population. No doubt, in the first instance, when these conquests have been made, there has been bloodshed, there has been loss of life among the native populations, loss of still more precious lives among those who have been sent out to bring these countries into some kind of disciplined order, but it must be remembered that that is the condition of the mission we have to fulfil. There are, of course, among us -- there always are among us, I think -- a very small minority of men who are ready to be the advocates of the most detestable tyrants, provided their skin is black -- men who sympathise with the sorrows of Prempeh and Lobengula, and who denounce as murderers those of their countrymen who have gone forth at the command of the Queen, and who have re-deemed districts as large as Europe from the barbarism and the superstition in which they had been steeped for centuries. I remember a picture by Mr. Selous of a philanthropist -- an imaginary philanthropist, I will hope -- sitting cosily by his fire-side and denouncing the methods by which British civilisation was promoted. This philanthropist complained of the use of Maxim guns and other instruments of warfare, and asked why we could not proceed by more conciliatory methods, and why the impis* of Lobengula could not be brought before a magistrate, and fined five shillings and bound over to keep the peace.

No doubt there is a humorous exaggeration in this picture, but there is gross exaggeration in the frame of mind against which it was directed. You cannot have omelettes without breaking eggs; you cannot destroy the practices of barbarism, of slavery, of superstition, which for centuries have desolated the interior of Africa, without the use of force; but if you will fairly contrast the gain to humanity with the price which we are bound to pay for it, I think you may well rejoice in the result of such expeditions as those which have been recently conducted with such signal success in Nyassaland, Ashanti, Benin, and Nupé -- expeditions which may have, and indeed have, cost valuable lives, but as to which we may rest assured that for one life lost a hundred will be gained, and the cause of civilisation and the prosperity of the people will in the long run be eminently advanced. But no doubt such a state of things, such a mission as I have described, in-volves heavy responsibility. In the wide dominions of the Queen the doors of the temple of Janus are never closed, and it is a gigantic task that we have undertaken when we have determined to wield the sceptre of empire. Great is the task, great is the responsibility, but great is the honour; and I am convinced that the conscience and the spirit of the country will rise to the height of its obligations, and that we shall have the strength to fulfil the mission which our history and our national character have imposed upon us.

---

*Impi: a band of tribal warriors.

Rudyard Kipling

The White Man's Burden

Take up the White Man's burden,
  Send forth the best ye breed,
Go bind your sons to exile
  To serve your captives' need;
To wait in heavy harness
  On fluttered folk and wild,
Your new-caught, sullen peoples,
  Half-devil and half-child.

Take up the White Man's burden
  In patience to abide,
To veil the threat of terror
  And check the show of pride;
By open speech and simple,
  An hundred times made plain,
To seek another's profit,
  And work another's gain.

Take up the White Man's burden,
  The savage wars of peace,
Fill full the mouth of Famine
  And bid the sickness cease;
And when your goal is nearest,
  The end for others sought,
Watch Sloth and heathen Folly
  Bring all your hope to nought.

Text: Rudyard Kipling's Verse: Inclusive Edition *(Garden City, N.Y.: Doubleday, Doran & Company, Inc., 1929), pp. 373-374.*

Take up the White Man's burden,
  No tawdry rule of kings,
But toil of serf and sweeper
  The tale of common things.
The ports ye shall not enter,
  The roads ye shall not tread,
Go make them with your living,
  And mark them with your dead.

Take up the White Man's burden
  And reap his old reward:
The blame of those ye better,
  The hate of those ye guard,
The cry of hosts ye humour
  (Ah, slowly!) toward the light;
"Why brought ye us from bondage,
  "Our loved Egyptian night?"

Take up the White Man's burden,
  Ye dare not stoop to less,
Nor call too loud on Freedom
  To cloak your weariness;
By all ye cry or whisper,
  By all ye leave or do,
The silent, sullen peoples
  Shall weigh your Gods and you.

Take up the White Man's burden,
  Have done with childish days,
The lightly proffered laurel,
  The easy, ungrudged praise,
Comes now, to search your manhood
  Through all the thankless years,
Cold, edged with dear-bought wisdom,
  The judgment of your peers!

Wilhelm II

Speeches

My Dear Henry:

As I rode into Kiel today I thought of the many times on which I had visited this city joyfully at your side and on my ships, either to be present at the sports or at some one of our military undertakings. On my arrival in the city today an earnest and deep feeling moved me, for I am perfectly conscious of the task which I have set before you and of the responsibility which I bear. But I am likewise conscious of the fact that it is my duty to build up and carry farther what my predecessors have bequeathed to me.

The journey which you are to undertake and the task which you are to accomplish indicate nothing new in themselves; it is merely the logical consequence of what my departed grandfather and his great Chancellor inaugurated politically and what our glorious father won with his sword on the field of battle. It is nothing more than the first expression of the newly united and newly arisen German Empire in its tasks beyond the seas. The empire has developed so astonishingly through the extension of its commercial interests that it is my duty to follow up the new German Hansa and to give it the protection which it has a right to expect from the empire and the Emperor.

Our German brothers of the church who have gone out to their quiet work and have not spared risking their lives in order to spread and make a home for our religion on foreign soil have placed themselves under my protection, and it is now a question of providing support and safety for these brothers who have been so often insulted and oppressed. For that reason the undertaking

---

Text: Christian Gauss, ed. and trans., The German Emperor as Shown in His Public Utterances *(New York: Charles Scribner's Sons, 1915), pp. 118-121, 181-182.*

which I intrust to you and which you must fulfil in company with your comrades and the ships which are already out there is really one of protection and not one of defiance. Under the protecting banner of our German flag of war we expect that the rights which we are justified in demanding will be guaranteed to our commerce, to the German merchant, and to German ships -- the same right which is vouchsafed by strangers to all other nations.

Our commerce is not new; in old times the Hanseatic League was one of the most powerful enterprises which the world has ever seen, and the German cities were able to build a fleet such as the sea's broad back had never carried in earlier days, but finally it came to naught because the one condition was lacking, namely that of an Emperor's protection. Now things have changed; the first condition, the German Empire, has been created; the second condition, German commerce, flourishes and develops, and it can only develop properly and securely if it feels itself safe under the power of the empire. Imperial power means sea power, and sea power and imperial power are so interdependent that the one cannot exist without the other.

As a token of this imperial sea power the squadron which has been strengthened by your division must now take its place, with all the comrades of the foreign fleet out there in close relationship and on good terms of friendship, but for the purpose of protecting our particular interests against every one who might be tempted to intrude upon the right of the Germans. That is your task and your mission.

Make it clear to every European there, to the German merchant, and, above all things, to the foreigner in whose country we are or with whom we have to deal, that the German *Michel** has set his shield, decorated with the imperial eagle, firmly upon the ground. Whoever asks him for protection will

---

*The German *Michel* was the proverbial representative of the German character, as Uncle Sam was of the American or John Bull of the English. He was usually pictured as a simple, good-natured fellow.

always receive it. And may our countrymen out there cherish the firm conviction, whether they are priests or merchants or whatever profession they follow, that the protection of the German Empire as exemplified in the Emperor's ships will continually be granted them. But if any one should undertake to insult us in our rights or to wish to harm us, then drive in with the mailed fist and, as God wills, bind about your young brow the laurels which no one in the entire German Empire will begrudge you!

In the firm conviction that you, following good examples -- and, God be praised, examples are not wanting in our house -- will carry out my thoughts and wishes, I raise my glass and drink it to your health, with the wish for a good voyage, for a happy issue to your task, and for a joyous return. Long live his Royal Highness, Prince Henry! Hurrah! Hurrah! Hurrah!

* * * * * * * *

In spite of the fact that we have no such fleet as we should have, we have conquered for ourselves a place in the sun. It will now be my task to see to it that this place in the sun shall remain our undisputed possession, in order that the sun's rays may fall fruitfully upon our activity and trade in foreign parts, that our industry and agriculture may develop within the state and our sailing sports upon the water, for our future lies upon the water. The more Germans go out upon the waters, whether it be in the races of regattas, whether it be in journeys across the ocean, or in the service of the battle-flag, so much the better will it be for us. For when the German has once learned to direct his glance upon what is distant and great, the pettiness which surrounds him in daily life on all sides will disappear. Whoever wishes to have this larger and freer outlook can find no better place than one of the Hanseatic cities . . . .

In the events which have taken place in China I see the indication that European peace is assured for many years to come; for the achievements of the particular contingents have brought about a mutual respect and feeling of comradeship that can only serve the furtherance of peace. But in this period of peace I hope that our Hanseatic cities will flourish. Our new

Hansa will open new paths and create and conquer new markets for them.

As head of the empire I therefore rejoice over every citizen, whether from Hamburg, Bremen, or Linbeck, who goes forth with this large outlook and seeks new points where we can drive in the nail on which to hang our armor.

Friedrich Nietzsche

The German philosopher Friedrich Nietzsche (1844-1900) has often been portrayed as a precursor of twentieth-century pessimistic thinking. His denunciation of democracy and Christianity and his extolling of the "will to power" sharply contrast with the general sense of optimism in late nineteenth-century Europe.

Beyond Good and Evil

Here one must think profoundly to the very basis and resist all sentimental weakness: life itself is essentially appropriation, injury, conquest of the strange and weak, suppression, severity, obtrusion of peculiar forms, incorporation, and at the least, putting it mildest, exploitation -- but why should one for ever use precisely these words on which for ages a disparaging purpose has been stamped? Even the organisation within which, as was previously supposed, the individuals treat each other as equal -- it takes place in every healthy aristocracy -- must itself, if it be a living and not a dying organisation, do all that towards other bodies, which the individuals within it refrain from doing to each other: it will have to be the incarnated Will to Power, it will endeavour to grow, to gain ground, attract to itself and acquire ascendency -- not owing to any morality or immorality, but because it lives, and because life is precisely Will to Power. On no point, however, is the ordinary consciousness of Europeans more unwilling to be corrected than on this matter; people now rave everywhere, even under the guise of science, about coming conditions of society in which "the exploiting character" is to be absent. That sounds to my ears as if they promised to invent a

Text: Friedrich Nietzsche, Complete Works *(New York: Russell and Russell, 1964), XII, pp. 226-227; XV, pp. 185-186, 295-298, 361-365. Reprint of 1909-1911 edition.*

mode of life which should refrain from all organic functions. "Exploitation" does not belong to a depraved, or imperfect and primitive society: it belongs to the nature of the living being as a primary organic function; it is a consequence of the intrinsic Will to Power, which is precisely the Will to Life. Granting that as a theory this is a novelty -- as a reality it is the fundamental fact of all history: let us be so far honest towards ourselves!

The Will to Power

Man has one terrible and fundamental wish; he desires power, and this impulse, which is called freedom, must be the longest restrained. Hence ethics has instinctively aimed at such an education as shall restrain the desire for power; thus our morality slanders the would-be tyrant, and glorifies charity, patriotism, and the ambition of the herd.

Impotence to power -- how it disguises itself and plays the hypocrite, as obedience, subordination, the pride of duty and morality, submission, devotion, love (the idolisation and apotheosis of the commander is a kind of compensation, and indirect self-enhancement). It veils itself further under fatalism and resignation, objectivity, self tyranny, stoicism, asceticism, self-abnegation, hallowing. Other disguises are: criticism, pessimism, indignation, susceptibility, "beautiful soul," virtue, self-deification, philosophic detachment, freedom from contact with the world (the realisation of impotence disguises itself as disdain).

There is a universal need to exercise some kind of power, or to create for one's self the appearance of some power, if only temporarily, in the form of intoxication.

There are men who desire power simply for the sake of the happiness it will bring; these belong chiefly to political parties. Other men have the same yearning, even when power means visible disadvantages, the sacrifice of their happiness, and well-being; they are the ambitious. Other men, again, are only like dogs in a manger, and will have power only to prevent its falling into the hands of others on whom they would then be dependent. In this age of universal suffrage, in which everybody is allowed to sit in judgment upon everything and everybody, I feel compelled to re-establish the order of rank.

* * * * * * * *

Quanta of power alone determine rank and distinguish rank: nothing else does.

* * * * * * * *

The will to power: How must those men be constituted who would undertake this transvaluation? The order of rank as the order of power: war and danger are the prerequisites which allow of a rank maintaining its conditions. The prodigious example: Man in Nature -- the weakest and shrewdest creature making himself master and putting a yoke upon all less intelligent forces.

* * * * * * * *

It is necessary for higher men to declare war upon the masses! In all directions mediocre people are joining hands in order to make themselves masters. Everything that pampers, that softens, and that brings the "people" or "woman" to the front, operates in favour of universal suffrage -- that is to say, the dominion of inferior men. But we must make reprisals, and draw the whole state of affairs (which commenced in Europe with Christianity) to the light of day and to judgment.

* * * * * * * *

The question, and at the same time the task, is approaching with hesitation, terrible as Fate, but nevertheless inevitable: how shall the earth as a whole be ruled? And to what end shall man as a whole -- no longer as a people or as a race -- be reared and trained?

Legislative moralities are the principal means by which one can form mankind, according to the fancy of a creative and profound will: provided, of course, that such an artistic will of the first order gets the power into its own hands, and can make its creative will prevail over long periods in the form of legislation, religions, and morals. At present, and probably for some time to come, one will seek such colossally creative men, such really great men, as I understand them, in vain: they will be lacking, until, after many disappointments, we are forced to begin to understand why it is they are lacking, and that nothing bars with greater hostility their rise and development, at present and for some time to come, than that which is now called *the* morality in Europe. Just as if there were no other kind of morality and could be no other kind, than the one we have already characterized as herd-morality. It is this morality which is now striving with all its power to attain to that green-meadow happiness on earth, which consists in security, absence of danger, ease, facilities for livelihood, and, last but not least, "if all goes well," even hopes to dispense with all kinds of shepherds and bell-wethers. The two doctrines which it preaches most universally are "equality of rights" and "pity for all sufferers" -- and it even regards suffering itself as something which must be got rid of absolutely. That such ideas may be modern leads one to think very poorly of modernity. He, however, who has reflected deeply concerning the question, how and where the plant man has hitherto grown most vigorously, is forced to believe that this has always taken place under the opposite conditions; that to this end the danger of the situation has to increase enormously, his inventive faculty and dissembling powers have to fight their way up under long oppression and compulsion, and his will to life has to be increased to the unconditioned will to power, to over-power: he believes that danger, severity, violence, peril in the street and in the heart, inequality of rights, secrecy, stoicism, seductive art, and devilry of every kind -- in short, the opposite of all gregarious desiderata -- are necessary for the elevation of man. Such a morality with opposite designs, which would rear man upwards instead of to comfort and mediocrity; such a morality, with the intention of producing a ruling caste -- the future lords of the earth -- must in order to be taught at all, introduce itself as if it were in some way correlated to the prevailing moral law, and must come forward under the cover of the latter's words and forms. But seeing that, to this end, a host of transitionary and deceptive measures must be discovered, and that the life of a single individual stands for almost nothing in view of the accomplishment of such lengthy tasks and aims, the first thing that must be done is to rear a new kind of man in whom the duration of the necessary will and the necessary instincts is guaranteed for many generations. This must be a new kind of ruling species and caste -- this ought to be quite as clear as the somewhat lengthy and not easily expressed consequences of this thought. The aim should be to prepare a transvaluation of values for a particularly strong kind of man, most highly gifted in intellect and will, and, to this end, slowly and cautiously to liberate in him a whole host of slandered instincts hitherto held in check: whoever meditates about this problem belongs to us, the free spirits -- certainly not to that kind of "free spirit" which has existed hitherto: for these desired practically the reverse. To this order, it seems to me, belong, above all, the pessimists of Europe, the poets and thinkers of a revolted idealism, in so far as their discontent with existence in general must consistently at least have led them to be dissatisfied with the man of the present; the same applies to certain insatiably ambitious artists who courageously and unconditionally fight against the gregarious animal for the special rights of higher men, and subdue all herd-instincts and precautions of more exceptional minds by their seductive art. Thirdly and lastly, we should include in this group all those critics and historians by whom the discovery of the Old World, which has begun so happily -- this was the work of the new Columbus, of German intellect -- will be courageously continued (for we still stand in the very first stages of this conquest). For in the Old World, as a matter of fact, a different and more lordly morality ruled than that of today; and the man of antiquity, under the educational ban of his morality, was a stronger and deeper man than the man of today-- up to the present he has been the only well-constituted man. The temptation, however, which from antiquity to the present day has always exercised its power on such lucky strokes of Nature, i.e., on strong and enterprising souls, is, even at the present day, the most subtle and most effective of antidemocratic and anti-Christian powers, just as it was in the time of the Renaissance.

I am writing for a race of men which does not yet exist: for "the lords of the earth."

L. T. Hobhouse

Liberalism

By the end of the nineteenth century, a number of theorists were attacking the traditional concept of liberalism as set forth by Adam Smith and Mill. One of these critics was L. T. Hobhouse (1864-1929), a professor of sociology at the University of London. Hobhouse contended that liberalism had to adjust to the times, and this included increased governmental involvement in the welfare of society. He insisted that he was not advocating socialism, but rather a new liberalism based on a sound compromise between individualism and collectivism.

That there are rights of property we all admit. Is there not perhaps a general right to property? Is there not something radically wrong with an economic system under which through the laws of inheritance and bequest vast inequalities are perpetuated? Ought we to acquiesce in a condition in which the great majority are born to nothing except what they can earn, while some are born to more than the social value of any individual of whatever merit? May it not be that in a reasoned scheme of economic ethics we should have to allow a true right of property in the member of the community as such which would take the form of a certain minimum claim on the public resources? A pretty idea, it may be said, but ethics apart, what are the resources on which the less fortunate is to draw? The British State has little or no collective property available for any such purpose. Its revenues are based on taxation, and in the end what all this means is that the rich are to be taxed for the benefit of the poor, which we may be told is neither justice nor charity but sheer spoliation. To this I would reply that the depletion of

Text: L. T. Hobhouse, Liberalism *(London: Oxford University Press, 1911), pp. 186-192, 195-198, 199-201, 202-204.*

public resources is a symptom of profound economic disorganization. Wealth, I would contend, has a social as well as a personal basis. Some forms of wealth, such as ground rents in and about cities, are substantially the creation of society, and it is only through the misfeasance of government in times past that such wealth has been allowed to fall into private hands. Other great sources of wealth are found in financial and speculative operations, often of distinctly anti-social tendency and possible only through the defective organization of our economy. Other causes rest in the partial monopolies which our liquor laws, on the one side, and the old practice of allowing the supply of municipal services to fall into private hands have built up. Through the principle of inheritance, property so accumulated is handed on; and the result is that while there is a small class born to the inheritance of a share in the material benefits of civilization, there is a far larger class which can say "naked we enter, naked we leave." This system, as a whole, it is maintained, requires revision. Property in this condition of things ceases, it is urged, to be essentially an institution by which each man can secure to himself the fruits of his own labour, and becomes an instrument whereby the owner can command the labour of others on terms which he is in general able to dictate. This tendency is held to be undesirable, and to be capable of a remedy through a concerted series of fiscal, industrial, and social measures which would have the effect of augmenting the common stock at the disposal of society, and so applying it as to secure the economic independence of all who do not forfeit their advantages by idleness, incapacity, or crime. There are early forms of communal society in which each person is born to his appropriate status, carrying its appropriate share of the common land. In destroying the last relics of this system economic individualism has laid the basis of great material advances, but at great cost to the happiness of the masses. The ground problem in economics is not to destroy property, but to restore the social conception of property to its right place under conditions suitable to modern needs. This is not to be done by crude measures of redistribution, such as those of which we hear in ancient history. It is to be done by distinguishing the social from the individual factors in wealth, by bringing the elements of social wealth into the public coffers, and by holding it at the disposal of society to administer to the prime needs of its members.

The basis of property is social, and that in two senses. On the one hand, it is the organized force of society that maintains the rights of owners by protecting them against thieves and depredators. In spite of all criticism many people still seem to speak of the rights of property as though they were conferred by Nature or by Providence upon certain fortunate individuals, and as though these individuals had an unlimited right to command the State, as their servant, to secure them by the free use of the machinery of law in the undisturbed enjoyment of their possessions. They forget that without the organized force of society their rights are not worth a week's purchase. They do not ask themselves where they would be without the judge and the policeman and the settled order which society maintains. The prosperous business man who thinks that he has made his fortune entirely by self help does not pause to consider what single step he could have taken on the road to his success but for the ordered tranquillity which has made commercial development possible, the security by road, and rail, and sea, the masses of skilled labour, and the sum of intelligence which civilization has placed at his disposal, the very demand for the goods which he produces which the general progress of the world has created, the inventions which he uses as a matter of course and which have been built up by the collective effort of generations of men of science and organizers of industry. If he dug to the foundations of his fortune he would recognize that, as it is society that maintains and guarantees his possessions, so also it is society which is an indispensable partner in its original creation.

This brings us to the second sense in which property is social. There is a social element in value and a social element in production. In modern industry there is very little that the individual can do by his unaided efforts. Labour is minutely divided; and in proportion as it is divided it is forced to be cooperative. Men produce goods to sell, and the rate of exchange, that is, price, is fixed by relations of demand and supply the rates of which are determined by complex social forces. In the methods of production every man makes use, to the best of his ability, of the whole available means of civilization, of the machinery which the brains of other men have devised, of the human apparatus which is the gift of acquired civilization. Society thus provides conditions or opportunities of which one man will make much better use than another, and the use to which they are put is the individual or personal element in production which is the basis of the personal claim to reward. To maintain and stimulate this personal effort is a necessity of good economic organization, and without asking here whether any particular conception of Socialism would or would not meet this need we may lay down with confidence that no form of Socialism which should ignore it could possibly enjoy enduring success. On the other hand, an individualism which ignores the social factor in wealth will deplete the national resources, deprive the community of its just share in the fruits of industry and so result in a one-sided and inequitable distribution of wealth. Economic justice is to render what is due not only to each individual but to each function, social or personal, that is engaged in the performance of useful service, and this due is measured by the amount necessary to stimulate and maintain the efficient exercise of that useful function. This equation between function and sustenance is the true meaning of economic equality.

* * * * * * * *

One important source of private wealth under modern conditions is speculation. Is this also a source of social wealth? Does it produce anything for society? Does it perform a function for which our ideal administration would think it necessary to pay? I buy some railway stock at 110. A year or two later I seize a favourable opportunity and sell it at 125. Is the increment earned or unearned? The answer in the single case is clear, but it may be said that my good fortune in this case may be balanced by ill luck in another. No doubt. But, to go no further, if on balance I make a fortune or an income by this method it would seem to be a fortune or an income not earned by productive service. To this it may be replied that the buyers and sellers of stocks are indirectly performing the function of adjusting demand and supply, and so regulating industry. So far as they are expert business men trained in the knowledge of a particular market this may be so. So far as they dabble in the market in the hope of profiting from a favourable turn, they appear rather as gamblers. I will not pretend to determine which of the two is the larger class. I would point out only that, on the face of the facts, the profits derived from this particular source appear to be rather of the nature of a tax which astute or fortunate individuals are able to levy on the producer than as the reward which they obtain for a definite contribution on their own part to production. There are two possible empirical tests of this view. One is that a form of collective organization should be devised which should diminish the importance of the speculative market. Our principle would suggest the propriety of an attempt in that direction whenever opportunity offers. Another would be the imposition of a special tax on incomes derived from this source, and experience would rapidly show whether any such tax would actually hamper the process of production and distribution at any stage. If not, it would justify itself. It would prove that the total profit now absorbed by individuals exceeds, at least by the amount of the tax, the remuneration necessary to maintain that particular economic function.

The other case I will take is that of inherited wealth. This is the main determining factor in the social and economic structure of our time. It is clear on our principle that it stands in quite a different position from that of wealth which is being created from day to day. It can be defended only on two grounds. One is prescriptive right, and the difficulty of disturbing the basis of the economic order. This provides an unanswerable argument against violent and hasty methods, but no argument at all against a gentle and slow-moving policy of economic reorganization. The other argument is that inherited wealth serves several indirect functions. The desire to provide for children and to found a family is a stimulus to effort. The existence of a leisured class affords possibilities for the free development of originality, and a supply of disinterested men and women for the service of the

State. I would suggest once again that the only real test to which the value of these arguments can be submitted is the empirical test. On the face of the facts inherited wealth stands on a different footing from acquired wealth, and Liberal policy is on the right lines in beginning the discrimination of earned from unearned income.

* * * * * * * *

If Liberal policy has committed itself not only to the discrimination of earned and unearned incomes but also to a super-tax on large incomes from whatever source, the ground principle, again, I take to be a respectful doubt whether any single individual is worth to society by any means as much as some individuals obtain. We might, indeed, have to qualify this doubt if the great fortunes of the world fell to the great geniuses. It would be impossible to determine what we ought to pay for a Shakespeare, a Browning, a Newton, or a Cobden. Impossible, but fortunately unnecessary. For the man of genius is forced by his own cravings to give, and the only reward that he asks from society is to be let alone and have some quiet and fresh air. Nor is he in reality entitled, notwithstanding his services, to ask more than the modest sufficiency which enables him to obtain those primary needs of the life of thought and creation, since his creative energy is the response to an inward stimulus which goads him on without regard to the wishes of any one else. The case of the great organizers of industry is rather different, but they, again, so far as their work is socially sound, are driven on more by internal necessity than by the genuine love of gain. They make great profits because their works reach a scale at which, if the balance is on the right side at all, it is certain to be a big balance, and they no doubt tend to be interested in money as the sign of their success, and also as the basis of increased social power. But I believe the direct influence of the lust of gain on this type of mind to have been immensely exaggerated; and as proof I would refer, first, to the readiness of many men of this class to accept and in individual cases actively to promote measures tending to diminish their material gain, and, secondly, to the mass of high business capacity which is at the command of the public administration for salaries which, as their recipient must be perfectly conscious, bear no relation to the income which it would be open to him to earn in commercial competition.

* * * * * * * *

But why should the proceeds of the tax go to the poor in particular? Granting that Peter is not robbed, why should Paul be paid? Why should not the proceeds be expended on something of common concern to Peter and Paul alike, for Peter is equally a member of the community? Undoubtedly the only just method of dealing with the common funds is to expend them in objects which subserve the common good, and there are many directions in which public expenditure does in fact benefit all classes alike. This, it is worth noting, is true even of some important branches of expenditure which in their direct aim concern the poorer classes. Consider, for example, the value of public sanitation, not merely to the poorer regions which would suffer first if it were withheld, but to the richer as well who, seclude themselves as they may, cannot escape infection. In the old days judge and jury, as well as prisoners, would die of gaol fever. Consider, again, the economic value of education, not only to the worker, but to the employer whom he will serve. But when all this is allowed for it must be admitted that we have throughout contemplated a considerable measure of public expenditure in the elimination of poverty. The prime justification of this expenditure is that the prevention of suffering from the actual lack of adequate physical comforts is an essential element in the common good, an object in which all are bound to concern themselves, which all have the right to demand and the duty to fulfil. Any common life based on the avoidable suffering even of one of those who partake in it is a life not of harmony, but of discord.

Emmeline Pankhurst

My Own Story

*One of the most dramatic features of the women's rights move-
ment early in the twentieth century was the attempt by suffragists
in Great Britain to obtain the vote. The leader of the crusade
was Emmeline Pankhurst (1858-1928). In her autobiography,
My Own Story (1913), she tells how she and others in the
Women's Social and Political Union became increasingly militant
in their struggle for the vote (which was finally granted in 1918
to women aged 30 and over, and in 1928 to women at the age of
21 -- the same as for men).*

It was in October, 1903, that I invited a number of women to
my house in Nelson street, Manchester, for purposes of organisation. We voted to call our new society the Women's Social
and Political Union, partly to emphasize its democracy, and
partly to define its object as political rather than propagandist.
We resolved to limit our membership exclusively to women, to
keep ourselves absolutely free from any party affiliation, and to
be satisfied with nothing but action on our question. Deeds, not
words, was to be our permanent motto.

To such a pass had the women's suffrage cause come in my
country that the old leaders, who had done such fine educational
work in the past, were now seemingly content with expressions
of sympathy and regret on the part of hypocritical politicians.
This fact was thrust upon me anew by an incident that occurred
almost at the moment of the founding of the Women's Social and
Political Union. In our Parliament no bill has a chance of becoming a law unless it is made a Government measure. Private

Text: Emmeline Pankhurst, My Own Story *(New York: Hearst's
International Library, 1914), pp. 38-39, 54-60, 98-103, 279-281,
323-324.*

members are at liberty to introduce measures of their own, but these rarely reach the second reading, or debatable stage. So much time is given to discussion of Government measures that very little time can be given to any private bills. About one day in a week is given over to consideration of private measures, to which, as we say, the Government give facilities; and since there are a limited number of weeks in a session, the members, on the opening days of Parliament, meet and draw lots to determine who shall have a place in the debates. Only these successful men have a chance to speak to their bills, and only those who have drawn early chances have any prospect of getting much discussion on their measures.

Now, the old suffragists had long since given up hope of obtaining a Government suffrage bill, but they clung to a hope that a private member's bill would some time obtain consideration. Every year, on the opening day of Parliament, the association sent a deputation of women to the House of Commons, to meet so-called friendly members and consider the position of the women's suffrage cause. The ceremony was of a most conventional, not to say farcical character. The ladies made their speeches and the members made theirs. The ladies thanked the friendly members for their sympathy, and the members renewed their assurances that they believed in women's suffrage and would vote for it when they had an opportunity to do so. Then the deputation, a trifle sad but entirely tranquil, took its departure, and the members resumed the real business of life, which was support of their party's policies.

* * * * * * * *

At length the opening of Parliament arrived. On February 19, 1906, occurred the first suffrage procession in London. I think there were between three and four hundred women in that procession, poor working-women from the East End, for the most part, leading the way in which numberless women of every rank were afterward to follow. My eyes were misty with tears as I saw them, standing in line, holding the simple banners which my daughter Sylvia had decorated, waiting for the word of command. Of course our procession attracted a large crowd of intensely amused spectators. The police, however, made no attempt to disperse our ranks, but merely ordered us to furl our banners. There was no reason why we should not have carried banners but the fact that we were women, and therefore could be bullied. So, bannerless, the procession entered Caxton Hall. To my amazement it was filled with women, most of whom I had never seen at any suffrage gathering before.

Our meeting was most enthusiastic, and while Annie Kenney was speaking, to frequent applause, the news came to me that the King's speech (which is not the King's at all, but the formally announced Government programme for the session) had been read, and that there was in it no mention of the women's suffrage question. As Annie took her seat I arose and made this announcement, and I moved a resolution that the meeting should at once proceed to the House of Commons to urge the members to introduce a suffrage measure. The resolution was carried, and we rushed out in a body and hurried toward the Strangers' Entrance. It was pouring rain and bitterly cold, yet no one turned back, even when we learned at the entrance that for the first time in memory the doors of the House of Commons were barred to women. We sent in our cards to members who were personal friends, and some of them came out and urged our admittance. The police, however, were obdurate. They had their orders. The Liberal government, advocates of the people's rights, had given orders that women should no longer set foot in their stronghold.

Pressure from members proved too great, and the government relented to the extent of allowing twenty women at a time to enter the lobby. Through all the rain and cold those hundreds of women waited for hours their turn to enter. Some never got in, and for those of us who did there was small satisfaction. Not a member could be persuaded to take up our cause.

Out of the disappointment and dejection of that experience I yet reaped a richer harvest of happiness than I had ever known before. Those women had followed me to the House of Commons. They had defied the police. They were awake at last. They were prepared to do something that women had never done before -- fight for themselves. Women had always fought for men, and for their children. Now they were ready to fight for their own human rights. Our militant movement was established.

To account for the phenomenal growth of the Women's Social and Political Union after it was established in London, to explain why it made such an instant appeal to women hitherto indifferent, I shall have to point out exactly wherein our society differs from all other suffrage associations. In the first place, our members are absolutely single minded; they concentrate all their forces on one object, political equality with men. No member of the W.S.P.U. divides her attention between suffrage and other social reforms. We hold that both reason and justice dictate that women shall have a share in reforming the evils that afflict society, especially those evils bearing directly on women themselves. Therefore, we demand, before any other legislation whatever, the elementary justice of votes for women.

There is not the slightest doubt that the women of Great Britain would have been enfranchised years ago had all the suffragists adopted this simple principle. They never did, and even today many English women refuse to adopt it. They are party members first and suffragists afterward; or they are suffragists part of the time and social theorists the rest of the time. We further differ from other suffrage associations, or from others existing in 1906, in that we clearly perceived the political situation that solidly inter-posed between us and our enfranchisement.

For seven years we had had a majority in the House of Commons pledged to vote favourably on a suffrage bill. The year before, they had voted favourably on one, yet that bill did not become law. Why? Because even an overwhelming majority of private members are powerless to enact law in the face of a hostile Government of eleven cabinet ministers. The private member of Parliament was once possessed of individual power and responsibility, but Parliamentary usage and a changed conception of statesmanship have gradually lessened the functions of members. At the present time their powers, for all practical purposes, are limited to helping to enact such measures as the Government introduces or, in rare instances, private measures approved by the Government. It is true that the House can revolt, can, by voting a lack of confidence in the Government, force them to resign. But that almost never happens, and it is less likely now than formerly to happen. Figureheads don't revolt.

This, then, was our situation: the Government all-powerful and consistently hostile; the rank and file of legislators impotent; the country apathetic; the women divided in their interests. The Women's Social and Political Union was established to meet this situation, and to overcome it. Moreover we had a policy which, if persisted in long enough, could not possibly fail to overcome it. Do you wonder that we gained new members at every meeting we held?

There was little formality about joining the Union. Any woman could become a member by paying a shilling, but at the same time she was required to sign a declaration of loyal adherence to our policy and a pledge not to work for any political party until the women's vote was won. This is still our inflexible custom. Moreover, if at any time a member, or a group of members, loses faith in our policy; if any one begins to suggest that some other policy ought to be substituted, or if she tries to confuse the issue by adding other policies, she ceases at once to be a member. Autocratic? Quite so. But, you may object, a suffrage organisation ought to be democratic. Well, the members of the W.S.P.U. do not agree with you. We do not believe in the effectiveness of the ordinary suffrage organisation. The W.S.P.U. is not hampered by a complexity of rules. We have no constitution and by-laws; nothing to be amended or tinkered with or quarrel led over at an annual meeting. In fact, we have no annual meeting, no business sessions, no elections of officers. The W.S.P.U. is simply a suffrage army in the field. It is purely a volunteer army, and no one is obliged to remain in it. Indeed we don't want anybody to remain in it who does not ardently believe in the policy of the army.

The foundation of our policy is opposition to a Government

who refuse votes to women. To support by word or deed a Government hostile to woman suffrage is simply to invite them to go on being hostile. We oppose the Liberal party because it is in power. We would oppose a Unionist government if it were in power and were opposed to woman suffrage. We say to women that as long as they remain in the ranks of the Liberal party they give their tacit approval to the Government's anti-suffrage policy. We say to members of Parliament that as long as they support any of the Government's policies they give their tacit approval to the anti-suffrage policy. We call upon all sincere suffragists to leave the Liberal party until women are given votes on equal terms with men. We call upon all voters to vote against Liberal candidates until the Liberal Government does justice to women.

* * * * * * * *

We had progressed as far as the entrance to Parliament Square, when two stalwart policemen suddenly grasped my arms on either side and told me that I was under arrest. My two companions, because they refused to leave me, were also arrested, and a few minutes later Annie Kenney and five other women suffered arrest. That night we were released on bail, and the next morning we were arraigned in Westminster police court for trial under the Charles II Act. But, as it turned out, the authorities, embarrassed by our readiness to test the act, announced that they had changed their minds, and would continue, for the present, to treat us as common street brawlers.

This was my first trial, and I listened with a suspicion that my ears were playing tricks with my reason to the most astonishing perjuries put forth by the prosecution. I heard that we had set forth from Caxton Hall with noisy shouts and songs, that we had resorted to the most riotous and vulgar behaviour, knocking off policemen's helmets, assaulting the officers right and left as we marched. Our testimony, and that of our witnesses, was ignored. When I tried to speak in my own defence, I was cut short rudely, and was told briefly that I and the others must choose between being bound over or going to prison in the second division for six weeks.

I remember only vaguely the long, jolting ride across London to Holloway Prison. We stopped at Pentonville, the men's prison, to discharge several men prisoners, and I remember shuddering at the thought of our women, many of them little past girlhood, being hauled to prison in the same van with criminal men. Arriving at the prison, we groped our way through dim corridors into the reception-ward, where we were lined up against the wall for a superficial medical examination. After that we were locked up in separate cells, unfurnished, except for low, wooden stools.

It seemed an endless time before my cell door was opened by a wardress, who ordered me to follow her. I entered a room where another wardress sat at a table, ready to take an inventory of my effects. Obeying an order to undress, I took off my gown, then paused. "Take off everything," was the next order. "Everything?" I faltered. It seemed impossible that they expected me to strip. In fact, they did allow me to take of my last garments in the shelter of a bath-room. I shivered myself into some frightful under-clothing, old and patched and stained, some coarse, brown woollen stockings with red stripes, and the hideous prison dress stamped all over with the broad arrow of disgrace. I fished a pair of shoes out of a big basket of shoes, old and mostly mismates. A pair of coarse but clean sheets, a towel, a mug of cold cocoa, and a thick slice of brown bread were given me, and I was conducted to my cell.

My first sensations when the door was locked upon me were not altogether disagreeable. I was desperately weary, for I had been working hard, perhaps a little too hard, for several strenuous months. The excitement and fatigue of the previous day, and the indignation I had suffered throughout the trial, had combined to bring me to the point of exhaustion, and I was glad to throw myself on my hard prison bed and close my eyes. But soon the relief of being alone, and with nothing to do, passed from me. Holloway Prison is a very old place, and it has the disadvantages of old places which have never known enough air and sunshine. It reeks with the odours of generations of bad ventilation, and it contrives to be at once the stuffiest and the draughtiest building I have ever been in. Soon I found myself sickening for fresh air. My head began to ache. Sleep fled. I lay all night suffering with cold, gasping for air, aching with fatigue, and painfully wide awake.

The next day I was fairly ill, but I said nothing about it. As a matter of fact, one's mental suffering is so much greater than any common physical distress that the latter is almost forgotten. The English prison system is altogether medieval and outworn. In some of its details the system has improved since they began to send the Suffragettes to Holloway. I may say that we, by our public denunciation of the system, have forced these slight improvements. In 1907 the rules were excessively cruel. The poor prisoner, when she entered Holloway, dropped, as it were, into a tomb. No letters and no visitors were allowed for the first month of the sentence. Think of it -- a whole month, more than four weeks, without sending or receiving a single word. One's nearest and dearest may have gone through dreadful suffering, may have been ill, may have died, meantime. One was given plenty of time to imagine all these things, for the prisoner was kept in solitary confinement in a narrow, dimly-lit cell, twenty-three hours out of the twenty-four. Solitary confinement is too terrible a punishment to inflict on any human being, no matter what his crime. Hardened criminals in the men's prisons, it is said, often beg for the lash instead. Picture what it must be to a woman who has committed some small offence, for most of the women who go to Holloway are small offenders, sitting alone, day after day, in the heavy silence of a cell -- thinking of her children at home -- thinking, thinking. Some women go mad. Many suffer from shattered nerves for a long period after release. It is impossible to believe that any woman ever emerged from such a horror less criminal than when she entered it.

Two days of solitary confinement, broken each day by an hour of silent exercise in a bitterly cold courtyard, and I was ordered to the hospital. There I thought I should be a little more comfortable. The bed was better, the food a little better, and small comforts, such as warm water for washing, were allowed. I slept a little the first night. About midnight I awoke, and sat up in bed, listening. A woman in the cell next mine was moaning in long, sobbing breaths of mortal pain. She ceased for a few minutes, then moaned again, horribly. The truth flashed over me, turning me sick, as I realised that a life was coming into being, there in that frightful prison. A woman, imprisoned by men's laws, was giving a child to the world. A child born in a cell! I shall never forget that night, nor what I suffered with the birth-pangs of that woman, who, I found later, was simply waiting trial on a charge which was found to be baseless.

The days passed very slowly, the nights more slowly still. Being in hospital, I was deprived of chapel, and also of work. Desperate, at last I begged the wardress for some sewing, and she kindly gave me a skirt of her own to hem, and later some coarse knitting to do. Prisoners were allowed a few books, mostly of the "Sunday-school" kind. One day I asked the chaplain if there were not some French or German books in the library, and he brought me a treasure, "Autour de mon Jardin," by Jules Janin. For a few days I was quite happy, reading my book and translating it on the absurd little slate they gave us in lieu of paper and pencil. That slate was, after all, a great comfort. I did all kinds of things with it. I kept a calendar, I wrote all the French poetry I could remember on it, I even recorded old school chorals and old English exercises. It helped wonderfully to pass the endless hours until my release. I even forget the cold, which was the harder to bear because of the fur coat, which I knew was put away, ticketed with my name. I begged them for the coat, but they wouldn't let me have it.

At last the time came when they gave me back all my things, and let me go free. At the door the Governor spoke to me, and asked me if I had any complaints to make. "Not of you," I replied, "nor of any of the wardresses. Only of this prison, and all of men's prisons. We shall raze them to the ground."

* * * * * * * *

The militants declared, and proceeded instantly to carry out, unrelenting warfare. We announced that either we must have a Government measure, or a Cabinet split -- those men in the Cabinet calling themselves suffragists going out -- or we would take up the sword again, never to lay it down until the enfranchisement of the women of England was won.

It was at this time, February, 1913, less than two years ago as I write these words, that militancy as it is now generally understood by the public began -- militancy in the sense of continued, destructive, guerilla warfare against the Government through injury to private property. Some property had been destroyed before this time, but the attacks were sporadic, and were meant to be in the nature of a warning as to what might become a settled policy. Now we indeed lighted the torch, and we did it with the absolute conviction that no other course was open to us. We had tried every other measure, as I am sure that I have demonstrated to my readers, and our years of work and suffering and sacrifice had taught us that the Government would not yield to right and justice, what the majority of members of the House of Commons admitted was right and justice, but that the Government would, as other governments invariably do, yield to expediency. Now our task was to show the Government that it was expedient to yield to the women's just demands. In order to do that we had to make England and every department of English life insecure and unsafe. We had to make English law a failure and the courts farce comedy theatres; we had to discredit the Government and Parliament in the eyes of the world; we had to spoil English sports, hurt business, destroy valuable property, demoralise the world of society, shame the churches, upset the whole orderly conduct of life.

That is, we had to do as much of this guerilla warfare as the people of England would tolerate. When they came to the point of saying to the Government: "Stop this, in the only way it can be stopped, by giving the women of England representation," then we should extinguish our torch.

* * * * * * * *

The two months of the summer of 1913 which were spent with my daughter in Paris were almost the last days of peace and rest I have been destined since to enjoy. I spent the days, or some hours of them, in the initial preparation of this volume, because it seemed to me that I had a duty to perform in giving to the world my own plain statement of the events which have led up to the women's revolution in England. Other histories of the militant movement will undoubtedly be written; in times to come when in all constitutional countries of the world, women's votes will be as universally accepted as men's votes are now; when men and women occupy the world of industry on equal terms, as coworkers rather than as cut-throat competitors; when, in a word, all the dreadful and criminal discriminations which exist now between the sexes are abolished, as they must one day be abolished, the historian will be able to sit down in leisurely fashion and do full justice to the strange story of how the women of England took up arms against the blind and obstinate Government of England and fought their way to political freedom. I should like to live long enough to read such a history, calmly considered, carefully analysed conscientiously set forth. It will be a better book to read than this one, written, as it were, in camp between battles. But perhaps this one, hastily prepared as it has been, will give the reader of the future a clearer impression of the strenuousness and the desperation of the conflict, and also something of the heretofore undreamed of courage and fighting strength of women, who, having learned the joy of battle, lose all sense of fear and continue their struggle up to and past the gates of death, never flinching at any step of the way.

Edward Bernstein

Evolutionary Socialism

As a leading German Marxist in the late nineteenth century, Edward Bernstein (1850-1932) questioned Marx's predictions regarding the intensification of the class struggle and imminent revolution. Instead of advocating a proletarian uprising, Bernstein argued for a "revisionist" Marxism, which would achieve socialist goals through non-revolutionary means.

It has been maintained in a certain quarter that the practical deductions from my treatises would be the abandonment of the conquest of political power by the proletariat organised politically and economically. That is quite an arbitrary deduction, the accuracy of which I altogether deny.

I set myself against the notion that we have to expect shortly a collapse of the bourgeois economy and that social democracy should be induced by the prospect of such an imminent, great, social catastrophe to adapt its tactics to that assumption. That I maintain most emphatically.

The adherents of this theory of a catastrophe base it especially on the conclusions of the *Communist Manifesto.* This is a mistake in every respect . . . .

Social conditions have not developed to such an acute opposition of things and classes as is depicted in the *Manifesto.* It is not only useless, it is the greatest folly to attempt to conceal this from ourselves. The number of members of the possessing classes is today not smaller but larger. The enormous increase of social wealth is not accompanied by a decreasing number of large capitalists but by an increasing number of capitalists of all

Text: Edward Bernstein, Evolutionary Socialism: A Criticism and Affirmation, *trans. Edith C. Harvey (New York: B. W. Huebsch, 1912), pp. x-xvi, 194-197.*

degrees. The middle classes change their character but they do not disappear from the social scale.

The concentration in productive industry is not being accomplished even today in all its departments with equal thoroughness and at an equal rate. In a great many branches of production it certainly justifies the forecasts of the socialist critic of society; but in other branches it lags even today behind them. The process of concentration in agriculture proceeds still more slowly. Trade statistics show an extraordinarily elaborated graduation of enterprises in regard to size. No rung of the ladder is disappearing from it. The significant changes in the inner structure of these enterprises and their inter-relationship cannot do away with this fact.

In all advanced countries we see the privileges of the capitalist bourgeoisie yielding step by step to democratic organisations. Under the influence of this, and driven by the movement of the working classes which is daily becoming stronger, a social reaction has set in against the exploiting tendencies of capital, a counteraction which, although it still proceeds timidly and feebly, yet does exist, and is always drawing more departments of economic life under its influence. Factory legislation, the democratising of local government, and the extension of its area of work, the freeing of trade unions and systems of cooperative trading from legal restrictions, the consideration of standard conditions of labour in the work undertaken by public authorities -- all these characterise this phase of the evolution.

But the more the political organisations of modern nations are democratised the more the needs and opportunities of great political catastrophes are diminished. He who holds firmly to the catastrophic theory of evolution must, with all his power, withstand and hinder the evolution described above, which, indeed, the logical defenders of that theory formerly did. But is the conquest of political power by the proletariat simply to be by a political catastrophe? Is it to be the appropriation and utilisation of the power of the State by the proletariat exclusively against the whole non-proletarian world?

* * * * * * * *

No one has questioned the necessity for the working classes to gain the control of government. The point at issue is between the theory of a social cataclysm and the question whether, with the given social development in Germany and the present advanced state of its working classes in the towns and the country, a sudden catastrophe would be desirable in the interest of social democracy. I have denied it and deny it again, because in my judgment a greater security for lasting success lies in a steady advance than in the possibilities offered by a catastrophic crash.

And as I am firmly convinced that important periods in the development of nations cannot be leapt over I lay the greatest value on the next tasks of social democracy, on the struggle for the political rights of the working man, on the political activity of working men in town and country for the interests of their class, as well as on the work of the industrial organisation of the workers . . . .

The conquest of political power by the working classes, the expropriation of capitalists, are no ends in themselves but only means for the accomplishment of certain aims and endeavours. As such they are demands in the programme of social democracy and are not attacked by me. Nothing can be said beforehand as to the circumstances of their accomplishment; we can only fight for their realisation. But the conquest of political power necessitates the possession of political *rights;* and the most important problem of tactics which German social democracy has at the present time to solve appears to me to be to devise the best ways for the extension of the political and economic rights of the German working classes.

Social democracy has today in Germany, besides the means of propaganda by speech and writing, the franchise for the Reichstag as the most effective means of asserting its demands. Its influence is so strong that it has extended even to those bodies which have been made inaccessible to the working class owing to a property qualification, or a system of class franchise; for parties must, even in these assemblies, pay attention to the electors for the Reichstag. If the right to vote for the Reichstag were protected from every attack, the question of treating the franchise for other bodies as a subordinate one could be justified to a certain extent, although it would be a mistake to make light of it. But the franchise for the Reichstag is not secure at all. Governments and government parties will certainly not resolve lightly on amending it, for they will say to themselves that such a step would raise amongst the masses of the German workers a hate and bitterness, which they would show in a very uncomfortable way on suitable occasions. The socialist movement is too strong, the political self-consciousness of the German workers is too much developed, to be dealt with in a cavalier fashion. One may venture, also, to assume that a great number even of the opponents of universal suffrage have a certain moral unwillingness to take such a right from the people. But if under normal conditions the curtailing of the franchise would create a revolutionary tension, with all its dangers for the governing classes, there can, on the other hand, be no doubt as to the existence of serious technical difficulties in the way of altering the franchise so as to allow, only as an exception, the success of independent socialist candidatures. It is simply political considerations which, on this question, determine the issue . . . .

Now social democracy depends not exclusively on the franchise and Parliamentary activity. A great and rich field exists for it outside Parliaments. The socialist working class movement would exist even if Parliaments were closed to it. Nothing shows this better than the gratifying movements among the Russian working classes. But with its exclusion from representative bodies the German working class movement would, to a great extent, lose the cohesion which today links its various sections; it would assume a chaotic character, and instead of the steady, uninterrupted forward march with firm steps, jerky forward motions would appear with inevitable back-slidings and exhaustions.

Such a development is neither in the interest of the working classes nor can it appear desirable to those opponents of social democracy who have become convinced that the present social order has not been created for all eternity but is subject to the law of change, and that a catastrophic development with all its horrors and devastation can only be avoided if in legislation consideration is paid to changes in the conditions of production and commerce and to the evolution of the classes. And the number of those who recognise this is steadily increasing. Their influence would be much greater than it is today if the social democracy could find the courage to emancipate itself from a phraseology which is actually outworn and if it would make up its mind to appear what it is in reality today: a democratic, socialistic party of reform.

Vladimir Ilich Lenin (1870-1924) joined the Russian Marxist movement during the 1890s and soon became the most prominent leader in the Social Democratic party. In What Is To Be Done? *(1902), he outlines his views on the type of party needed to accomplish the revolution. In* State and Revolution, *written at the time of the October Revolution in 1917, he describes the political and economic characteristics of the new order, particularly the intermediate stages in the transformation from capitalism to communism.*

V. I. Lenin

What is to be Done?

The history of all countries shows that the working class, exclusively by its own effort, is able to develop only trade-union consciousness, i.e., the conviction that it is necessary to combine in unions, fight the employers, and strive to compel the government to pass necessary labour legislation, etc. The theory of socialism, however, grew out of the philosophic, historical, and economic theories elaborated by educated representatives of the propertied classes, by intellectuals. By their social status, the founders of modern scientific socialism, Marx and Engels, themselves belonged to the bourgeois intelligentsia. In the very same way, in Russia, the theoretical doctrine of Social-Democracy arose altogether independently of the spontaneous growth of the working-class movement; it arose as a natural and inevitable outcome of the development of thought among the revolutionary socialist intelligentsia.

The political struggle of Social-Democracy is far more

Text: V. I. Lenin, Collected Works *(Moscow: Progress Publishers, 1964), V, pp. 375-376, 452-453, 464-467.*

extensive and complex than the economic struggle of the workers against the employers and the government. Similarly (indeed for that reason), the organisation of the revolutionary Social Democratic Party must inevitably be of a kind different from the organisation of the workers designed for this struggle. The workers' organisation must in the first place be a trade-union organisation; secondly, it must be as broad as possible; and thirdly, it must be as public as conditions will allow (here and further on, of course, I refer only to absolutist Russia). On the other hand, the organisation of the revolutionaries must consist first and foremost of people who make revolutionary activity their profession (for which reason I speak of the organisation of revolutionaries, meaning revolutionary Social-Democrats). In view of this common characteristic of the members of such an organisation, all distinctions as between workers and intellectuals, not to speak of distinctions of trade and profession, in both categories, must be effaced. Such an organisation must perforce not be very extensive and must be as secret as possible . . . .

I assert: (1) that no revolutionary movement can endure without a stable organisation of leaders maintaining continuity; (2) that the broader the popular mass drawn spontaneously into the struggle, which forms the basis of the movement and participates in it, the more urgent the need for such an organisation, and the more solid this organisation must be (for it is much easier for all sorts of demagogues to side-track the more backward sections of the masses); (3) that such an organisation must consist chiefly of people professionally engaged in revolutionary activity; (4) that in an autocratic state, the more we confine the membership of such an organisation to people who are professionally trained in the art of combating the political police, the more difficult will it be to unearth the organisation; and (5) the greater will be the number of people from the working class and from the other social classes who will be able to join the movement and perform active work in it . . . .

The question as to whether it is easier to wipe out "a dozen wise men" or "a hundred fools" reduces itself to the question, above considered, whether it is possible to have a mass organisation when the maintenance of strict secrecy is essential. We can never give a mass organisation that degree of secrecy without which there can be no question of persistent and continuous struggle against the government. To concentrate all secret functions in the hands of as small a number of professional revolutionaries as possible does not mean that the latter will "do the thinking for all" and that the rank and file will not take an active part in the movement. On the contrary, the membership will promote increasing numbers of the professional revolutionaries from its ranks; for it will know that it is not enough for a few students and for a few working men waging the economic struggle to gather in order to form a "committee," but that it takes years to train oneself to be a professional revolutionary; and the rank and file will "think" not only of amateurish methods but of such training. Centralisation of the secret functions of the organisation by no means implies centralisation of all the functions of the movement. Active participation of the widest masses in the illegal press will not diminish because a "dozen" professional revolutionaries centralise the secret functions connected with this work; on the contrary, it will increase tenfold. In this way, and in this way alone, shall we ensure that reading the illegal press, writing for it, and to some extent even distributing it will almost cease to be secret work, for the police will soon come to realise the folly and impossibility of judicial and administrative red-tape procedure over every copy of a publication that is being distributed in the thousands. This holds not only for the press but for every function of the movement, even for demonstrations. The active and widespread participation of the masses will not suffer; on the contrary, it will benefit by the fact that a "dozen" experienced revolutionaries, trained professionally no less than the police, will centralise all the secret aspects of the work -- the drawing up of leaflets, the working out of approximate plans, and the appointing of bodies of leaders for each urban district, for each factory district, and for each educational institution, etc. (I know that exception will be taken to my "undemocratic" views, but I shall reply below fully to this anything but intelligent objection.)

Centralisation of the most secret functions in an organisation of revolutionaries will not diminish, but rather increase the extent and enhance the quality of the activity of a large number of other organisations, that are intended for a broad public and are therefore as loose and as non-secret as possible, such as workers' trade unions; workers' self-education circles and circles for reading illegal literature; and socialist, as well as democratic, circles among all other sections of the population, etc., etc. We must have such circles, trade unions, and organisations everywhere in as large a number as possible and with the widest variety of functions; but it would be absurd and harmful to confound them with the organisation of revolutionaries, to efface the borderline between them, to make still more hazy the all too faint recognition of the fact that in order to "serve" the mass movement we must have people who will devote themselves exclusively to Social-Democratic activities, and that such people must train themselves patiently and steadfastly to be professional revolutionaries.

Yes, this recognition is incredibly dim. Our worst sin with regard to organisation consists in the fact that by our primitiveness we have lowered the prestige of revolutionaries in Russia. A person who is flabby and shaky on questions of theory, who has a narrow outlook, who pleads the spontaneity of the masses as an excuse for his own sluggishness, who resembles a trade-union secretary more than a spokesman of the people, who is unable to conceive of a broad and bold plan that would command the respect even of opponents, and who is inexperienced and clumsy in his own professional art -- the art of combating the political police -- such a man is not a revolutionary, but a wretched amateur!

Let no active worker take offense at these frank remarks, for as far as insufficient training is concerned, I apply them first and foremost to myself. I used to work in a study circle that set itself very broad, all-embracing tasks; and all of us, members of the circle, suffered painfully and acutely from the realisation that we were acting as amateurs at a moment in history when we might have been able to say, varying a well-known statement: "Give us an organisation of revolutionaries, and we will overturn Russia!" The more I recall the burning sense of shame I then experienced, the bitterer become my feelings towards those pseudo-Social Democrats whose preachings "bring disgrace on the calling of a revolutionary," who fail to understand that our task is not to champion the degrading of the revolutionary to the level of an amateur, but to raise the amateurs to the level of revolutionaries.

V. I. Lenin

State and Revolution

Engels' words regarding the "withering away" of the state are so widely known, they are so often quoted, and so clearly reveal the essence of the customary adaptation of Marxism to opportunism that we must deal with them in detail. We shall quote the whole argument from which they are taken.

The proletariat seizes state power and turns the means of production into state property to begin with. But thereby it abolishes itself as the proletariat, abolishes also the state as state. Society thus far, operating amid class antagonisms, needed the state, that is, an organisation of the particular exploiting class, for the maintenance of its external conditions of production, and, therefore, especially, for the purpose of forcibly keeping the exploited class in the conditions of oppression determined by the given mode of production (slavery, serfdom or bondage, wage-labour). The state was the official representative of society as a whole, its concentration in a visible corporation. But it was this only insofar as it was the state of that class which itself represented, for its own time, society as a whole: in ancient times, the state of slave-owning citizens; in the Middle Ages, of the feudal nobility; in our own time, of the bourgeoisie. When at last it becomes the real representative of the whole of society, it renders itself unnecessary. As soon as there is no longer any social class to be held in subjection, as soon as class rule, and the individual struggle for existence based upon the present anarchy in production, with the collisions and excesses arising from this struggle, are removed, nothing more remains to be held in subjection -- nothing necessitating a special coercive

Text: V. I. Lenin, Collected Works (Moscow: Progress Publishers, 1964), XXV, pp. 395-396, 459-463, 465-467, 470-474.

force, a state. The first act by which the state really comes forward as the representative of the whole of society -- the taking possession of the means of production in the name of society -- is also its last independent act as a state. State interference in social relations becomes, in one domain after another, superfluous, and then dies down of itself. The government of persons is replaced by the administration of things, and by the conduct of processes of production. The state is not 'abolished.' It withers away.

* * * * * * * *

The first fact that has been established most accurately by the whole theory of development, by science as a whole a fact that was ignored by the utopians, and is ignored by the present-day opportunists, who are afraid of the socialist revolution -- is that, historically, there must undoubtedly be a special stage, or a special phase, of transition from capitalism to communism.

Marx continued:

Between capitalist and communist society lies the period of the revolutionary transformation of the one into the other. Corresponding to this is also a political transition period in which the state can be nothing but the revolutionary dictatorship of the proletariat.

Marx bases this conclusion on an analysis of the role played by the proletariat in modern capitalist society, on the data concerning the development of this society, and on the irreconcilability of the antagonistic interests of the proletariat and the bourgeoisie.

Previously the question was put as follows: to achieve its emancipation, the proletariat must overthrow the bourgeoisie, win political power, and establish its revolutionary dictatorship.

Now the question is put somewhat differently: the transition from capitalist society -- which is developing towards communism -- to communist society is impossible without a "political transition period," and the state in this period can only be the revolutionary dictatorship of the proletariat.

What, then, is the relation of this dictatorship to democracy?

We have seen that the *Communist Manifesto* simply places side by side the two concepts: "to raise the proletariat to the position of the ruling class" and "to win the battle of democracy." On the basis of all that has been said above, it is possible to determine more precisely how democracy changes in the transition from capitalism to communism.

In capitalist society, providing it develops under the most favourable conditions, we have a more or less complete democracy in the democratic republic. But this democracy is always hemmed in by the narrow limits set by capitalist exploitation, and consequently always remains, in effect, a democracy for the minority, only for the propertied classes, only for the rich. Freedom in capitalist society always remains about the same as it was in the ancient Greek republics: freedom for the slave-owners. Owing to the conditions of capitalist exploitation, the modern wage slaves are so crushed by want and poverty that "they cannot be bothered with democracy" -- "cannot be bothered with politics"; in the ordinary, peaceful course of events, the majority of the population is debarred from participation in public and political life.

* * * * * * * *

And the dictatorship of the proletariat, i.e., the organisation of the vanguard of the oppressed as the ruling class for the purpose of suppressing the oppressors, cannot result merely in an expansion of democracy. Simultaneously with an immense expansion of democracy, which for the first time becomes democracy for the poor, democracy for the people, and not democracy for the money-bags, the dictatorship of the proletariat imposes a series of restrictions on the freedom of the oppressors, the exploiters, the capitalists. We must suppress them in order to free humanity from wage slavery, their resistance must be crushed by force; it is clear that there is no freedom and no democracy where there is suppression and where there is violence.

Engels expressed this splendidly in his letter to Bebel when he said, as the reader will remember, that "the proletariat needs the state, not in the interests of freedom but in order to hold down its adversaries, and as soon as it becomes possible to speak of freedom the state as such ceases to exist."

Democracy for the vast majority of the people, and suppression by force, i.e., exclusion from democracy, of the exploiters and oppressors of the people -- this is the change democracy undergoes during the transition from capitalism to communism.

Only in communist society, when the resistance of the capitalists has been completely crushed, when the capitalists have disappeared, when there are no classes (i.e., when there is no distinction between the members of society as regards their relation to the social means of production), only then the "state . . . ceases to exist," and "it becomes possible to speak of freedom." Only then will a truly complete democracy become possible and be realised, a democracy without any exceptions whatever. And only then will democracy begin to wither away, owing to the simple fact that, freed from capitalist slavery, from the untold horrors, savagery, absurdities and infamies of capitalist exploitation, people will gradually become accustomed to observing the elementary rules of social intercourse that have been known for centuries and repeated for thousands of years in all copy-book maxims. They will become accustomed to observing them without force, without coercion, without subordination, without the special apparatus for coercion called the state.

The expression "the state withers away" is very well chosen, for it indicates both the gradual and the spontaneous nature of the process. Only habit can, and undoubtedly will, have such an effect; for we see around us on millions of occasions how readily people become accustomed to observing the necessary rules of social intercourse when there is no exploitation, when there is nothing that arouses indignation, evokes protest and revolt, and creates the need for suppression.

And so in capitalist society we have a democracy that is curtailed, wretched, false, a democracy only for the rich, for the minority. The dictatorship of the proletariat, the period of transition to communism, will for the first time create democracy for the people, for the majority, along with the necessary suppression of the exploiters, of the minority. Communism alone is capable of providing really complete democracy, and the more complete it is, the sooner it will become unnecessary and wither away of its own accord.

In other words, under capitalism we have the state in the proper sense of the word, that is, a special machine for the suppression of one class by another, and, what is more, of the majority by the minority. Naturally, to be successful, such an undertaking as the systematic suppression of the exploited majority by the exploiting minority calls for the utmost ferocity and savagery in the matter of suppressing, it calls for seas of blood, through which mankind is actually wading its way in slavery, serfdom, and wage labour.

Furthermore, during the transition from capitalism to communism suppression is still necessary, but it is now the suppression of the exploiting minority by the exploited majority. A special apparatus, a special machine for suppression, the "state," is still necessary, but this is now a transitional state. It is no longer a state in the proper sense of the word; for the suppression of the minority of exploiters by the majority of the wage slaves of yesterday is comparatively so easy, simple and natural a task that it will entail far less bloodshed than the suppression of the risings of slaves, serfs or wage-labourers, and it will cost mankind far less. And it is compatible with the extension of democracy to such an overwhelming majority of the population that the need for a special machine of suppression will begin to disappear.

* * * * * * * *

It is this communist society, which has just emerged into the light of day out of the womb of capitalism and which is in every respect stamped with the birthmarks of the old society, that Marx terms the "first," or lower, phase of communist society.

The means of production are no longer the private property of individuals. The means of production belong to the whole of society. Every member of society, performing a certain part of the socially necessary work, receives a certificate from society to the effect that he has done a certain amount of work. And with this certificate he receives from the public store of consumer goods a corresponding quantity of products. After a deduction is made of the amount of labour which goes to the public fund, every worker, therefore, receives from society as much as he has given to it . . . .

The first phase of communism, therefore, cannot yet provide justice and equality: differences, and unjust differences, in wealth will still persist, but the exploitation of man by man will have become impossible because it will be impossible to seize the means of production the factories, machines, land, etc. -- and make them private property . . . .

And so, in the first phase of communist society (usually called socialism) "bourgeois right" is not abolished in its entirety, but only in part, only in proportion to the economic revolution so far attained, i.e., only in respect of the means of production. "Bourgeois right" recognises them as the private property of individuals. Socialism converts them into common property. To that extent -- and to that extent alone -- "bourgeois right" disappears.

* * * * * * * *

Until the "higher" phase of communism arrives, the socialists demand the strictest control by society and by the state over the measure of labour and the measure of consumption; but this control must start with the expropriation of the capitalists, with the establishment of workers' control over the capitalists, and must be exercised not by a state of bureaucrats, but by a state of armed workers . . . .

But the scientific distinction between socialism and communism is clear. What is usually called socialism was termed by Marx the "first," or lower, phase of communist society. Insofar as the means of production become common property, the word "communism" is also applicable here, providing we do not forget that this is not complete communism. The great significance of Marx's explanations is that here, too, he consistently applies materialist dialectics, the theory of development, and regards communism as something which develops out of capitalism.

Instead of scholastically invented, "concocted" definitions and fruitless disputes over words (What is socialism? What is communism?), Marx gives an analysis of what might be called the stages of the economic maturity of communism.

In its first phase, or first stage, communism cannot as yet be fully mature economically and entirely free from traditions or vestiges of capitalism. Hence the interesting phenomenon that communism in its first phase retains "the narrow horizon of bourgeois right." Of course, bourgeois right in regard to the distribution of consumer goods inevitably presupposes the existence of the bourgeois state, for right is nothing without an apparatus capable of enforcing the observance of the standards of right.

It follows that under communism there remains for a time not only bourgeois right, but even the bourgeois state, without the bourgeoisie!

* * * * * * * *

Democracy means equality. The great significance of the proletariat's struggle for equality and of equality as a slogan will be clear if we correctly interpret it as meaning the abolition of classes. But democracy means only formal equality. And as soon as equality is achieved for all members of society in relation to ownership of the means of production, that is, equality of labour and wages, humanity will inevitably be confronted with the question of advancing farther, from formal equality to actual equality, i.e., to the operation of the rule "from each according to his ability, to each according to his needs." By what stages, by means of what practical measures humanity will proceed to this supreme aim we do not and cannot know. But it is important to realise how infinitely mendacious is the ordinary bourgeois conception of socialism as something lifeless, rigid, fixed once and for all, whereas in reality only socialism will be the beginning of a rapid, genuine, truly mass forward movement, embracing first the majority and then the whole of the population, in all spheres of public and private life.

Democracy is a form of the state, one of its varieties. Consequently, it, like every state, represents, on the one hand, the organised, systematic use of force against persons; but, on the other hand, it signifies the formal recognition of equality of citizens, the equal right of all to determine the structure of, and to administer, the state. This, in turn, results in the fact that, at a certain stage in the development of democracy, it first welds together the class that wages a revolutionary struggle against capitalism -- the proletariat, and enables it to crush, smash to atoms, wipe off the face of the earth the bourgeois, even the republican-bourgeois, state machine, the standing army, the police and the bureaucracy and to substitute for them a more democratic state machine, but a state machine nevertheless, in the shape of armed workers who proceed to form a militia involving the entire population.

* * * * * * * *

Accounting and control -- that is mainly what is needed for the "smooth working," for the proper functioning, of the first phase of communist society. All citizens are transformed into hired employees of the state, which consists of the armed workers. All citizens become employees and workers of a single country-wide state "syndicate." All that is required is that they should work equally, do their proper share of work, and get equal pay. The accounting and control necessary for this have been simplified by capitalism to the utmost and reduced to the extraordinarily simple operations -- which any literate person can perform -- of supervising and recording, knowledge of the four rules of arithmetic, and issuing appropriate receipts.

When the majority of the people begin independently and everywhere to keep such accounts and exercise such control over the capitalists (now converted into employees) and over the intellectual gentry who preserve their capitalist habits, this control will really become universal, general and popular; and there will be no getting away from it, there will be "nowhere to go."

The whole of society will have become a single office and a single factory, with equality of labour and pay.

But this "factory" discipline, which the proletariat, after defeating the capitalists, after overthrowing the exploiters, will extend to the whole of society, is by no means our ideal, or our ultimate goal. It is only a necessary step for thoroughly cleaning society of all the infamies and abominations of capitalist exploitation and for further progress.

From the moment all members of society, or at least the vast majority, have learned to administer the state themselves, have taken this work into their own hands, have organised control over the insignificant capitalist minority, over the gentry who wish to preserve their capitalist habits and over the workers who have been thoroughly corrupted by capitalism -- from this moment the need for government of any kind begins to disappear altogether. The more complete the democracy, the nearer the moment when it becomes unnecessary. The more democratic the "state" which consists of the armed workers, and which is "no longer a state in the proper sense of the word," the more rapidly every form of state begins to wither away.

For when all have learned to administer and actually do independently administer social production, independently keep accounts and exercise control over the parasites, the sons of the wealthy, the swindlers and other "guardians of capitalist traditions," the escape from this popular accounting and control will inevitably become so incredibly difficult, such a rare exception, and will probably be accompanied by such swift and severe punishment (for the armed workers are practical men and not sentimental intellectuals, and they will scarcely allow anyone to trifle with them), that the necessity of observing the simple, fundamental rules of the community will very soon become a habit.

Then the door will be thrown wide open for the transition from the first phase of communist society to its higher phase and with it to the complete withering away of the state.

Woodrow Wilson

The Fourteen Points

President Woodrow Wilson announced his famous "Fourteen Points" in an address to the United States Congress on January 8, 1918, in response to the new Russian Bolshevik government's proposal of a status quo conclusion to World War I. These "Fourteen Points" became the basis on which the western Allies eventually negotiated peace with the Central Powers. After the war, lack of specificity in Wilson's statements caused a great deal of controversy at the Paris Peace Conference.

We entered this war because violations of right had occurred which touched us to the quick and made the life of our own people impossible unless they were corrected and the world secured once for all against their recurrence. What we demand in this war, therefore, is nothing peculiar to ourselves. It is that the world be made fit and safe to live in; and particularly that it be made safe for every peace-loving nation which, like our own, wishes to live its own life, determine its own institutions, be assured of justice and fair dealings by the other peoples of the world, as against force and selfish aggression. All the peoples of the world are in effect partners in this interest, and for our own part we see very clearly that unless justice be done to others it will not be done to us.

The program of the world's peace, therefore, is our program, and that program, the only possible program, as we see it, is this:

I. -- Open covenants of peace, openly arrived at, after which there shall be no private international understandings of any kind, but diplomacy shall proceed frankly and in the public view.

Text: A Compilation of the Messages and Papers of the Presidents *(New York: Bureau of National Literature, Inc., n.d.),* XVIII, 8423-8426.

II. -- Absolute freedom of navigation upon the seas, outside territorial waters, alike in peace and in war, except as the seas may be closed in whole or in part by international action for the enforcement of international covenants.

III. -- The removal, so far as possible, of all economic barriers and the establishment of an equality of trade conditions among all the nations consenting to the peace and associating themselves for its maintenance.

IV. -- Adequate guarantees given and taken that national armaments will be reduced to the lowest point consistent with domestic safety.

V. -- Free, open-minded, and absolutely impartial adjustment of all colonial claims, based upon a strict observance of the principle that in determining all such questions of sovereignty the interests of the population concerned must have equal weight with the equitable claims of the Government whose title is to be determined.

VI. -- The evacuation of all Russian territory and such a settlement of all questions affecting Russia as will secure the best and freest cooperation of the other nations of the world in obtaining for her an unhampered and unembarrassed opportunity for the independent determination of her own political development and national policy, and assure her of a sincere welcome into the society of free nations under institutions of her own choosing; and, more than a welcome, assistance also of every kind that she may need and may herself desire. The treatment accorded Russia by her sister nations in the months to come will be the acid test of their good-will, of their comprehension of her needs as distinguished from their own interests, and of their intelligent and unselfish sympathy.

VII. -- Belgium, the whole world will agree, must be evacuated and restored, without any attempt to limit the sovereignty which she enjoys in common with all other free nations. No other single act will serve as this will serve to restore confidence among the nations in the laws which they have themselves set and determined for the government of their relations with one another. Without this healing act the whole structure and validity of international law is forever impaired.

VIII. -- All French territory should be freed and the invaded portions restored, and the wrong done to France by Prussia in 1871 in the matter of Alsace-Lorraine, which has unsettled the peace of the world for nearly fifty years, should be righted, in order that peace may once more be made secure in the interest of all.

IX. -- A readjustment of the frontiers of Italy should be effected along clearly recognizable lines of nationality.

X. -- The peoples of Austria-Hungary, whose place among the nations we wish to see safeguarded and assured, should be accorded the freest opportunity of autonomous development.

XI. -- Rumania, Serbia, and Montenegro should be evacuated; occupied territories restored; Serbia accorded free and secure access to the sea; and the relations of the several Balkan States to one another determined by friendly counsel along historically established lines of allegiance and nationality; and international guarantees of the political and economic independence and territorial integrity of the several Balkan States should be entered into.

XII. -- The Turkish portions of the present Ottoman Empire should be assured a secure sovereignty, but the other nationalities which are now under Turkish rule should be assured an undoubted security of life and an absolutely unmolested opportunity of autonomous development, and the Dardanelles should be permanently opened as a free passage to the ships and commerce of all nations under international guarantees.

XIII. -- An independent Polish State should be erected which should include the territories inhabited by indisputably Polish populations, which should be assured a free and secure access to the sea, and whose political and economic independence and territorial integrity should be guaranteed by international covenant.

XIV. -- A general association of nations must be formed under specific covenants for the purpose of affording mutual guarantees of political independence and territorial integrity to great and small states alike.

In regard to these essential rectifications of wrong and assertions of right, we feel ourselves to be intimate partners of all the governments and peoples associated together against the imperialists. We cannot be separated in interest or divided in purpose. We stand together until the end.

For such arrangements and covenants we are willing to fight and to continue to fight until they are achieved; but only because we wish the right to prevail and desire a just and stable peace, such as can be secured only by removing the chief provocations to war, which this program does remove. We have no jealousy of German greatness, and there is nothing in this program that impairs it. We grudge her no achievement or distinction of learning or of pacific enterprise such as have made her record very bright and very enviable. We do not wish to injure her or to block in any way her legitimate influence or power. We do not wish to fight her either with arms or with hostile arrangements of trade, if she is willing to associate herself with us and the other peace-loving nations of the world in covenants of justice and law and fair dealing. We wish her only to accept a place of equality among the peoples of the world -- the new world in which we now live -- instead of a place of mastery.

Neither do we presume to suggest to her any alteration or modification of her institutions. But it is necessary, we must frankly say, and necessary as a preliminary to any intelligent dealings with her on our part, that we should know whom her spokesmen speak for when they speak to us, whether for the Reichstag majority or for the military party and the men whose creed is imperial domination.

We have spoken now, surely, in terms too concrete to admit of any further doubt or question. An evident principle runs through the whole program I have outlined. It is the principle of justice to all peoples and nationalities, and their right to live on equal terms of liberty and safety with one another, whether they be strong or weak. Unless this principle be made its foundation, no part of the structure of international justice can stand. The people of the United States could act upon no other principle, and to the vindication of this principle they are ready to devote their lives, their honor, and everything that they possess. The moral climax of this, the culminating and final war for human liberty, has come, and they are ready to put their own strength, their own highest purpose, their own integrity and devotion to the test.

The following two selections include portions of the Treaty of Versailles -- the peace treaty between Germany and the western powers after World War I -- and John Maynard Keynes' criticism of the Treaty. Keynes (1883-1946), a member of the British delegation to the Paris Peace Conference, who later became one of the foremost economic theorists of the twentieth century, was disturbed by the economic clauses of the Treaty, which he believed were not conducive to a stable peace. Many Germans, including Adolf Hitler, thought that Keynes had not gone far enough and attacked all aspects of the "dictated" peace settlement.

The Treaty of Versailles

The High Contracting Parties, in order to promote international cooperation and to achieve international peace and security:

by the acceptance of obligations not to resort to war, by the prescription of open, just and honourable relations between nations,

by the firm establishment of the understandings of international law as the actual rule of conduct among Governments, and

by the maintenance of justice and a scrupulous respect for all treaty obligations in the dealings of organised peoples with one another,

Agree to this Covenant of the League of Nations.

Text: United States, Department of State, Foreign Relations of the United States: Paris Peace Conference, 1919 *(Washington: United States Government Printing Office, 1947), XIII, pp. 72-73, 83-85, 159, 162, 182-183, 198, 202, 208, 272-276, 319, 325, 413, 425, 428, 720, 725.*

Article 10

The Members of the League undertake to respect and preserve as against external aggression the territorial integrity and existing political independence of all Members of the League. In case of any such aggression or in case of any threat or danger of such aggression the Council shall advise upon the means by which this obligation shall be fulfilled.

Article 12

The Members of the League agree that, if there should arise between them any dispute likely to lead to a rupture, they will submit the matter either to arbitration or judicial settlement or to inquiry by the Council, and they agree in no case to resort to war until three months after the award by the arbitrators or the judicial decision, or the report by the Council.

Article 13

The Members of the League agree that, whenever any dispute shall arise between them which they recognize to be suitable for submission to arbitration or judicial settlement, and which cannot be satisfactorily settled by diplomacy, they will submit the whole subject matter to arbitration or judicial settlement . . . .

The Members of the League agree that they will carry out in full good faith any award or decision that may be rendered and that they will not resort to war against a Member of the League which complies therewith. In the event of any failure to carry out such an award or decision, the Council shall propose what steps should be taken to give effect thereto.

Article 42

Germany is forbidden to maintain or construct any fortifications either on the left bank of the Rhine or on the right bank to the west of a line drawn 50 kilometres to the East of the Rhine.

Article 43

In the area defined above the maintenance and the assembly of armed forces, either permanently or temporarily, and military manoeuvres of any kind, as well as the upkeep of all permanent works for mobilization, are in the same way forbidden.

Article 45

As compensation for the destruction of the coal-mines in the north of France and as part payment towards the total reparation due from Germany for the damage resulting from the war, Germany cedes to France in full and absolute possession, with exclusive rights of exploitation, unencumbered and free from all debts and charges of any kind, the coal-mines situated in the Saar Basin . . . .

Article 51

The High Contracting Parties, recognising the moral obligation to redress the wrong done by Germany in 1871 both to the rights of France and to the wishes of the population of Alsace and Lorraine . . . .

The territories which were ceded to Germany in accordance with the Preliminaries of Peace signed at Versailles on February 26, 1871, and the Treaty of Frankfort of May 10, 1871, are restored to French sovereignty as from the date of the Armistice of November 11, 1918.

Article 80

Germany acknowledges and will respect strictly the independence of Austria, within the frontiers which may be fixed in a Treaty between that State and the Principal Allied and Associated Powers; she agrees that this independence shall be inalienable, except with the consent of the Council of the League of Nations.

Article 81

Germany, in conformity with the action already taken by the Allied and Associated Powers, recognizes the complete independence of the Czecho-Slovak State which will include the autonomous territory of the Ruthenians to the south of the Carpathians. Germany hereby recognizes the frontiers of this State as determined by the Principal Allied and Associated Powers and the other interested States.

Article 87

Germany, in conformity with the action already taken by the Allied and Associated Powers, recognizes the complete independence of Poland . . . .

The provisions of this Article do not, however, apply to the territories of East Prussia and the Free City of Danzig.

Article 116

Germany acknowledges and agrees to respect as permanent and inalienable the independence of all the territories which were part of the former Russian Empire on August 1, 1914.

Article 117

Germany undertakes to recognize the full force of all treaties or agreements which may be entered into by the Allied and Associated Powers with States now existing or coming into existence in future in the whole or part of the former Empire of Russia as it existed on August 1, 1914, and to recognize the frontiers of any such States as determined therein.

Article 118

In territory outside her European frontiers as fixed by the present Treaty, Germany renounces all rights, ties and privileges whatever in or over territory which belonged to her or to her allies, and all rights, titles and privileges whatever their origin which she held as against the Allied and Associated Powers.

Article 119

Germany renounces in favour of the Principal Allied and Associated Powers all her rights and titles over her oversea possessions.

Article 159

The German military forces shall be demobilized and reduced as prescribed hereinafter.

Article 160

By a date which must not be later than March 31, 1920, the German Army must not comprise more than seven divisions of infantry and three divisions of cavalry.

After that date the total number of effectives in the Army of the States constituting Germany must not exceed one hundred thousand men, including officers and establishments of depots. The Army shall be devoted exclusively to the maintenance of order within the territory and to the control of the frontiers.

The total effective strength of officers, including the personnel of staffs, whatever their composition, must not exceed four thousand.

Article 168

The manufacture of arms, munitions, or any war material, shall only be carried out in factories or works the location of which shall be communicated to and approved by the Governments of the Principal Allied and Associated Powers, and the number of which they retain the right to restrict.

Article 231

The Allied and Associated Governments affirm and Germany accepts the responsibility of Germany and her Allies for causing all the loss and damage to which the Allied and Associated Governments and their nationals have been subjected as a consequence of the war imposed upon them by the aggression of Germany and her allies.

Article 232

The Allied and Associated Governments recognize that the resources of Germany are not adequate, after taking into account permanent diminutions of such resources which will result from other provisions of the present Treaty, to make complete reparation for all such loss and damage.

The Allied and Associated Governments, however, require, and Germany undertakes, that she will make compensation for all damage done to the civilian population of the Allied and Associated Powers and to their property during the period of the belligerency of each as an Allied or Associated Power against Germany by such aggression by land, by sea and from the air.

Article 233

The amount of the above damage for which compensation 15 to be made by Germany shall be determined by an Inter-Allied Commission, to be called the Reparation Commission . . . .

The findings of the Commission as to the amount of damage defined as above shall be concluded and notified to the German Government on or before May 1, 1921, as representing the extent of that Government's obligations.

Article 428

As a guarantee for the execution of the present Treaty by Germany, the German territory situated to the west of the Rhine, together with the bridgeheads, will be occupied by Allied and Associated troops for a period of fifteen years from the coming into force of the present Treaty.

Article 431

If before the expiration of the period of fifteen years Germany complies with all the undertakings resulting from the present Treaty, the occupying forces will be withdrawn immediately.

John Maynard Keynes

The Economic Consequences of the Peace

In November 1918 the armies of Foch and the words of Wilson had brought us sudden escape from what was swallowing up all we cared for. The conditions seemed favourable beyond any expectation. The victory was so complete that fear need play no part in the settlement. The enemy had laid down his arms in reliance on a solemn compact as to the general character of the peace, the terms of which seemed to assure a settlement of justice and magnanimity and a fair hope for a restoration of the broken current of life. To make assurance certain the President was coming himself to set the seal on his work.

When President Wilson left Washington he enjoyed a prestige and a moral influence throughout the world unequal led in history. His bold and measured words carried to the peoples of Europe above and beyond the voices of their own politicians. The enemy peoples trusted him to carry out the compact he had made with them; and the Allied peoples acknowledged him not as a victor only but almost as a prophet.

Yet the causes were very ordinary and human. The President was not a hero or a prophet; he was not even a philosopher; but a generously intentioned man, with many of the weaknesses of other human beings, and lacking that dominating intellectual equipment which would have been necessary to cope with the subtle and dangerous spellbinders whom a tremendous clash of forces and personalities had brought to the top as triumphant

Text: John Maynard Keynes, The Collected Writings of John Maynard Keynes *(London: Macmillan for the Royal Economic Society, 1971), pp. 23-25, 27-28, 41-44, 51, 95, 117-118, 143. Reprinted with permission of the Royal Economic Society and the Keynes trustees. Originally published in 1920.*

master in the swift game of give and take, face to face in council -- a game of which he had no experience at all.

He not only had no proposals in detail, but he was in many respects, perhaps inevitably, ill-informed as to European conditions. And not only was he ill-informed -- that was true of Mr. Lloyd George also -- but his mind was slow and unadaptable. The President's slowness amongst the Europeans was noteworthy. He could not, all in a minute, take in what the rest were saying, size up the situation with a glance, frame a reply, and meet the case by a slight change of ground; and he was liable, therefore, to defeat by the mere swiftness, apprehension, and agility of a Lloyd George. There can seldom have been a statesman of the first rank more incompetent than the President in the agilities of the council chamber. A moment often arrives when substantial victory is yours if by some slight appearance of a concession you can save the face of the opposition or conciliate them by a restatement of your proposal helpful to them and not injurious to anything essential to yourself. The President was not equipped with this simple and usual artfulness. His mind was too slow and unresourceful to be ready with any alternatives. The President was capable of digging his toes in and refusing to budge, as he did over Fiume. But he had no other mode of defence, and it needed as a rule but little maneuvering by his opponents to prevent matters from coming to such a head until it was too late . . . .

The German economic system as it existed before the war depended on three main factors: I. Overseas commerce as represented by her mercantile marine, her colonies, her foreign investments, her exports, and the overseas connection of her merchants. II. The exploitation of her coal and iron and the industries built upon them. III. Her transport and tariff system. Of these the first, while not the least important, was certainly the most vulnerable. The treaty aims at the systematic destruction of all three, but principally of the first two.

(1) Germany has ceded to the Allies all the vessels of her mercantile marine exceeding 1,600 tons gross, half the vessels between 1,000 tons and 1,600 tons, and one-quarter of her

trawlers and other fishing boats! The cession is comprehensive, including not only vessels flying the German flag, but also all vessels owned by Germans but flying other flags, and all vessels under construction as well as those afloat. Further, Germany undertakes, if required, to build for the Allies such types of ships as they may specify up to 200,000 tons annually for five years, the value of these ships being credited to Germany against what is due for her reparation.

Thus the German mercantile marine is swept from the seas and cannot be restored for many years to come on a scale adequate to meet the requirements of her own commerce . . . .

(2) Germany has ceded to the Allies "all her rights and titles over her oversea possessions." This cession not only applies to sovereignty but extends on unfavourable terms to government property, all of which, including railways, must be surrendered without payment, while, on the other hand, the German government remains liable for any debt which may have been incurred for the purchase or construction of this property, or for the development of the colonies generally.

In distinction from the practice ruling in the case of most similar cessions in recent history, the property and persons of private German nationals, as distinct from their government, are also injuriously affected. The Allied government exercising authority in any former German colony "may make such provisions as it thinks fit with reference to the repatriation from them of German nationals and to the conditions upon which German subjects of European origin shall, or shall not, be allowed to reside, hold property, trade or exercise a profession in them." All contracts and agreements in favour of German nationals for the construction or exploitation of public works lapse to the Allied governments as part of the payment due for reparation . . . .

(3) The provisions just outlined in regard to the private property of Germans in the ex-German colonies apply equally to private German property in Alsace-Lorraine, except insofar as the French government may choose to grant exceptions. This is of much greater practical importance than the similar expropriation

overseas because of the far higher value of the property involved and the closer interconnection, resulting from the great development of the mineral wealth of these provinces since 1871, of German economic interests there with those in Germany itself. Alsace-Lorraine has been part of the German empire for nearly fifty years -- a considerable majority of its population is German-speaking -- and it has been the scene of some of Germany's most important economic enterprises. Nevertheless, the property of those Germans who reside there, or who have invested in its industries, is now entirely at the disposal of the French government without compensation, except in so far as the German government itself may choose to afford it. The French government is entitled to expropriate without compensation the personal property of private German citizens and German companies resident or situated within Alsace-Lorraine, the proceeds being credited in part satisfaction of various French claims. The severity of this provision is only mitigated to the extent that the French government may expressly permit German nationals to continue to reside, in which case the above provision is not applicable. Government, state, and municipal property, on the other hand, is to be ceded to France without any credit being given for it. This includes the railway system of the two provinces, together with its rolling-stock. But while the property is taken over, liabilities contracted in respect of it in the form of public debts of any kind remain the liability of Germany. The provinces also return to French sovereignty free and quit of their share of German war or pre-war dead-weight debt; nor does Germany receive a credit on this account in respect of reparation.

The provision relating to coal and iron are more important in respect of their ultimate consequences on Germany's internal industrial economy than for the money value immediately involved. The German empire has been built more truly on coal and iron than on blood and iron. The skilled exploitation of the great coal fields of the Ruhr, Upper Silesia, and the Saar, alone made possible the development of the steel, chemical, and electrical industries which established her as the first industrial nation of continental Europe. One-third of Germany's population lives in towns of more than 20,000 inhabitants, an industrial concentration which is only possible on a foundation of coal and iron. In striking, therefore, at her coal supply, the French politicians were not mistaking their target . . . .

It is evident that Germany's pre-war capacity to pay an annual foreign tribute has not been unaffected by the almost total loss of her colonies, her overseas connections, her mercantile marine, and her foreign properties, by the cession of ten per cent of her territory and population, of one-third of her coal and of three-quarters of her iron ore, by two million casualties amongst men in the prime of life, by the starvation of her people for four years, by the burden of a vast war debt, by the depreciation of her currency to less than one-seventh its former value, by the disruption of her allies and their territories, by revolution at home and Bolshevism on her borders, and by all the unmeasured ruin in strength and hope of four years of all-swallowing war and final defeat . . . .

The treaty includes no provisions for the economic rehabilitation of Europe -- nothing to make the defeated Central empires into good neighbours, nothing to stabilize the new states of Europe, nothing to reclaim Russia; nor does it promote in any way a compact of economic solidarity amongst the Allies themselves; no arrangement was reached at Paris for restoring the disordered finances of France and Italy or to adjust the systems of the Old World and the New.

The Council of Four paid no attention to these issues, being preoccupied with others -- Clemenceau to crush the economic life of his enemy, Lloyd George to do a deal and bring home something which would pass muster for a week, the President to do nothing that was not just and right. It is an extraordinary fact that the fundamental economic problem of a Europe starving and disintegrating before their eyes was the one question in which it was impossible to arouse the interest of the Four. Reparation was their main excursion into the economic field, and they settled it as a problem of theology, of politics, of electoral chicane, from every point except that of the economic future of the states whose destiny they were handling.

Adolf Hitler

Mein Kampf

Adolf Hitler (1889-1945) wrote most of Mein Kampf *during a period of imprisonment in 1924, and it quickly became the cornerstone of the National Socialist movement. Despite his turgid writing style and pseudo-Darwinistic ideas, Hitler's notion of a superior race and the need for territorial expansion struck a responsive chord among those Germans who felt the humiliation of defeat in World War I and the general desire for recognition and self-worth in the impersonal world of the twentieth century.*

Any crossing of two beings not exactly at the same level produces an offspring between the level of both parents. That is, the offspring will probably stand higher than the racially inferior half of the two parents, but not as high as the higher one. Consequently, it will later be overcome in the struggle against this higher one. But such a mating is contrary to the will of nature for a higher breeding of life. The prerequisite for this lies not in joining the stronger with the weaker, but in the total victory of the former. The stronger must dominate and not blend with the weaker so as to sacrifice his own greatness. Only the born weakling can feel this as cruel, for after all he is only a weak and limited man; for if this law did not prevail, then any conceivable higher development of organic living beings would be unthinkable.

The consequence of this racial purity, which is a universally valid urge in nature, is not only the sharp outward differentiation of individual races, but also its uniform character in itself. The fox is always a fox, the goose a goose, the tiger a tiger, etc., and

Text: Adolf Hitler, Mein Kampf *(Muenchen: Franz Eher Nachf., GmbH, 1939), pp. 312-314, 316-318, 324, 329-331, 334, 357, 493, 496-497, 499-501, 739-742. Translation by Alan Wilt.*

the difference can lie uppermost in the varying amount of force, strength, intelligence, dexterity, endurance, etc. of the individual specimens. But one will never find a fox who in his inner disposition might possibly show humane impulses toward geese, as similarly there is no cat with a friendly affection toward mice.

Therefore, here also the struggle one with another arises less from an inner aversion than from hunger and love. In both cases nature looks on calmly, even contentedly. The struggle for daily bread lets those who are weak and sickly or less determined succumb, while the struggle of males for females accords only to the healthiest the right or the possibility of procreating. And the struggle is always a means for improving the health and power of resistance of a species and, therefore, a source of its higher development.

If the process were different, all further and higher development would cease and the opposite would take place. For, since the inferior always predominate over the best, if both had the possibility of preserving life and propagating, the inferior would increase so much more rapidly that in the end the best would inevitably be driven to the background. A correction in favor of the better type must therefore be undertaken. Nature provides for this by subjecting the weaker part to such severe living conditions that by them alone the number is limited, and by not permitting the rest to increase indiscriminately but by making a new, ruthless choice according to strength and health.

As little as nature desires a mating of weaker with stronger beings, even less does she desire the blending of a higher with a lower race, since, if she did, her entire work of higher breeding, over perhaps hundreds of thousands of years, would fail in one blow.

* * * * * * * *

Historical experience offers countless proofs of this. It shows with terrifying clarity that every mixing of Aryan blood with lower peoples resulted in the end of the upholders of culture. North America, whose population consists of by far the largest part of Germanic elements, who mixed but very little with lower colored peoples, shows a different humanity and culture than

Central and South America, where the predominantly Latin immigrants often mixed with the original inhabitants on a large scale. By this one example we recognize clearly and distinctly the effect of racial mixing. The racially pure and unmixed German inhabitant of the American continent rose to be master of the continent; he will remain the master so long as he does not also fall victim to defilement of the blood.

The result of all racial crossing is therefore in brief always the following:

(a) Lowering of the level of the higher race.

(b) Physical and mental regression and with it the beginning of a slow but sure progressing sickness.

Such a development brings about then nothing other than to sin against the will of the eternal creator.

* * * * * * * *

Everything we admire on this earth today -- science and art, technology and inventions -- is only the creative product of a few people and perhaps originally of one race. On them depends even the existence of this entire culture. If they perish, then the beauty of this earth will sink into the grave with them.

However much the soil, for example, might influence men, so will the result of the influence always be different depending on the races in question. The low fertility of a living space may stimulate one race to the highest achievement; in others it will only be the cause of bitterest poverty and endless undernourishment with all its consequences. The inner nature of peoples is always the determinant for the type of effect of external influences. Whatever leads one to starvation trains the other to hard work.

All great cultures of the past perished only because the originally creative race died out from blood poisoning.

The ultimate cause of such a decline was always forgetting that all culture depends on man and not the opposite. Therefore, to preserve a certain culture the man who creates it must be saved.

This preservation is bound up with the early law of necessity and the right to victory of the best and strongest.

Whoever wants to live let him struggle, and whoever does not want to fight in this world of eternal struggle does not deserve to live.

Even though this is hard -- that is how it is! Assuredly, however, by far the hardest fate is that which affects the man who believes he can overcome nature and actually mocks her. Misery, misfortune, and diseases are then her answer.

* * * * * * * *

The man who misjudges and disregards the racial laws actually forfeits the good fortune which appears certain for him. He is prevented the triumphal march with the best race and with it also the precondition for all human progress. He proceeds as a consequence burdened with the sensibility of man into the realm of the helpless beast . . . .

If one were to divide mankind into three types, the culture founders, the culture bearers, and the culture destroyers, then probably only the Aryan could be considered as the representative of the first group. From him originate the foundations and walls of all human creation, and only the outward form and color are determined by the changing character traits of various peoples. He provides the mightiest building stones and plans for all human progress, and only the realization corresponds to the character of the carious races. In a few decades, for example, all of East Asia will possess a culture, whose ultimate basis will be the Hellenistic spirit and Germanic technology, as is the case with us. Only the outward form will -- at least in part -- bear the features of Asiatic character. It is not true, as many believe, that Japan takes European technology to its culture, but European science and technology are embellished with Japanese characteristics. The basis of actual life is no longer special Japanese culture, although it determines the color of life -- because outwardly as a consequence of inner difference it is more conspicuous for the Europeans -- but the mighty scientific-technical achievements of Europe and America, and therefore of Aryan peoples. On these achievements alone can the Orient follow general human progress . . . .

Therefore, the way which the Aryan had to take was clearly

marked. As a conqueror he subjected the lower beings and regulated their practical activity under his command, according to his will and for his goals. But in directing them to a useful, if difficult activity, he not only spared the life of the subjected, but also gave them perhaps a fate that was better than their earlier so-called "freedom." So long as he ruthlessly upheld the master attitude, not only did he actually remain master, but also the preserver and increaser of culture. For this culture was based exclusively on his abilities and thus on his own survival. As soon as the subjected people began to raise themselves up and possibly approached the conqueror in language, the sharp division between master and servant fell. The Aryan gave up the purity of his blood and hence lost his stay in paradise which he had created for himself. He sank into the racial mixture, and gradually more and more lost his cultural abilities, until at last not only mentally, but also physically he began to resemble more the subjected and original inhabitants than his own ancestors. For a long time he could still live on with the existing cultural benefits, but then numbness set in and he fell ultimately into oblivion.

Thus cultures and empires collapse to make place for new formations.

The blood mixing and the resultant drop in the racial level is the sole cause of the dying out of all culture; for man does not perish as a result of lost wars, but by the loss of that strength of resistance which is contained only in pure blood.

* * * * * * * *

The mightiest opposition to the Aryan is represented by the Jew. In scarcely any people in the world is the instinct for self-preservation developed more strongly than in the so-called chosen ones. The best proof of this may be considered the simple fact of the survival of this race. Where is the people who in the last two thousand years has been exposed to so few changes of inner disposition, character, etc., as the Jewish people? What people ultimately has gone through greater upheavals than this one -- and nevertheless come forth unchanged from the mightiest catastrophes of mankind? What an infinitely tenacious will to live and to preserve the species speaks from these facts!

The intellectual qualities of the Jew have been schooled in the course of thousands of years. Today he passes as "clever," and this has been in a certain sense at all times. But his intelligence is not the result of his own development, but of visual instructions from foreigners. For the human mind cannot climb to the top without steps; he needs for each step upward the foundation of the past, and this in the comprehensive sense in which it can be revealed only in general culture. All thinking is based only in small part on inherent knowledge, and mostly on the experiences of the time that has preceded it.

The general cultural level provides the individual man, without his generally noticing it, with such a profusion of preliminary knowledge that he, thus armed, can take more easily further steps of his own. The boy of today, for example, grows up among a truly enormous number of technical achievements of the last centuries, so that he takes for granted and no longer pays attention to much that a hundred years ago was a riddle to even the greatest minds, although it is for him of decisive importance for following and understanding our progress in the area in question. If a true genius of twenty years of the past century should suddenly leave his grave today, it would be harder for him at present even intellectually to find his way than would be the case for an average fifteen year old boy of today. For he would lack all the infinite preliminary education, which the contemporary of today assimilates unconsciously, so to speak, while growing up in the midst of the manifestations of present general culture.

Since the Jew -- on the basis of which will become apparent immediately -- was never in possession of his own culture, the foundations of his intellectual work were always provided by others. His intellect has at all times developed through the cultural world surrounding him.

At no time did the reverse process take place.

For if the instinct of self-preservation of the Jewish people is not smaller but larger than that of other peoples, if also his intellectual qualities can easily arouse the impression that they are equal to the intellectual gifts of other races, then he still lacks completely the essential prerequisite for a cultured people, the idealistic disposition.

The will to self-sacrifice in the Jewish people does not go beyond the naked instinct of self-preservation of the individual. Their apparently great sense of solidarity is based on a very primitive herd instinct as is shown by many other living creatures in this world. Noteworthy thereby is the fact that the herd instinct leads to mutual support only so long as a common danger makes this appear useful or inevitable. The same pack of wolves which has just fallen together on its prey is dissolved by weakening hunger in its single animals. The same is true of horses which seek to defend themselves against attackers in a group but scatter again as soon as the danger is overcome.

It is similar with the Jew. His sense of sacrifice is only an appearance. It exists only so long as the existence of the individual makes it absolutely necessary. However, as soon as the common enemy is conquered, the all threatening danger averted, and the booty hidden, the apparent harmony of the Jews ceases among themselves in order to make way again for their subjective existing tendencies. The Jew is only united when a common danger forces him to be or a common prey entices him; if these two bases are lacking, then the qualities of the crassest egoism come into their own, and out of a united people comes in a twinkling of an eye a horde of rats fighting bloodily among themselves.

If the Jews were alone in this world, then they would stifle just as much in filth and garbage as in the attempt to exterminate and get ahead of each other in hate-filled struggle is so far as the absolute absence of all sense of self-sacrifice, expressing itself in their cowardice, did not turn the struggle into theater here too.

Therefore, it is absolutely false to infer any ideal sense of sacrifice in the Jews from the fact that they stand together in the struggle, or better expressed, in the plundering of their fellow man.

Also here leading the Jews is nothing more than the naked egoism of the individual.

Therefore, the Jewish state -- which should be the living

organism for preserving and increasing a race -- is completely unlimited as to territory. For a created state to have a definite spatial setting always presupposed an idealistic sense of the state race, and especially a correct interpretation of the concept of work. In the exact measure in which this attitude is lacking, any attempt at forming, even of preserving, a spatially delimited state fails. With it falls the basis on which a culture alone can arise.

Therefore the Jewish people, despite all the apparent intellectual qualities, is without any true culture, and especially without even their own. For what occupies the Jew today is sham culture, which is the property of other peoples, and which is ruined in his hands . . . .

* * * * * * * *

He is and remains the typical parasite, a sponger who spreads more and more like a noxious bacillus as soon as a favorable medium invites him in. And the effect of his presence is also like that of spongers; wherever he appears, the host people dies out after a shorter or longer time.

Therefore the Jew lived at all times in the states of other people and formed there his own state, which, to be sure, habitually sailed under the disguise of a "religious community" so long as the outward circumstances did not make a complete revelation of his nature seem advisable. But as soon as he believed himself strong enough to do without the protective cover, then he always dropped the veil and suddenly became what so many of the others previously did not want to believe and see: the Jew . . . .

With satanic joy in his face, the black-haired Jewish youth lurks in wait for the unsuspecting girl whom he defames with his blood, and thus takes her away from her people. With every means he seeks to destroy the racial basis of the people to be subjugated. Just as he himself systematically destroys women and girls, he also does not shirk back from pulling down even on a large scale the blood barrier for others. It was and is Jews who bring Negroes to the Rhineland, always with the same hidden thought and clear goal of destroying the hated white race by the necessarily resulting bastardization, throwing it down from its cultural and political height, and himself rising to be its master.

A philosophy which strives for the rejection of mass democratic thinking and gives this earth the best people, that is the highest man, must logically obey the same aristocratic principle within this people and make sure that the leadership and the highest influence fall to the best minds. Thus, it builds not on the idea of the majority, but on the idea of personality . . . .

A human community appears well organized only if it facilitates the labors of these creative forces in every possible helpful way and applies them in a manner advantageous to all. The most worthwhile thing about the invention itself, whether it lies in the material world or the world of thought, is primarily the inventor as a personality. To employ him therefore, in a way benefiting all is the first and highest task in the organization of a national community. Indeed, the organization itself must be a realization of this principle. Thus, also, it is redeemed from the curse of mechanism and becomes a living thing. It must itself be the embodiment of the endeavor to place thinking individuals above the masses and hence to subordinate them to the thinkers.

The organization must, therefore, not only not prevent the emergence of thinking individuals from the masses, but also it must in the highest degree make this possible and easy by the nature of its own being. It has thereby proceeded on the basis that the salvation of mankind has never lain in the masses, but in the creative thinkers, who therefore are to be regarded actually as the benefactors of the human race. To assure them of the most decisive influence and to facilitate their work is in the interest of all. Certainly this interest is not satisfied and is not served by the domination of the unintelligent or incompetent, in any case the uninspired masses, but solely by the leadership of those to whom nature has given special gifts for this purpose.

The selection of these thinkers, as said before, is primarily accomplished by the hard struggle for existence. Many break and die, thus showing they are not destined for the ultimate, and in the end only a few appear to be chosen.

* * * * * * * *

The folkish philosophy is basically distinguished from Marxist philosophy by the fact that it not only recognizes the value of race, but also with it the importance of personality, which it therefore makes one of the pillars of the entire edifice. These are the enduring factors of our philosophy.

If the National Socialist movement did not understand the fundamental significance of this basic realization, but instead merely performed superficial patchwork on the present-day state, or even adopted the mass standpoint as its own, then it would only constitute a party in competition with Marxism; in that case it would not possess the right to call itself a philosophy. If the social program of the movement consisted only in pushing aside the personality and putting the masses in its place, then National Socialism itself would be corroded by the poison of Marxism, as is the case with our bourgeois parties.

The folkish state must care for the welfare of its citizens by recognizing in all and everything the significance of the value of personality and thus in all fields preparing the way for that highest measure of productive performance which grants to the individual the highest measure of participation.

And the folkish state, accordingly, must free the entire leadership and especially the highest, that is the political leadership, from the parliamentary principle of majority rule, meaning mass rule, in order to guarantee absolutely in its place the right to the personality.

Out of this the following realization results: The best state constitution and state form is that which, with the most unquestioned certainty, brings the best minds in the national community to leading importance and leading influence.

But as in economic life, the able men cannot be determined from above, but must struggle through for themselves, and just as here endless schooling, ranging from the smallest business to the largest enterprise, occurs, since life alone gives the examinations, then obviously political minds cannot be "discovered" suddenly. Extraordinary geniuses allow no consideration for normal mankind.

The state in its organization must have the personality principle anchored from the smallest community cell to the highest leadership of the entire nation.

There are no majority decisions, but only responsible persons, and the word "council" must be restored again to its original meaning. Certainly every man will have advisors by his side, but the decisions will be made by one man alone.

The principle which made the Prussian army in its time into the most wonderful instrument of the German people must some day, in a transferred sense, become the foundation of the construction of our whole state conception: authority of every leader downward and responsibility upward.

Even then one will not be able to dispense with those corporations, which we designate today as parliament. But then councillors will actually give counsel, and responsibility can and ought to be borne more and more only by one bearer and consequently this one alone may possess the authority and the right to command.

* * * * * * * *

We National Socialists must hold immovably to foreign policy goals, namely to secure for the German people the land and soil entitled to them on this earth. And this action is the only one which, before God and our German posterity, makes any sacrifice of blood seem justified: before God in so far as we have been placed in this world with the mission of eternal struggle for our daily bread, as beings who have received nothing, and who owe their position as lords of the earth only to the genius and the courage with which they know to conquer and defend it; and before our German posterity in so far as we have shed no citizen's blood out of which a thousand others were not bestowed to posterity. The land and soil on which some day German generations of peasants can beget powerful sons will sanction the investment of the sons of today, and responsible statesmen, even if persecuted by their contemporaries, will some day absolve themselves of blood-guilt and sacrifice of the people.

I must, moreover, sharply attack those folkish penpushers who claim to regard such an acquisition of soil as a "breach of sacred human rights" and attack it as such in their scribblings. One never knows who stands behind such fellows. It is only certain that the confusion which they can create is desirable and convenient for the enemies of our people. Through such an attitude they help to weaken and destroy the will of our people from within for the only correct way of defending their vital needs. For no people on this earth possesses so much as a square meter of land and soil on the strength of a higher will or a higher right. Just as Germany's boundaries are accidental boundaries, momentary boundaries in the current political arena of any period, so also are the boundaries of other nations' living space. And just as the shape of our earth's surface can seem as immovable as granite only to the thoughtless imbecile, in reality it only represents for each period an apparent pause in a continuous development, created in a process of continuous growth by the mighty forces of nature only to be transformed or destroyed tomorrow by greater forces, likewise in the boundaries of living space in the life of the nation.

State boundaries are made by men and changed by men. The fact a nation succeeds in acquiring an undue amount of soil constitutes no higher obligation for eternal recognition itself. It proves at most the strength of the conqueror and the weakness of the sufferer. And only in this strength alone lies the right. If the German nation today, packed together into an impossible area, faces a miserable future, this is no more a commandment of fate than a revolt against this state of affairs constitutes an affront to fate. No more has any higher power promised another nation more land and soil than the German nation or is offended by the fact of this unjust distribution of soil. Just as our ancestors did not receive the soil on which we live today as sent from heaven, but had to fight for it at the risk of their lives, so in the future no Godlike grace will win for us the soil and with it life for our people but only the might of a victorious sword.

Much as all of us today recognize the necessity of a reckoning with France, it would remain ineffectual in the long run if it represented the whole of our foreign policy aim. It can and will be maintained only if it offers rear cover for an enlargement of the living space of our people in Europe. For we do not perceive in colonial acquisitions a solution to this problem, but exclusively in the gaining of settlement area, which will enhance the basis of the motherland, and thus not only maintain the new settlers in the most intimate community with the land of their origin, but also secure for the entire area those advantages which lie in its unified largeness.

The folkish movement must not be the champion of other peoples, but the vanguard fighter of our own people. Otherwise it is superfluous and above all has no right to sulk about the past. For in that case it is behaving in exactly the same way. Just as the old German policy was wrongly determined by dynastic considerations, so must future policy not be directed by cosmopolitan folkish drivel. Especially we are not the policemen of the well-known "poor little nations," but soldiers of our own nation.

But we National Socialists must go further. The right to possess land and soil becomes a duty if without extension of its soil a great nation appears doomed to destruction. And most especially not if some little nigger nation or other is involved, but the German mother of life, which has given today's world its cultural picture. Germany will either be a world power or will not be at all. And for world power she needs that largeness which will give her at the present time the necessary position and life to her citizens.

And so we National Socialists consciously draw a line under the foreign policy direction of our pre-World War I period. We take up where we broke off six hundred years ago. We stop the endless German movement to the south and west in Europe and turn our glance to the land in the east. We break off finally from the colonial and commercial policy of the future.

And if we speak of land and soil in Europe today, we can primarily have in mind only Russia and her vassal border states.

By the mid-1930s, Nazi Germany, disregarding the Versailles Treaty, began to rearm and to pursue an aggressive foreign policy. After remilitarizing the Rhineland in 1936 and concluding a quasi-legal union with Austria in 1938, Hitler proposed the annexation of the Sudetenland, that section of Czechoslovakia bordering Germany, which was inhabited mainly by ethnic Germans. By treaty France had guaranteed Czechoslovakia's territorial integrity; and presumably Great Britain, an ally of France, also supported the Czechs. But with the horrors of the Great War imprinted in their memories, the British and French hoped to halt Hitler's expansionist intentions without resorting to military action. In September 1938, British Prime Minister Neville Chamberlain and French Premier Édouard Daladier, meeting with Hitler in Munich, conceded to his annexation of the Sudetenland, which he assured them was his last territorial demand.

Below is Chamberlain's speech upon returning to London, followed by portions of two speeches by Winston Churchill, already a prominent political figure in Great Britain, who succeeded Chamberlain as Prime Minister in May 1940. The sentiments found in these addresses epitomize the long-lasting debate over whether the policy of "appeasement" was the best course of action for avoiding war.

Neville Chamberlain

Speech after the Munich Conference

(September 27, 1938)

Tomorrow Parliament is going to meet, and I shall be making a full statement of the events which have led up to the present anxious and critical situation.

Text: The Times *(London), September 28, 1938, p. 10.*

An earlier statement would not have been possible when I was flying backwards and forwards across Europe, and the position was changing from hour to hour. But today there is a lull for a brief time, and I want to say a few words to you, men and women of Britain and the Empire, and perhaps to others as well.

First of all I must say something to those who have written to my wife or myself in these last weeks to tell us of their gratitude for my efforts and to assure us of their prayers for my success. Most of these letters have come from women -- mothers or sisters of our own countrymen. But there are countless others besides -- from France, from Belgium, from Italy, even from Germany, and it has been heartbreaking to read of the growing anxiety they reveal and their intense relief when they thought, too soon, that the danger of war was past.

If I felt my responsibility heavy before, to read such letters has made it seem almost overwhelming. How horrible, fantastic, incredible it is that we should be digging trenches and trying on gas-masks here because of a quarrel in a far away country between people of whom we know nothing. It seems still more impossible that a quarrel which has already been settled in principle should be the subject of war.

I can well understand the reasons why the Czech Government have felt unable to accept the terms which have been put before them in the German memorandum. Yet I believe after my talks with Herr Hitler that, if only time were allowed, it ought to be possible for the arrangements for transferring the territory that the Czech Government has agreed to give to Germany to be settled by agreement under conditions which would assure fair treatment to the population concerned.

You know already that I have done all that one man can do to compose this quarrel. After my visits to Germany I have realized vividly how Herr Hitler feels that he must champion other Germans, and his indignation that grievances have not been met before this. He told me privately, and last night he repeated publicly, that after the Sudeten German question is settled, that is the end of Germany's territorial claims in Europe.

After my first visit to Berchtesgaden I did get the assent of the Czech Government to proposals which gave the substance of what Herr Hitler wanted, and I was taken completely by surprise when I got back to Germany and found that he insisted that the territory should be handed over to him immediately, and immediately occupied by German troops without previous arrangements for safeguarding the people within the territory who were not Germans, or did not want to join the German Reich.

I must say that I find this attitude unreasonable. If it arises out of any doubts that Herr Hitler feels about the intentions of the Czech Government to carry out their promises and hand over the territory, I have offered on the part of the British Government to guarantee their words, and I am sure the value of our promise will not be underrated anywhere.

I shall not give up the hope of a peaceful solution, or abandon my efforts for peace, as long as any chance for peace remains. I would not hesitate to pay even a third visit to Germany if I thought it would do any good. But at this moment I see nothing further that I can usefully do in the way of mediation.

Meanwhile there are certain things we can and shall do at home. Volunteers are still wanted for air raid precautions, for the fire brigade and police services, and for the Territorial units. I know that all of you, men and women alike, are ready to play your part in the defence of the country, and I ask you all to offer your services, if you have not already done so, to the local authorities, who will tell you if you are wanted and in what capacity.

Do not be alarmed if you hear of men being called up to man the anti-aircraft defences or ships. These are only precautionary measures such as a Government must take in times like this. But they do not necessarily mean that we have determined on war or that war is imminent.

However much we may sympathize with a small nation confronted by a big and powerful neighbor, we cannot in all circumstances undertake to involve the whole British Empire in war simply on her account. If we have to fight it must be on larger issues than that. I am myself a man of peace to the depths of my soul. Armed conflict between nations is a nightmare to me; but if I were convinced that any nation had made up its mind to dominate the world by fear of its force, I should feel that it must be resisted. Under such a domination life for people who believe in liberty would not be worth living; but war is a fearful thing, and we must be very clear, before we embark on it, that it is really the great issues that are at stake, and that the call to risk everything in their defence, when all the consequences are weighed, is irresistible.

For the present I ask you to await as calmly as you can the events of the next few days. As long as war has not begun, there is always hope that it may be prevented, and you know that I am going to work for peace to the last moment. Good night.

Winston Churchill

Speeches on the Czech Crisis

(September 21, 1938)

It is necessary that the nation should realize the magnitude of the disaster into which we are being led.   The partition of Czechoslovakia under Anglo-French pressure amounts to a complete surrender by the Western Democracies to the Nazi threat of force. Such a collapse will not bring peace or safety to Great Britain and France.   On the contrary, it will bring both countries into a position of ever-increasing weakness and danger.

The neutralization of Czechoslovakia alone means the liberation of 25 German divisions to threaten the Western Front.   The path to the Black Sea will be laid wide open to triumphant Nazism.

Acceptance of Herr Hitler's terms involves the prostration of Europe before the Nazi power, of which the fullest advantage will certainly be taken.   The menace, therefore, is not to Czechoslovakia, but to the cause of freedom and democracy in every country.

The idea that safety can be purchased by throwing a small State to the wolves is a fatal delusion.   The German war power will grow faster than the French and British can complete their preparations for defence.

If peace is to be preserved on a lasting basis it can only be by combination of all the Powers whose convictions and whose vital interests are opposed to Nazi domination.   A month ago this would have been possible.   But all was cast away.

Parliament should be called together without further delay and duly informed upon these grievous matters which affect the whole life and future of our country.

Text: The Times *(London), September 22, 1938, p. 15.*

(October 5, 1938)

I venture to think that in future the Czechoslovak State cannot be maintained as an independent entity. You will find that in a period of time which may be measured by years, but may be measured only by months, Czechoslovakia will be engulfed in the Nazi regime. Perhaps they may join it in despair or in revenge. At any rate, that story is over and told. But we cannot consider the abandonment and ruin of Czechoslovakia in the light only of what happened only last month. It is the most grievous consequence which we have yet experienced of what we have done and of what we have left undone in the last five years five years of futile good intention, five years of eager search started for the line of least resistance, five years of uninterrupted retreat of British power, five years of neglect of our air defences. Those are the features which I stand here to declare and which marked an improvident stewardship for which Great Britain and France have dearly to pay. We have been reduced in those five years from a position of security so overwhelming and so unchallenge-able that we never cared to think about it. We have been reduced from a position where the very word "war" was considered one which would be used only by persons qualifying for a lunatic asylum. We have been reduced from a position of safety and power -- power to do good, power to be generous to a beaten foe, power to make terms with Germany, power to give her proper redress for her grievances, power to stop her arming if we chose, power to take any step in strength or mercy or justice which we thought right -- reduced in five years from a position safe and unchallenged to where we stand now.

When I think of the fair hopes of a long peace which still lay before Europe at the beginning of 1933 when Herr Hitler first obtained power, and of all the opportunities of arresting the growth of the Nazi power which have been thrown away, when

Text: Parliamentary Debates. House of Commons. *Fifth Series. Vol. 339, cols. 365-367.*

I think of the immense combinations and resources which have been neglected or squandered, I cannot believe that a parallel exists in the whole course of history. So far as this country is concerned the responsibility must rest with those who have the undisputed control of our political affairs. They neither prevented Germany from rearming, nor did they rearm ourselves in time. They quarrelled with Italy without saving Ethiopia. They exploited and discredited the vast institution of the League of Nations and they neglected to make alliances and combinations which might have repaired previous errors, and thus they left us in the hour of trial without adequate national defence or effective international security.

Albert Camus

The Myth of Sisyphus

One of the more prominent philosophical currents in the mid-twentieth century was that of existentialism. Its proponents addressed themselves to the question of meaning in a chaotic and seemingly irrational world. Their solution was that the starting point is the fact of one's existence. From this recognition a person has the freedom and responsibility to choose the meaning of one's own life. Albert Camus (1913-1960), a French novelist born in Algeria, and an existentialist, explores this theme in The Myth of Sisyphus, *published in 1942.*

The gods had condemned Sisyphus to ceaselessly rolling a rock to the top of a mountain, whence the stone would fall back of its own weight. They had thought with some reason that there is no more dreadful punishment than futile and hopeless labor.

If one believes Homer, Sisyphus was the wisest and most prudent of mortals. According to another tradition, however, he was disposed to practice the profession of highwayman. I see no contradiction in this. Opinions differ as to the reasons why he became the futile laborer of the underworld. To begin with, he is accused of a certain levity in regard to the gods. He stole their secrets. Aegina, the daughter of Aesopus was carried off by Jupiter. The father was shocked by that disappearance and complained to Sisyphus. He, who knew of the abduction, offered to tell about it on condition that Aesopus would give water to the citadel of Corinth. To the celestial thunderbolts he preferred the benediction of water. He was punished for this in

---

Text: Albert Camus, The Myth of Sisyphus and Other Essays, *trans. by Justin O'Brien. Copyright © 1955 by Alfred Knopf, Inc., New York, pp. 119-123. Reprinted with permission of the publisher.*

the underworld. Homer tells us also that Sisyphus had put Death in chains. Pluto could not endure the sight of his deserted, silent empire. He dispatched the god of war, who liberated Death from the hands of her conqueror.

It is also said that Sisyphus, being near to death, rashly wanted to test his wife's love. He ordered her to cast his unburied body into the middle of the public square. Sisyphus woke up in the underworld. And there, annoyed by an obedience so contrary to human love, he obtained from Pluto permission to return to earth in order to chastise his wife. But when he had seen again the face of this world, enjoyed water and sun, warm stones and the sea, he no longer wanted to go back to the infernal darkness. Recalls, signs of anger, warnings were of no avail. Many years more he lived facing the curve of the gulf, the sparking sea, and the smiles of earth. A decree of the gods was necessary. Mercury came and seized him from his joys, led him forcibly back to the underworld, where his rock was ready for him.

You have already grasped that Sisyphus is the absurd hero. He is, as much through his passions as through his torture. His scorn of the gods, his hatred of death, and his passion for life won him that unspeakable penalty in which the whole being is exerted toward accomplishing nothing. This is the price that must be paid for the passions of this earth. Nothing is told us about Sisyphus in the underworld. Myths are made for the imagination to breathe life into them. As for this myth, one sees merely the whole effort of a body straining to raise the huge stone, to roll it and push it up a slope a hundred times over; one sees the face screwed up, the cheek tight against the stone, the shoulder bracing the clay-covered mass, the foot wedging it, the fresh start with arms outstretched, the wholly human security of two earth-clotted hands. At the very end of his long effort measured by skyless space and time without depth, the purpose is achieved. Then Sisyphus watches the stone rush down in a few moments toward that lower world whence he will have to push it up again toward the summit. He goes back down to the plain.

It is during that return, that pause, that Sisyphus interests me. A face that toils so close to stones is already stone itself. I see that man going back down with a heavy yet measured step toward the torment of which he will never know the end. That hour like a breathing-space which returns as surely as his suffering, that is the hour of consciousness. At each of those moments when he leaves the heights and gradually sinks toward the lairs of the gods, he is superior to his fate. He is stronger than his rock.

If this myth is tragic, that is because its hero is conscious. Where would his torture be, indeed, if at every step the hope of succeeding upheld him? The workman of today works every day in his life at the same tasks, and this fate is no less absurd. But it is tragic only at the rare moments when it becomes conscious. Sisyphus, proletarian of the gods, powerless and rebellious, knows the whole extent of his wretched condition: it is what he thinks of during his descent. The lucidity that was to constitute his torture at the same time crowns his victory. There is no fate that cannot be surmounted by scorn.

* * * * * * * *

If the descent is thus sometimes performed in sorrow, it can also take place in joy. This word is not too much. Again I fancy Sisyphus returning toward his rock, and the sorrow was in the beginning. When the images of earth cling too tightly to memory, when the call of happiness becomes too insistent, it happens that melancholy rises in man's heart: this is the rock's victory, this is the rock itself. The boundless grief is too heavy to bear. These are our nights of Gethsemane. But crushing truths perish from being acknowledged. Thus, Oedipus at the outset obeys fate without knowing it. But from the moment he knows, his tragedy begins. Yet at the same moment, blind and desperate, he realizes that the only bond linking him to the world is the cool hand of a girl. Then a tremendous remark rings out: "Despite so many ordeals, my advanced age and the nobility of my soul make me conclude that all is well." Sophocles' Oedipus, like Dostoevsky's Kirilov, thus gives the recipe for the absurd victory. Ancient wisdom confirms modern heroism.

One does not discover the absurd without being tempted to write a manual of happiness. "What.! By such narrow ways?" There is but one world, however. Happiness and the absurd are two sons of the same earth. They are inseparable. It would be a mistake to say that happiness necessarily springs from the absurd discovery. It happens as well that the feeling of the absurd springs from happiness. "I conclude that all is well," says Oedipus, and that remark is sacred. It echoes in the wild and limited universe of man. It teaches that all is not, has not been, exhausted. It drives out of this world a god who had come into it with dissatisfaction and a preference for futile sufferings. It makes of fate a human matter, which must be settled among men.

All Sisyphus' silent Joy is contained therein. His fate belongs to him. His rock is his thing. Likewise, the absurd man, when he contemplates his torment, silences all the idols. In the universe suddenly restored to its silence, the myriad wondering little voices of the earth rise up. Unconscious, secret calls, invitations from all the faces, they are the necessary reverse and price of victory. There is no sun without shadow, and it is essential to know the night. The absurd man says yes and his effort will henceforth be unceasing. If there is a personal fate, there is no higher destiny, or at least there is but one which he concludes is inevitable and despicable. For the rest, he knows himself to be the master of his days. At that subtle moment when man glances backward over his life, Sisyphus returning toward his rock, in that slight pivoting he contemplates that series of unrelated actions which becomes his fate, created by him, combined under his memory's eye and soon sealed by his death. Thus, convinced of the wholly human origin of all that is human, a blind man eager to see who knows that the night has no end, he is still on the go. The rock is still rolling.

I leave Sisyphus at the foot of the mountain! One always finds one's burdens again. But Sisyphus teaches the higher fidelity that negates the gods and raises rocks. He too concludes that all is well. This universe henceforth without a master seems to him neither sterile nor futile. Each atom of that stone, each mineral flake of that nightfilled mountain, in itself forms a world. The struggle itself toward the heights is enough to fill a man's heart. One must imagine Sisyphus happy.

Vaclav Havel

The Future of Europe

The movement of Eastern Europe and the Soviet Union toward liberal democratic systems has been one of the most far-reaching developments in recent times. Epitomizing this trend is the former dissident and Czech playwright, Vaclav Havel. Although jailed on several occasions for his criticisms of the Communist regime, Havel eventually became president of a rejuvenated Czech Republic in December 1989. Two months later, he traveled to the United States and addressed a joint session of Congress. His speech has been hailed as an optimistic yet realistic appraisal of prospects for the future.

(The following address was delivered in Czech, with a simultaneous translation in English.)

President HAVEL. Dear Mr. Speaker, dear Mr. President, dear Senators and Members of the House, ladies and gentlemen:

My advisers advised me to speak on this important occasion in Czech. I don't know why. Perhaps they wanted you to enjoy the sweet sounds of my mother tongue.

The last time they arrested me, on October 27 of last year, I didn't know whether it was for two days or two years.

Exactly one month later, when the rock musician Michael Kocab told me that I would probably be proposed as a presidential candidate, I thought it was one of his usual jokes.

On the 10th of December 1989, when my actor friend Jirl Bartoska, in the name of the Civic Forum, nominated me as a candidate for the office of President of the Republic, I

Text: Congressional Record, *Vol. 136, February 21, 1990, H392-395.*

thought it was out of the question that the Parliament we had inherited from the previous regime would elect me.

Nineteen days later, when I was unanimously elected President of my country, I had no idea that two months later I would be speaking in front of this famous and powerful assembly, and that what I say would be heard by millions of people who have never heard of me and that hundreds of politicians and political scientists would study every word I say.

When they arrested me on October 27, I was living in a country ruled by the most conservative Communist government in Europe, and our society slumbered beneath the pall of a totalitarian system. Today, less than four months later, I am speaking to you as the representative of a country that has set out on the road to democracy, a country where there is complete freedom of speech, which is getting ready for free elections, and which wants to create a prosperous market economy and its own foreign policy.

It is all very extraordinary.

But I have not come here to speak for myself or my feelings, or merely to talk about my own country. I have used this small example of something I know well, to illustrate something general and important.

We are living in very extraordinary times. The human face of the world is changing so rapidly that none of the familiar political speedometers are adequate.

We playwrights, who have to cram a whole human life or an entire historical era in a two-hour play, can scarcely understand this rapidity ourselves. And if it gives us trouble, think of the trouble it must give to political scientists, who spend their whole lives studying the realm of the probable, and have even less experience with the realm of the improbable than us, the playwrights.

Let me try to explain why I think the velocity of the changes in my country, in Central and Eastern Europe, and of course in the Soviet Union itself, has made such a significant impression on the face of the world today, and why it concerns the fate of all, including you Americans. I would like to look at this, first from the political point of view, and then from a point of view that we might call philosophical.

* * * * * * * *

And now what is happening is happening: the totalitarian system in the Soviet Union and in most of its satellites is breaking down and our nations are looking for a way to democracy and independence. The first act in this remarkable drama began when Mr. Gorbachev and those around him, faced with the sad reality of their country, initiated their policy of "perestroika." Obviously they had no idea either what they were setting in motion or how rapidly events would unfold. We knew a lot about the enormous number of growing problems that slumbered beneath the honeyed, unchanging mask of socialism. But I don't think any of us knew how little it would take for these problems to manifest themselves in all their enormity, and for the longings of these nations to emerge in all their strength. The mask fell away so rapidly that, in the flood of work, we have literally no time even to be astonished.

What does all this mean for the world in the long run? Obviously a number of things. This is, I am firmly convinced, a historically irreversible process, and as a result Europe will begin again to seek its own identity without being compelled to be a divided armory any longer. Perhaps this will create the hope that sooner or later your boys will no longer have to stand on guard for freedom in Europe, or come to our rescue, because Europe will at last be able to stand guard over itself. But that is still not the most important thing: the main thing is, it seems to me, that these revolutionary changes will enable us to escape from the rather antiquated straitjacket of this bipolar view of the world, and to enter at last into an era of multipolarity. That is, into an era in which all of us -- large and small -- former slaves and former masters -- will be able to create what your great President Lincoln called the "family of man."

* * * * * * * *

Ladies and gentlemen, I've only been president for two months and I haven't attended any schools for presidents. My only school was life itself. Therefore I don't want to burden you any longer with my political thoughts, but instead I will move on to an area that is more familiar to me, to what I would call the philosophical aspect of those changes that still concern everyone, although they are taking place in our corner of the world.

As long as people are people, democracy in the full sense of the word will always be no more than an ideal; one may approach it as one would a horizon in ways that may be better or worse, but it can never be fully attained. In this sense you too are merely approaching democracy. You have thousands of problems of all kinds, as other countries do. But you have one great advantage: You have been approaching democracy uninterruptedly for more than 200 years, and your journey toward the horizon has never been disrupted by a totalitarian system. Czechs and Slovaks, despite their humanistic traditions that go back to the first millennium, have approached democracy for a mere 20 years, between the two world wars, and now for the 3-1/2 months since the 17th of November of last year.

The advantage that you have over us is obvious at once.

The Communist type of totalitarian system has left both our nations, Czechs and Slovaks -- as it has all the nations of the Soviet Union subjugated in its time -- a legacy of countless dead, an infinite spectrum of human suffering, profound economic decline, and above all enormous human humiliation. It has brought us horrors that fortunately you have not known.

At the same time, however -- unintentionally, of course -- it have given us something positive: a special capacity to look, from time to time, somewhat further than someone who has not undergone this bitter experience. A person who cannot move and live a somewhat normal life because he is pinned under a boulder has more time to think about his hopes than someone who is not trapped that way.

What I am trying to say is this: we must all learn many things from you, from how to educate our offspring, how to elect our representatives, all the way to how to organize our economic life so that it will lead to prosperity and not to poverty. But it doesn't have to be merely assistance from the well-educated, the powerful and the wealthy to someone who has nothing and therefore has nothing to offer in return.

We too can offer something to you: our experience and the knowledge that has come from it.

This is a subject for books, many of which have already been written and many of which have yet to be written. I shall therefore limit myself to a single idea.

The specific experience I'm talking about has given me one great certainty: Consciousness precedes Being, and not, the other way around, as the Marxists claim.

For this reason, the salvation of this human world lies nowhere else than in the human heart, in the human power to reflect, in human meekness and in human responsibility.

Without a global revolution in the sphere of human consciousness, nothing will change for the better in the sphere of our Being as humans, and the catastrophe toward which this world is headed, be it ecological, social, demographic or a general break - down of civilization, will be unavoidable. If we are no longer threatened by world war, or by the danger that the absurd mountains of accumulated nuclear weapons might blow up the world, this does not mean that we have definitively won. We are in fact far from the final victory.

We are still a long way from that "family of man"; in fact, we seem to be receding from the ideal rather than drawing closer to it. Interests of all kinds: personal, selfish, state, national, group, and, if you like, company interests still considerably outweigh genuinely common and global interests. We are still under the sway of the destructive and vain belief that man is the pinnacle of creation, and not just a part of it, and that therefore everything is permitted. There are still many who say they are concerned not for themselves, but for the cause, while they are demonstrably out for themselves and not for the cause at all. We are still destroying the planet that was entrusted to us, and its environment. We still close our eyes to the growing social, ethnic and cultural conflicts in the world. From time to time we say that the anonymous megamachinery we have created for ourselves no longer serves us, but rather has enslaved us, yet we still fail to do anything about it.

In other words, we still don't know how to put morality ahead of politics, science and economics. We are still incapable of understanding that the only genuine backbone of all our actions -- if they are to be moral -- is responsibility. Responsibility to something higher than my family, my country, my company, my success. Responsibility to the order of Being, where all our actions are indelibly recorded and where, and only where, they will be properly judged.

The interpreter or mediator between us and this higher authority is what is traditionally referred to as human conscience.

If I subordinate my political behavior to this imperative mediated to me by my conscience, I can't go far wrong. If on the contrary I were not guided by this voice, not even ten presidential schools with 2,000 of the best political scientists in the world could help me.

This is why I ultimately decided -- after resisting for a long time -- to accept the burden of political responsibility.

I am not the first, nor will I be the last, intellectual to do this. On the contrary, my feeling is that there will be more and more of them all the time. If the hope of the world lies in human consciousness, then it is obvious that intellectuals cannot go on forever avoiding their share of responsibility for the world and hiding their distaste for politics under an alleged need to be independent.

It is easy to have independence in your program and then leave others to carry that program out. If everyone thought that way, pretty soon no one would be independent.

I think that you Americans should understand this way of thinking. Wasn't it the best minds of your country, people you could call intellectuals, who wrote your famous Declaration of Independence, your Bill of Human Rights and your Constitution, and who -- above all took upon themselves the practical responsibility for putting them into practice? The worker from Branik in Prague that your President referred to in his State of the Union message this year is far from being the only person in

Czechoslovakia, let alone in the world, to be inspired by those great documents. They inspire us all. They inspire us to despite the fact that they are over 200 years old. They inspire us to be citizens.

When Thomas Jefferson wrote that "Governments are instituted among Men deriving their just Powers from the Consent of the Governed," it was a simple and important act of the human spirit.

What gave meaning to that act, however, was the fact that the author backed it up with his life. It was not just his words, it was his deeds as well.

I will end where I began: history has accelerated. I believe that once again, it will be the human mind that will notice this acceleration, give it a name, and transform those words into deeds.

Thank you.